Translation Theory and Development Studies

This book aims to provide a philosophical underpinning to translation and relate translation to development. The second aim flows from the first part's argument that societies emerge out of, among others, complex translational interactions amongst individuals. It will do so by conceptualizing translation from a complexity and emergence point of view and relating this view on emergent semiotics to some of the most recent social research. It will further fulfill its aims by providing empirical data from the South African context concerning the relationship between translation and development. The book intends to be interdisciplinary in nature and to foster interdisciplinary research and dialogue by relating the newest trends in translation theory, that is, agency theory in the sociology of translation, to development theory within sociology. Data in the volume are drawn from fields that have received very little if any attention in translation studies, that is, local economic development, the knowledge economy, and the informal economy.

Kobus Marais is Senior Lecturer in Translation Studies in the Department of Linguistics and Language Practice at the University of the Free State, South Africa.

Routledge Advances in Translation Studies

1 **Applying Luhmann to Translation Studies**
Translation in Society
Sergey Tyulenev

2 **Interpreting Justice**
Ethics, Politics and Language
Moira Inghilleri

3 **Translation and Web Searching**
Vanessa Enríquez Raído

4 **Translation Theory and Development Studies**
A Complexity Theory Approach
Kobus Marais

Translation Theory and Development Studies
A Complexity Theory Approach

Kobus Marais

NEW YORK AND LONDON

First published 2014
by Routledge
711 Third Avenue, New York, NY 10017

Simultaneously published in the UK
by Routledge
2 Park Square, Milton Park, Abingdon, Oxfordshire OX14 4RN

First issued in paperback 2015

*Routledge is an imprint of the Taylor & Francis Group,
an informa business*

© 2014 Taylor & Francis

The right of Kobus Marais to be identified as author of this work has been asserted in accordance with sections 77 and 78 of the Copyright, Designs and Patents Act 1988.

All rights reserved. No part of this book may be reprinted or reproduced or utilized in any form or by any electronic, mechanical, or other means, now known or hereafter invented, including photocopying and recording, or in any information storage or retrieval system, without permission in writing from the publishers.

Trademark Notice: Product or corporate names may be trademarks or registered trademarks, and are used only for identification and explanation without intent to infringe.

Library of Congress Cataloging-in-Publication Data
Marais, Kobus.
 Translation theory and development studies : a complexity theory approach / By Kobus Marais.
  pages cm. — (Routledge Advances In Translation Studies ; 4)
 Includes bibliographical references and index.
1. Translating and interpreting. I. Title.
 P306.M36 2013
 418'.02—dc23
 2013013349

ISBN 13: 978-1-138-94081-9 (pbk)
ISBN 13: 978-0-415-84035-4 (hbk)

Typeset in Sabon
by Apex CoVantage, LLC

I dedicate this book to my colleague Jackie Naudé, for never having pulled rank on me.

Contents

List of Tables ix
List of Figures xi
Acknowledgements xiii

Introduction 1

PART I

1 Toward a Philosophy of Complexity 15
   1. Introduction 15
   2. Situating Complexity 17
   3. A Framework for an Epistemology of Complexity 19
   4. Complex Adaptive Systems 26
   5. Toward a Complexity Framework for Translation 43

2 Emergent Semiotics 46
   1. Introduction 46
   2. Conceptualizing Emergence 47
   3. Social Emergence 54
   4. The Semiotic Substratum for the Emergence of Social Reality 62
   5. The Role of Semiotics in the Emergent Social 69
   6. Conclusion 72

3 Developing Translation Studies 74
   1. Introduction 74
   2. An Analysis of Philosophical Underpinnings in Translation Studies 77
   3. Toward a Philosophy of Translation 95
   4. Conclusion 114

PART II

4	**Translation and Development**	119
	1. Introduction	119
	2. Conceptualizing Development	121
	3. Critical Perspectives on Development	138
	4. Translation and Development	143
5	**Translation, Local Economic Development, and Border**	146
	1. Introduction	146
	2. Translating Policy Documents for Local Economic Development	151
	3. Findings of Open-Ended Interviews	160
	4. Theoretical Implications	167
	Addendum	170
6	**Translation, the Knowledge Economy, and Development**	171
	1. Introduction	171
	2. The Knowledge Economy	171
	3. Learning Regions	175
	4. The Network Economy	178
	5. Translation, the Knowledge Economy, and Agriculture Development	179
	6. Conclusion	184
	Addendum	185
7	**Translation in the Informal Economy**	187
	1. Introduction	187
	2. Defining the Informal Economy	188
	3. Conceptualizing the Informal Economy	189
	4. The Relevance of the Informal Economy for Translation Studies	193
	5. Translation in the Informal Economy in South Africa	196
	6. Conclusion	203
	Conclusion: Developing Translation, Translating Development	205
	1. Present	205
	2. Future	207
	3. Past	208
	Notes	211
	References	213
	Index	225

Tables

5.1	Table of contents of the Ukhahlamba IDP	155
5.2	Table of contents of the Pixley Ka Seme IDP	156
5.3	Table of contents of the !Xhariep IDP	157
5.4	Comparison of points of interest in IDPs	159

Figures

3.1	Emergent reality	96
3.2	A schematic representation of inter-ness	101
3.3	The emergent semiotic	101
3.4	The complexity of inter- and intra-semiosis	102
3.5	The emergence of translation	107
3.6	The role of translation in the emergence of social reality	108
3.7	Agency, translation, and emergence	109
5.1	Provinces of South Africa	148
5.2	District municipalities in the Free State	149
5.3	Provinces, municipalities, and towns around the Gariep Dam	150

Acknowledgements

According to the well-known African proverb, it takes a village to raise a child. Relating this wisdom to my own experience, I have rephrased it: It takes a world to write a book. Apart from the few people I am able to thank by name in this section, my thinking is connected to all of those I have quoted in the book and to many more whose work I have read and who have benefited me with their time and intellect at conferences and during other discussions. Especially when I came toward the end of the writing process, I became increasingly aware of how many people had contributed in various ways.

By name, I wish to thank my employer, the University of the Free State (UFS) and, in particular, the Faculty of the Humanities and the Department of Linguistics and Language Practice, not only for paying my salary on time but also for providing me with six months of sabbatical time to focus on this book. Furthermore, Doreen Atkinson from the Cluster for Sustainable Development at the University of the Free State not only provided two rounds of funding, the means by which the empirical work for Chapters 6, 7 and 8 was done, but she also made me feel at home in an interdisciplinary group and boosted my self-confidence, which prevented me from ending my efforts prematurely. I am hugely grateful toward her and other colleagues in the Cluster. Mark Ingle, Jan Cloete, Deidre van Rooyen, and Doreen herself read chapters and provided invaluable feedback.

Closer colleagues Munene Mwaniki and Mariana Kriel have not only been warm and supportive colleagues but also critical and constructive conversation partners. In particular, Sergey Tyulenev, who spent some time as a postdoctoral research fellow in our department, contributed much to my own fledgling thoughts on expanding notions of translation studies. And Marlie van Rooyen, my colleague in translation studies, provided intellectual and moral support beyond expectation and shared her deep humanness freely. At the UFS Library, Ronet Vrey has rendered invaluable and friendly service over a number of years.

My colleague Ilse Feinauer from the University of Stellenbosch, who cooperated in arranging the Spring School for Translation Studies in Africa, contributed through many discussions on various aspects of translation studies. Christiane Nord and Anthony Pym, who were the plenary speakers at the first two Spring Schools, also provided me with excellent opportunities for trying out my ideas. I am also grateful towards my colleagues at Katholieke Universiteit Leuven, Luc van Doorslaer, Peter Flynn, and Reine Meylaerts, who have over a number of mutual visits and conference debates kept me honest, intellectually. Jenny Lake made a huge contribution to my work by editing the final manuscript.

Edgard Sienaert became not only an intellectual father figure to me over the past five years, but he also shared his ample wisdom and humor freely, guiding me along many hazardous intellectual and social routes.

Sandra Halverson proved to be an invaluable colleague as we discovered the extent to which we were interested in similar subjects. It has been wonderful for me to simply dive into matters without first having to explain my ideas to her.

Johann Visagie played a major part in helping me tease out my ideas on semiotics, systems theory, and emergence. His philosophical expertise, coupled with a deep sense of humanness, provided a safe laboratory—on the carpet of his living room—for me to experiment conceptually.

Last, I wish to thank Jackie Naudé and Cynthia Miller-Naudé for their support, belief and encouragement. The idea for this book started out in Melbourne in 2008 when Jackie and I attended the International Association of Translation and Intercultural Studies Conference. Because I could not afford upmarket accommodation, Jackie graciously, although clearly apprehensive, agreed to share a room with me in a youth hostel. As we expected, the nights were quite boisterous. One night, a group of youngsters came in at about two o'clock, totally inebriated, sitting with their backs against the dry wall of our room, conversing as only the drunk can. Jackie and I obviously were woken, but he did not complain. Rather, at that hour, we started discussing notions of "translation as" because I was reading Theo Hermans's *The Conference of the Tongues* at the time. I am eternally grateful for what he has taught me about translation studies, for the broadness in scope of his thinking and for his unceasing belief in and support of me. My hope is that this book will honor his tireless belief in excellence and that it will be some recompense for the lonely, unacknowledged road he often had to travel.

I am not sure how to thank my wife and three children because the usual thanks to family members for their patience and for managing without the author often seems so paternalistic. Perhaps, I just want to thank them here, in public, for enriching my life with the richness of theirs. Through their deep humanity and biting wit, they kept me as sane and connected to material life as is humanly possible, for which I thank and honor them.

Introduction

I first met Meshack Masuku towards the end of 2001. At that stage, I was recently retrenched and had set up a small bonsai nursery in order to provide an income for my family. Part of my vision for the nursery was to indigenize the art of bonsai by developing African bonsai styles, working with African tree species and finding a potter who would be able to design African bonsai pots. This is where Meshack entered in. He was a lecturer in ceramics at the then Port Elizabeth Technikon (currently the Nelson Mandela Metropolitan University). A Swazi of origin, he left school to herd cattle where he spent his days working with clay. Somehow, as part of a development program that ran during the 1990s, the details of which I cannot recall, he received the opportunity to study ceramics at the PE Technikon where he was appointed as a lecturer in his second year "because they had nothing more to teach me". He agreed to work on the design of African bonsai pots with me and immediately started off with a lecture on African art. I immediately felt an attachment to this huge guy, always with a guineafowl feather or porcupine quill in his hair, with his boisterous laugh and his deep sense of humanity.

It must have been during our second or third meeting that the discussion turned towards politics. He told me that he had attended some UN meeting as a student representative. One day, I asked Meshack why black South Africans had been so tolerant under apartheid rule. I indicated that I would probably have been much more militant than most black people I knew. His answer came from an angle I never expected. "Africa is the mother of humanity," he told me. "And if a mother sees her children going astray, she looks at them with love and compassion, understanding that they do not know better. And she absorbs the wrongdoing of the children in her own soul and body because she loves them and she understands that they need time to grow and come to a point where they themselves understand what it means to be human. She absorbs the pain that they inflict on her because she understands that they need time."

Since that day I have pondered over his words time and time again. I am aware that, philosophically, Meshack's view is not without grave problems. And I do not intend to make his views the basis of my

2 Translation Theory and Development Studies

> theorization in this book. By means of his narrative, I wish to illustrate that which fascinates me and what motivated the quest on which I have embarked. As a Euro-African, I am a hybrid human, neither European nor African, and yet both European and African, to use essentialist terms. As a hybrid human, I wish to gain some understanding of the context in which I exist. I wish to understand both sides of my hybridity—European and African—as well as the newness emerging from this complex hybridity. As a hybrid child of history, living in Africa, this book is in itself complex—both a scholarly treatise and a personal odyssey. It is both an argument and a pondering.
>
> Awe and respect have become powerfully unfashionable in our confused postmodern society. But has not our Baconian tradition, which celebrates science as the power to predict and control, also brought us a secular loss of awe and respect? If nature were truly ours to command and control, then we might well afford the luxury of contempt. Power corrupts, after all. (Kauffman, 1995, p. 302)

Masuku and Kauffman are the kinds of people I am trying to engage with in this book. I shall not be able to answer the questions they pose, but I shall talk to them, listen to them, and engage with them and with others like them. The conceptual framework I have attempted to open up in this book will hopefully make it possible to interpret Kauffman in terms of Masuku in future, as opposed to the reversed interpretation seen in the current situation. Is Maria Tymoczko correct when she suggests that different cultures and continents should make their voices heard in translation studies? Can Africa be heard in this debate? Does Africa have something to say? Can I understand what Africa wants to say? Under what conditions can the African voice be heard in this debate?

My quest in this book is to answer the following: What does it mean to do translation or study translation phenomena in South Africa as a development context?

This question entails a number of suppositions to which I shall attend in due course. First, I wish to explain that the study of translation in Africa has become somewhat of an intellectual and even existential quest for me. Being an African is complex because it means that, among other things, one has to deal with a history of colonization. It also means being far away from the intellectual center of the academe and being part of a troubled society, a multiply broken society (Maathai, 2009). Living and dealing with this kind of social posttraumatic stress disorder depletes one's intellectual and emotional energy. Being an African with a European ancestry makes the situation even more complex. It implies that you are not "pure," that you are forced to deal with your own hybrid identity, and that you are suspected of being a bastard by "the pure" on both sides. Forming part of a group of people that has been both colonized and colonizer makes it even more complex because it leaves you, among other things, with guilt issues. Having to grapple with an identity that could be construed as both an enemy to and a child from the soil of

Africa is what drives me to understand my context, not myself but my context. Well, maybe myself too. However, my aim is not to ponder my existence as semi-African or Euro-African or settler—or whichever name one could come up with. Being an Afrikaans-speaking South African, my being is African. Afrikaans means language from Africa. Afrikaner, the group to which I belong, means people of Africa. I am an African—no qualms about it.

Because this study is ultimately about the unsolvable paradox of locality and universality, I have to factor in my own locality in space and time as part of the (re)presentation. I do not mean that I shall follow the methodology of auto-ethnography. What I do mean is that my existence, my hopes, my history is the context in which I live, work and write. Although trying to conduct good science in this book and acknowledging that good science requires a meta-stance, also as far as one's own situatedness is concerned, I also need to acknowledge that this book is somewhat of an odyssey—searching for myself, my people, my place in the globe, and the cosmos. Or perhaps it is a construction site—constructing myself, my people, and my place as a paradox of here and not here, of African and non-African. In fact, it is probably more. It is searching for Africa, its people, its place. So perhaps it is both. Searching for Africa in myself and myself in Africa. Searching for Africa in humanity and humanity in Africa.

I hope that this book offers more than merely theoretical insight. I hope that it will become an agenda, a motivation for scholars and translators on the continent who want to contribute to make this continent work. However, the "making work" part is related to an "understanding" part. I am well aware of how complex an endeavor attempting to change a society can be. I know that it takes generations. I know that it takes a village to raise a child, but I do not know what it takes to raise a village and, for that matter, a continent, a society. I hope that this effort at understanding aspects of translation in South Africa could play a small role in helping people make Africa better, whatever that may entail. Imposing some kind of change on moral or other ideological grounds is not what I have in mind. I must admit that I am not always sure what I have in mind. What I do know is that the kind of moral outrage about everything that is wrong, as is currently found in South Africa, does little more than to make people feel guilty. Although it is true that guilt could play a role in motivating people to do things or to stop doing them, this does not help us to understand why they did or did not do these things in the first place. My primary interest is thus to understand. I do not believe that understanding can solve all problems, but I do know that if there is something that I can contribute to the African project, it is scholarly understanding, however little and however limited. I am very well aware of the limitations of rationality, as I am of the Western bias underlying my belief in the power of rationality for solving social problems. But, as I have argued earlier, I am of a hybrid nature, so it should not come as a surprise that my scholarship is similarly hybrid. Thus, by contributing what I can, with the assumption that others are contributing what they can,

I hope that through pooling our knowledge and resources, we can try to make a difference—we can try to raise a continent. In this sense, this book entails a challenge to translation scholars in Africa: Let us focus our powers of understanding on our context. Let our scholarship be about our context within the larger context of humanity.

But what does it mean to translate in South Africa? To be a translator in Africa? To study translation in Africa? I am deliberately considering both South Africa and Africa, not because I believe that I speak on behalf of Africa but because I am trying to consider my South African context within larger contexts, that is, Africa, the Global South, the world. The notion of complex adaptive systems that are open to other systems, which I put forward in the next chapter, precludes me from viewing my context as isolated from other contexts. Although Africa is varied, in a larger sense it is part of my context. Translation scholars these days tend to think that "doing it" in Africa is different from "doing it" in Europe, or anywhere else; a position eloquently advocated by scholars such as Maria Tymoczko (ironically not from Africa). In fact, what she claims is that doing translation anywhere should be different from doing it anywhere else. Locality or space[1] has become one of the defining factors in conceptualizing translation. This means that geography has become a factor in translation. Whether this argument holds true in all cases remains to be seen, but what needs to be done in the meantime, and what I intend to do in this book, is to investigate the influence of a particular locality in conceptualizing translation. This I shall do in dialogue with other spaces. In the process, space itself should be theorized as a factor in translation and in translation studies. It should be clear to the reader that this is a postmodern view of science. In attaching significance to space, one steps out of the Enlightenment ideal of universal knowledge. One immediately gives up knowledge for knowledges. Both radical universalism and radical particularism have rightfully been criticized. This book will thus be yet another endeavor at walking the tightrope between these -isms by using complexity as the balancing rod. Whether I will fall myself to a pitiful pulp remains to be seen.

On a very deep level, the seminal work done by Susam-Sarajeva (2002) on the power configurations in global translation studies informs this book. I face the real possibility of my book becoming data for some other translation scholar who is smarter than I am, or who is closer to the center of production, or who is a more astute rhetorician. However, because I am aware of this danger (if it is a danger), I am trying not only to present data, but also to theorize the data. I am, thus, if you can call it that, claiming the data for my own theory first before putting it out in the public domain where others will retheorize it. Whether I can have enough weight behind my theory to prevent it from becoming mere data in someone else's theory will be out of my hands once the book has been published. Perhaps living at the periphery, living in a context in which you do not have the power to influence how people think, providing data that do not influence the major world powers is part of what this book is about. Finding life, in particular academic and human life, meaningful while being powerless seems to run counter to current dominant, constructionist views of science. Practicing science has become a production race, chasing after promotion, recognition, and funding. In a sense, it has lost its nature as a common human search for understanding our common dilemma. So, let me be clear: I am not in the race. I think because I like it. I think because I believe that any life is worth understanding and that any society is worth understanding. Frankly, I cannot but think. What I am thus trying to do is to present data on translation practices in South Africa and to theorize those data with a view of engaging, first, fellow African translation scholars. I am not sure whether this can be done. I am not sure that it will lead us anywhere, but I do believe that it should be done even if it will only later lead us to conclude that it should not have been done in the first place. My perspective is thus paradoxically Africanist and globalist, entertaining a dialogue between these perspectives.

But what is the difference between here and elsewhere? The problem with difference is that it is very difficult to talk about it without essentializing it. Saying what something is generally also entails saying what it is not, or at least implying what it is not. Whether it is possible to hold mutually inclusive views on here and elsewhere remains to be seen. Could one think about here and elsewhere in ways that neither essentialize nor relativize either? On one hand, we have seen that universalizing does not provide us with all the answers we need, especially in the social sciences. Some phenomena are not the same everywhere, as Tymoczko (2006) has pointed out about translation. On the other hand, elevating locality and difference to the level of principle could lead to essentializing particular views on culture and society, which have been shown throughout history to have a devastating effect on human relationships. This effect has perhaps nowhere been more clearly demonstrated than in my own country, that is, through the history of apartheid South Africa. Having read Sturge's (2007) insightful work on other and self and similarity and difference in ethnographic studies, I have my doubts about whether the tension could be resolved. This is another reason why I am opting for a complexity perspective. I suspect we stand to gain from holding mutually exclusive notions in an insurmountable tension.

Despite the dangers inherent in my attempted balancing act, I believe it necessary to try to understand the context in which I work. I have to find a way of looking at the particular without losing sight of the universal, and vice versa. I believe that some kind of emic view could, in this regard, add value to studies that have been conducted on the topic from the outside. I acknowledge that my own emic-ness is contestable. Being an African of European descent, I am an African of the soil and not of the blood (as some African thinkers conceptualize it). How "into" Africa am I? Well, my question is, How deep is deep enough? Because if you go too deep in your requirements for "real" Africans, you essentialize us/me. As an African of the soil, I thus believe that I dare take part in talking about Africa, asking about Africa, trying to understand Africa. In the fashion of the case studies presented in Milton and Bandia (2009a), I am attempting to ask how translation can serve the development of society in Africa.

I should clarify yet some more points at this stage. First, I am not claiming to talk on behalf of Africa. I am talking about South Africa and only by some kind of tenuous extension about Africa. Second, I am actually talking about facets of translation phenomena in South Africa. My claims to be talking about Africa are thus a polemic strategy. In this strategy, I assume that the rest of Africa can also be considered as development contexts, but I am not assuming one, undifferentiated Africa. Thus, my notion of "Africa" actually means "Africa, as a geographical space and as a development context". For the debate in this book, I am using what could be called a comparative methodology. For the sake of this book, I am thus constructing the nature of the phenomena I am comparing. One of these constructions is the space within which I am studying translation phenomena, and this space is arbitrarily, but with good reason, constructed as Africa. Over and against Africa, I shall construct comparative spaces such as the West, Europe, the Americas, Asia, well knowing that these spaces could be constructed alternatively, that they do not denote anything essential, and that they are in no sense unified (Flynn & Van Doorslaer, 2011). I could, for example, also perform a study in which I compare African countries with one another. Such a comparison would be fraught with the same dangers as my current one, because any African country, for example, Kenya, can easily become essentialized when thought of as a unified whole. The spatial designations I use are thus epistemological tools to help me understand and communicate, nothing more. Third, what I am writing about could also have implications for development contexts outside of Africa, that is, what is known as the third world or the Global South. Fourth, well aware of the dangers of essentializing the notion of Africa, I am not trying to essentialize, but rather to understand difference and similarity.

I am interested to see whether one could conceptualize the nature of translation in Africa. This means seeing difference based on sameness and sameness based on difference. I would like to see, once there is sufficient data for comparison, whether there are differences with other contexts and, most important, what these differences are. Simultaneously, I would like to find out more about the similarities with other contexts. At this moment, I am positing that one could conceptualize the African context in which translation takes place as a development context. As I pondered over the difference between doing translation in the United States or Belgium and doing it in South Africa or Cameroon, I was confronted with various categories in which to conceptualize the difference. One could use the notions of West and Africa, first and third world, modern and premodern, rich and poor, and so on. None of these satisfied because they were, first, binary and, second, categories of critical theory. Also, notions of modern and premodern have racist undertones that I would like to avoid. I do think it necessary to discuss ideological differences, if there are any, between contexts in translation, and

I shall do so in future. However, I want to escape from the somewhat sterile categories of the critical paradigm, that is, the haves and the have-nots, the colonizers and the colonized, the oppressors and the oppressed. For what I am trying to do, I thought that development could be a category that would give me scope to start conceptualizing the landscape of translation in Africa without forcing my conceptualization into a straitjacket. I do not want to escape from criticality; I want to open critical thinking to more complex categories.

By calling the African context of translation developmental, I am connecting translation to the motion of society as a whole. Development studies usually comprises an interdisciplinary field connecting political science, economics and sociology, all three of which are seen as fields of study interested in the driving factors behind the development of societies. In Africa, a wide-ranging debate is raging on the direction the continent should take on the issue of development. One of the prominent African philosophers of our time, Achille Mbembe, put it as follows: In Africa, we need a debate on alternative ways of being modern (see also Maathai 2009, p. 162). This quest is the motivation behind my book. It seeks to place translation studies within the broader quest for developing a society, in this case the South African society and, by extension, other developing contexts. Taking this position frees translation studies from its overdependence on literary texts as objects of study when investigating agency (Gentzler, 2008) and from its bias toward professional and formal expressions of translational actions (Tymoczko, 2006). It situates translation as a factor in the political economy of the day, the day-to-day efforts of people to adapt to the power configurations within which they were born or had been forced. In this book, I shall argue that the semiotic interaction of people involved in the development of societies needs to be factored into the equation of development and that development should be considered as a contextual factor influencing semiotic interactions such as translation. In this endeavor, I shall build on the work done by social emergentists, philosophers such as John Searle, and development anthropologists such as Olivier de Sardan. One of the main advantages opened up by this approach is that one is able to shift the attention to include translation phenomena in the informal economy into the purview of translation studies. This does not mean that I want to characterize translation studies in Africa as focusing only on the informal, but rather that the one-sided focus on the formal economy and translation has to be supplemented by perspectives from the informal economy.

What makes my point of view difficult is that development and development studies are highly contested notions. Not only is the definition of development contested, but scholars and practitioners also strongly disagree about philosophies, approaches, goals and methods of development. In itself, this is no different from other fields of study. The problem is just that one has to tread very carefully when you start out for the first time bringing together notions such as development and translation. The road is full of potholes, it does not appear on the global positioning system (GPS), and it is the roaming space of hijackers (to use well-known South African images). I am thus setting out on this effort expecting to make mistakes, to get things wrong. I do this in the hope that, if the project is deemed worth the while, others will continue to navigate the road more clearly and effectively.

For the sake of this study, I make the choice of focusing on local development matters. Although acknowledging the ideological and theoretical implications of this choice, I have to make it for the sake of time and space, in other words, to provide my study with a necessary focus. I do not think that I can claim with integrity to write about the entire development field. Ideologically, I will only touch on global development debates, leaving these for future work or for other scholars. For now, to keep the project manageable, I have conceptualized my suggestions in such a way that they do not exclude macro issues of development, and my fieldwork focuses on local and micro-developmental issues. There is another reason for this choice. I wish to follow Latour's (2007) suggestion to conduct social science like an ant, following the local traces that construct the social links in a myopic way.

I believe that development is a value-laden notion. It is about making society better, and better is a value. Part of the debate we should keep going in the African context is about the kind of society that we would like to see. Do we all want to become filthy rich? Do we all believe economic power to be the savior of humanity? Do we believe that advanced medicine will cure the human condition? Do we believe that driving fast cars will make us treat women with respect? I have not aimed to answer these questions here or elsewhere in the book. Rather, I consider options and try to understand not only how translation plays a role in developing a society, but also how the values of a society are negotiated by translation. What I am sure about is that development, that is, changing a society, is a hermeneutic exercise. I do not claim that it is only a hermeneutic exercise, but I do claim that the change needs to be internalized hermeneutically to be sustainable. The most perfect macro-economic conditions would lead to naught if people do not "buy into" the possibilities at hand. Too many development projects have failed for us not to be sensitive about it. For example, the church in Africa is an example of a success story as far as social change is concerned (for the moment ignoring its negative impact) for the very reason that it translated its documents. If one then assumes that development is, among others, a hermeneutic exercise, understanding becomes pivotal, which means that semiotics becomes pivotal, which means that language becomes pivotal, which means that translation becomes pivotal in multilingual contexts.

I thus posit development as yet another border where "cultures" meet, where ideas that have travelled from elsewhere meet the local, where new, hybrid forms of culture result from this meeting, where the "other" has to be represented. Similar to the ethnographic encounter, it is a meeting place between the "other" and the "self". It is a site of contestation between the new and the old. It is a site where one can neither relentlessly cling to the old nor unreservedly accept the new. It is a site of judgment where information, worldviews and cultures need to be considered, reviewed, weighed, and translated. In fact, in this encounter at the border of "developed" and "un(der)developed," the power differential is even more distorted than in purely ethnographic work. Where development projects take place, it has already been decided that what "they" have to offer is good. The encounter already takes place under a clear value choice—not necessarily made by the recipients or beneficiaries of this project. And usually, this change comes in a foreign language, with foreign terminology, foreign technology, and foreign values. In these cases, translation takes place or should take place both literally and metaphorically (Lewis & Mosse, 2006). How are people at grassroots level to judge the appropriateness or not of development initiatives if it comes to them in foreign tongues? The indigenization of foreign ideas is a translation process, in all senses of the word.

So why am I taking the long and arduous route of complexity philosophy to talk about translation and development? Well, I am wondering about the following: If I want to understand a particular context, can I understand it with the logic of another context? Or perhaps what I am asking is whether there is only one kind of logic for understanding the world. I know that I am treading on thin ice here, but I have to ask these questions, although it will be asked in a very preliminary way (also see Marais, 2011). Can I challenge Western notions of translation by means of Western notions of science? Can I challenge Western paradigms of development by means of Western notions of science? I am thus looking for notions of science or logic that are somehow also critical of both modernist and postmodernist notions of science. In this regard, a philosophy of complexity, though undoubtedly born from Western thought, is also open to alternative conceptualizations such as Eastern (and perhaps African) worldviews (Hofstadter, 1979).

One of the central tenets of the Western scientific project that I shall contest in this book constitutes the notion of reductionism. Now, contesting reductionism is not an African endeavor. It is being done by Western scientists themselves, although I suspect that it contains a flavor of Eastern philosophy. However, in this book, I would like to investigate the possibility that the breakdown of reductionism, in certain fields of study and to some extent, may open up new vistas for alternative forms of logic or philosophy of science or sociology of science. This could, in theory, open a conceptual space for thinking about locality and difference in a paradoxical relationship with global philosophies. Reductionism, being a totalizing idea, seems to me radically opposed to locality and difference, as argued by Tymoczko (2007). What I am experimenting with is that a philosophy of complexity may provide us with more adequate conceptual tools for looking at and for thinking about Africa as a context for translation practice. At least, a philosophy of complexity would create a space in which Africa and Europe need not be conceptual binaries or opposites, but instead subsumed in a larger human quest.

This book thus entails an effort to propose a philosophy of translation, which may or may not have implications for contexts besides Africa. This philosophy proposes a view of translation from the perspective of complexity. The argument is thus that translation cannot be reduced to any one of its constituent phenomena or any combination of these. Translation is inherently a complex phenomenon caused by factors too complex to compute. Furthermore, the influence of translation, that is, its effects, is also too complex to compute. Translation is thus both caused by a complexity of phenomena and causes complex phenomena; that is, it is an emergent phenomenon. In closed systems, were the initial conditions identical, that is, were two identical brains to tackle the same translation job, with the same brief, at the same time, under the same conditions, one could imagine having identical translations. However, in open systems, with the slightest difference in initial conditions, one cannot predict the outcome; that is, one could not have identical translations. Also, rather than reducing translation to linguistics or literature or text, a complexity perspective will assume that translation is caused by multiple substructures.

The conceptualization of translation that I propose thus entails that translation is both an emergent phenomenon, emerging from lower-level constituent phenomena, and a lower-level phenomenon out of which higher-level social phenomena emerge. I explain in Chapter 2 that one could conceptualize it as both a supervenient and a subvenient phenomenon. Emergence, explained in greater detail later, is a concept that gained currency in an effort to escape from a reductionist approach to doing science. It aims at conceptualizing a view of reality that is neither monist nor dualist, by conceptualizing reality as a hierarchy of levels of ontology. This world is physical, out of which emerge chemical, biological, psychological, and social phenomena. The notion of emergence conceptualizes reality as one in the sense that the physical is the basic; there is no "spirit" or "soul" or "culture" apart from the physical. As Searle (1995, p. 227) claims, "Culture is the form biology takes." The approach I take in the book is thus radically ecological. I view the universe as one and humanity as a physical, chemical, biological, psychological, social phenomenon that is part of the whole of the universe. I do not subscribe to views of human dominance. In fact, I shall argue that extreme forms of constructivism philosophically negate the ecological model of reality. This view, which conceives of humanity as dominating over nature, in the fashion of fundamentalist Christianity or, for that matter, fundamentalist constructivism, is part of what causes the destruction of the universe. Humans may be unique beings in the universe, but so are baobabs and viruses. They can do things humans cannot do. The view that "nothing but constructions" exists thus seems to me connected to views on human dominance and a conceptualization that refuses to see itself as part of the universe. Humans are not the creators. They have wonderful powers of creation, true. But they are also creations (if you believe in a God) or products of creative processes. Their very human creations, such as language, are always material, which is a condition from which humanity can never escape, as argued by Jousse (2000).

I thus structured the book as follows: In Chapter 1, I explore a philosophy of complexity in which I argue that reductionism, though effective in some cases as an explanatory tool, does not suffice in all cases to explain phenomena in (especially) social reality. I argue, instead, in favor of a multi-level, hierarchical view of reality in which causality is a nonlinear, complex phenomenon.

This is followed by Chapter 2, in which I investigate the notion of emergence as it applies to translation. The framework that I propose conceptualizes the relationship between the lower-level entities from which translation emerge, as well as the relationship between translation and other social facts and institutions to which translation may contribute. Thus, translation is both an emergent semiotic phenomenon and a lower-level semiotic phenomenon in the emergence of other social phenomena.

Chapter 3 explicates the implications of the philosophy of complexity and emergence for translation studies. It focuses in particular on conceptualizing translation and translation studies and on the agency role of translators, currently highly contested debates in translation studies. I suggest that conceptualizing translation as a factor in the emergence of social facts and institutions provides a philosophical perspective from which to deal with issues of agency. If my argument, that social reality emerges out of the semiotic interactions of humans, holds, this implies that translators are indeed agents in the emergence of social reality in multilingual groups or in cases where groups come into contact with one another.

In Chapter 4, I introduce the notion of development as a contextual factor in translation. Having conceptualized development, I ask how translation is a factor in development, that is, how new social ties emerge out of translation acts. I also enquire into the contextual constraints that developing contexts may have on translation.

The next three chapters present data from different developing contexts. In Chapter 5, I look at the role of translation in local economic development and the role that local borders play in this process.

In Chapter 6, I explore the role of translation in the knowledge economy and in the distribution of knowledge.

Chapter 7 is focused on the informal economy as a particular context within which translation acts take place.

The conclusion draws certain implications, theoretical, practical, and educational, from the book.

Part I

1 Toward a Philosophy of Complexity

1. INTRODUCTION

In their introduction to their new journal, *Translation,* Arduini and Nergaard (2011, pp. 9–10) argue that, despite its apparent success, translation studies is facing a crisis. They define the nature of this crisis as one of epistemology, arguing that translation studies is caught up in a "repetition of theories and a plethora of stagnant approaches." They argue that new ways of "what we know and how we know" are on the cards and then make the point that these ways have to do with complexity and multiplicity, nonlinearity and hybridity (Arduini & Nergaard, 2011, pp. 9–10). Although I am hesitant about the rhetorical strategy of terming the problems I see as a "crisis," I do agree with them on their analysis that we need a new epistemology in translation studies, and I wish to take their argument further. To my mind, what these researchers are putting up for discussion is the Western scientific program, in general, and reductionism, in particular, and the way in which it influences the nature of translation studies.

In this chapter, I intend to show that theirs is not an isolated argument. In numerous fields of study, one finds a questioning of the Western scientific program and of the impasses it has left in these fields of study (Heylighen et al., 2007). This questioning pertains to both modernism and postmodernism, which can both be said to be reductionist, the first to structure, logic, and construct and the latter to anti-structure, non-logic and deconstruct (M. Taylor, 2001, pp. 47–72). In other words, both modernism and postmodernism can be said to be unable to hold alternative, paradoxical, complex views of reality. What scholars all over the spectrum seem to be looking for is an epistemology of complexity, not necessarily to replace reductionism but to supplement it or to subsume it within a philosophy of complexity. Complexity philosophy has shown that replacing one perspective by another, which is assumed to be better but which is equally reductive, does not solve the kind of problems scholars are faced with in both the natural and social sciences. A consensus seems to be emerging that what is needed is the ability to embrace paradoxical perspectives to supplement new insights to existing ones without replacing what may be of use in the existing perspectives. Realizing that reality is complex and that scholarly activity has to deal with this complexity is becoming a zeitgeist. Thus, this chapter sets out to propose the framework of a philosophy of complexity within which to think about translation.

A second motivation for this chapter is that, to my mind, translation studies is in need of a philosophical foundation. As a field of study, it lacks a philosophical underpinning. Despite much having been written about how to conceptualize translation studies as a scientific field of study (Gambier & Van Doorslaer, 2009; Hermans, 2007; Holmes, 2002; Jakobson, 2004; Toury, 1995; Tymoczko, 2007), I contend that not enough has been done philosophically to conceptualize the field. Except for Tymoczko, the discussions have mostly been of a technical or theoretical nature, as in Holmes's map of translation studies. Also, the discussions tended to be attempts to define translation in terms of other fields of studies, for example, Hermans and Jakobson, who both make use of linguistic approaches. What one does not find is a philosophy of translation as one would with a philosophy of history or a philosophy of mathematics. As I understand it, when the question, "What is x?" is asked of a field of study, x, one moves into the domain of philosophy or philosophy of science. These are the meta-questions concerning each field, which are not strictly questions concerning the content of the field itself but are questions that have moved into probing the nature of the field itself. Thus, discussing the nature of translation is a philosophical endeavor, not a translation studies endeavor. Answering the question, "What is translation?" means that one moves to a meta-theoretical or philosophical level of conceptualizing. To my mind, this has not yet been done for translation studies. Translation has, to my mind, not yet been conceptualized within the larger philosophical framework of Western science, which may be one reason why it is suffering from an epistemological crisis, as claimed by Arduini and Nergaard (2011). The result is that translation studies has been conceptualized either "as" something else, that is, linguistics, literature, pragmatics, culture, sociology, ideology, or as in competition with something else, in order to defend the field against borrowing from or encroaching on other disciplines. I suggest that the time has come to conceptualize translation as translation, an effort started by Tymoczko (2007) but, to my mind, not completed by her. I take this effort up again in Chapter 3.

In this chapter, I first provide a brief historical overview of the development of complexity philosophy/theory. Then I consider some of the major lines of thought in a philosophy of complexity. This is followed by a section on complex systems theory, and the chapter concludes with a broad overview of the implications of this philosophical position for translation studies.

Before proceeding, I need to point out a problem I had in writing this chapter. I found myself caught between a number of demands. On one hand, I had to provide a thorough discussion on complexity for the sake of intellectual honesty and for the sake of not falling into the first trap of transdisciplinary work: shallowness. On the other hand, I had to provide an understandable overview of complexity. If the discussion becomes too technical, I may lose the translation studies audience. Also, I have not been trained as a complexity theorist, so I cannot claim the depth of knowledge and insight that experts in the field have. I thus acknowledge that I am probably the fool storming in where the more expert angels fear to tread. I cannot, however, refrain from writing about this mode of thinking that has gripped my imagination.

2. SITUATING COMPLEXITY

The philosophical roots of complexity have been with humanity for a very long time. The philosophical tensions between Plato and Aristotle, one focusing on the universal and the unchanging and another focusing on the contingent and change, bear testimony to this tension (see, for instance, Mitchell, 2009, pp. 15–22; Stumpf, 1975, pp. 48–113). In a sense, the modernism/postmodernism debate is still based on this tension. Modernism claims to be able to explain reality by reducing it to some universal, unchanging principle(s), which is obviously a reduction, while postmodernism claims to explain it by considering everything as contingent and context dependent, which is just another reduction. This kind of binary thinking has permeated all of scholarly reality. In philosophy, one finds the binaries of subject and object, universalism and individualism, constancy, and change. In anthropology, the battle rages between the self and the other. In sociology, the individual and society are posited against one another, and in translation studies, source and target remain in tension, to name but a few. All of these tensions are based on a logic that is not able to deal with complexity, such as that source and target are both needed and related to one another in a complex way for a theory of translation. It is also based on a fear of uncertainty (see Callon et al., 2011), such as that the exact relationship between the two components of the binary will forever remain a complex matter which scholars may not be able to explain in detail and that this inability to provide exact knowledge may lead to academics losing face. Also, these tensions are not able to deal with the complex nature of translation as a phenomenon that has its roots in language, literature, culture, society and power—and all of this at the same time.

A philosophy of complexity thus represents an attempt to solve these tensions by taking some kind of meta-stance (Hofstadter, 1979, pp. 103–152), standing back at least one level—and possible many more—and viewing the universal and the contingent, consistency and change as constituent factors of reality. In this sense, it moves away from linear logic toward paradoxical or nonlinear or complex logic to be able to do justice to the complexity of reality. Also, through this stance, it hopes to do justice to the wholeness and interrelatedness of reality. In this sense, the interest in complexity can be seen as an epistemological effort which tries to see whether some of the age-old binaries and tensions cannot be resolved if one looks at them from a different point of view, or a different level of view. At the same time, it would not suffice to call complexity theory a shift in perspective only. As will become clear from the chapter, the interest in complexity has also been sparked by advancements in computing power (Mitchell, 2009, pp. 56–70) and the development of network culture (Castells, 2000a; Latour, 2007; Taylor, 2001). Before computers, most complex problems were merely inaccessible to scholars. One cannot build mathematical models of weather prediction by hand. So, it was the work of Alan Turing and John von Neumann that provided much of the technological backup that is necessary to study systems (Coveny & Highfield, 1995, pp. 43–88). To this, one can add developments that have led to the demise of the Newtonian ideal of reductionism such as Einstein's relativity theory, Heisenberg's uncertainty principle, and Gödel's incompleteness theorem.

In a sense, complexity thinking seems to be inevitable. The whole program of Western science has focused on analyzing the parts of reality in order to understand them better (Johnson, 2009, pp. 4–16; Van Kooten Niekerk & Buhl, 2004b). Now, the realization is dawning on scholars that analysis can only take you so far, because only a small part of reality is to be explained by the way parts are, or only a small part of reality can be understood by understanding the parts of it. Much of reality is to be explained not by the parts themselves but by the way in which they relate to one another or by the way in which they are becoming, the way in which constituent parts form wholes (Latour, 2007; Van Huyssteen, 2004). The focus has thus shifted from an analysis of parts to a focus on the relationships and connections between parts and between parts and wholes. Also, the focus has shifted from an interest in phenomena to an interest in processes, that is, the way in which phenomena are the result of the interaction of their constituent parts. The philosophical problems of stasis and movement, and of how both constitute reality, are what are within the purview of complexity thinking. Let me hurry to say that I do not suggest replacing analysis with synthesis or being with process. I hope to incorporate these binaries in a complexity view in which both sides of the binary find their rightful place in thinking about a particular phenomenon.

Another historical pointer is the late nineteenth century when basic ideas of (chaotic) systems thinking came to be (Heylighen et al., 2007; Sawyer [2005] also provides an interesting overview of this history in the first half of his book). Scholars such as Maxwell and Poincaré started questioning the implications of Newtonian science (Mitchell, 2009, pp. 20–21). Sawyer (2005) provides quite a detailed overview of what he calls the three waves of social systems thinking, that is, structural functionalism, general systems theory and chaos theory and emergence and complexity, as well as the historical roots of emergence and complexity. Although not everybody will agree with his division, he clearly indicates that complexity thinking did not suddenly arise on the scene; it has been in the making for at least a century. Sawyer (2005, pp. 31–33) also points to the role that British emergentists played in the development of complexity studies by focusing their efforts on the role of part and whole in society. In the South African context, the then prime minister, Jan Smuts (1926), wrote an influential book called *Holism and Evolution*. In this book, he argued that evolution is driven by the needs or requirements of a whole, not the parts, and that one thus has to focus your interest on understanding wholes. The initial phase of systems thinking was followed by Von Bertalanffy's general systems theory in the second half of the twentieth century (see, for instance, Sawyer, 2005, pp. 14–19).

It was chaos theory in the 1970s and 1980s, however, which provided a huge impetus to complexity theory (Coveny & Highfield, 1995; Mitchell, 2009, pp. 15–39). Out of this development, came the Santa Fe Institute in the mid-1980s, which became the first institutionalized brand of complexity studies (Cohen & Stewart, 1994; Waldrop, 1992), though not the only one. Complexity studies is thus a transdisciplinary field that brings together insights from philosophy, mathematics, physics, chemistry, biology, psychology, linguistics, sociology, economics and other fields in an effort to understand reality as a complex phenomenon.

3. A FRAMEWORK FOR AN EPISTEMOLOGY OF COMPLEXITY

My argument in this section is that the Western scientific project has been dominated by "a paradigm of simplification" (Morin, 2008, p. 3), which "mutilates" (Montuori, 2008, p. ix; Morin, 2008, p. 51) reality by imposing a simple conceptualization on a complex reality. This paradigm attempts to provide simple laws underlying complex reality, which is the reductionist (and covertly religious) ideal of explaining all of reality by means of one cause. I do not have space here to go into all the philosophical motives behind this search for simplicity. Suffice to say that this Newtonian paradigm believes that, behind the chaos, there is order, simplicity, and oneness. Implied in this approach is the notion of determinism. Being subjected to precise, simple laws, reality unfolds in a predetermined, mechanical way. Having started in the natural sciences, this paradigm has also taken root in the social sciences or humanities (Latour, 2007) and, I argue, underlies some of the conceptualizations in translation studies. The problem with this paradigm is not that it is wrong in all cases, but rather that it cannot explain all cases, especially in the social sciences and humanities. As indicated earlier, my aim is not to replace it, but to amend it, to make it more complex.

The theory and, to a much lesser extent, the philosophy of complexity have mushroomed over the last three decades to the extent that one chapter does not really do justice to the complexity of the debates among complexity theorists themselves and among proponents and antagonists of the approach.

I shall not represent complexity studies as a homogenous field, but I can also not go into all the minute differences in point of view. Hopefully, this representation will honor both difference and similarity in a sufficient way to avoid both chaos and sterile equilibrium, but, being an overview, it will most probably be more biased towards a picture of equilibrium.

In my view, the paradigm of simplicity is the cause of the binary thinking that dominates the reductionist paradigm. As Morin (2008, p. 39) argues, this paradigm can see the one and the many, but it cannot see that the one is simultaneously the many. It can see phenomena, but it cannot see, or at least it cannot theorize, the interrelatedness of all phenomena (Morin, 2008, p. 84). Put differently, it can see parts and it can see wholes, but it cannot see the interrelationships between parts and parts and between parts and wholes. The simplicity paradigm cannot see that difference is similarity and that the universal is the particular. In short, it cannot deal with complexity, or paradox. In this sense, a philosophy of complexity has a synthesizing aim based on analysis. As Latour (2007) claims, a phenomenon such as the social cannot be thought of in terms of parts and wholes, but in terms of the relationships between nodes. The focus needs to move from things to what is in between things, to how things are related. The focus needs to change from things to movements of things.

As a meta-philosophical approach (Morin, 2008, p. 48), complexity philosophy tries to deal with all kinds of complexities in reality. Rather than trying to reduce complexity to simpler, more manageable notions, complexity theory attempts to face complexity head-on. Philosophically speaking, a philosophy of complexity tries to think about reality without choosing any one explanation thereof. To give a few examples, thought assuming a complexity perspective will refuse to give priority to either part or whole, to either the universal or the particular, to either rationality or irrationality, to either modernism or postmodernism. In this sense, it is a unifying idea claiming that there may be some unifying ideas and that not all unifying ideas hold true. In a sense, it turns recursivity into its logic (Hofstadter, 1979; Morin, 2008, p. 61). The universal is produced by the particular which is produced by the universal or, in Morin's (2008, p. 61) example, individuals create society which produces the individuals that produce society.

Morin (2008, p. 85) further argues that the Western scientific paradigm is disjunctive and reductive, separating or isolating a phenomenon from its environment. Latour (2007) also argues against the tendency to separate the natural and the social, while arguing that they are connected with various links (see also Atkinson et al., 2008). With this way of thinking, analytical thinking, the Newtonian paradigm believes that it will eliminate the problem of complexity. This paradigm is concerned with dominance, in particular with human dominance over nature and thus with control. One of the principles of Newtonian science is predictability, which complexity science argues does not hold in all cases, especially in the humanities (see

Heylighen et al., 2007). By building conceptual structures that are able to predict, humanity, according to the Newtonian ideal, remains in control of the chaotic nature of the future. The Newtonian world assumes that complexity is only apparent; what is real is simple (Heylighen et al., 2007). If one can thus break through the complexity, you can get to a point where you are in control, managing reality and constructing reality. Western science has deep religious roots, putting humanity in control of reality. Prigogine (1996, p. 38) argues that one of the reasons why it has taken Western science so long to arrive at theories that deal with irreversibility and probability is that Western science was dominated by a quasi-divine point of view. Admitting the possibility of irreversibility and probability also meant letting go of this quasi-divine point of view. When Western science stepped down from the point of view that the future is determined, certainty came to an end (Prigogine, 1996, p. 183). One could thus argue that the Western scientific ideal is inherently un-ecological, not willing to see itself as part of an infinitely large, infinitely complex system. On his part, Morin advises scholars to conceptualize complexity rather than eliminate it. The implication of this argument is that scholarly thought needs to be able to live with disorder, complexity, paradox, or, as Latour (2007) suggests, it should follow reality like an ant, through all the particular, complex labyrinths to and through which it leads.

Rather than think it out of our theories and philosophies, we need to include complexity and deal with it. Complexity theory tries to deal with complexity by posing a meta-meta-narrative allowing for a complex array of meta-narratives. As a meta-meta-narrative, it is aware of the fact that it cannot know everything about the meta-narratives it is studying (Hofstadter, 1979, pp. 15–27). It attempts to hold onto a complex view of reality while paradoxically conceptualizing a hierarchical view of reality. This hierarchy is not a separating or isolating hierarchy, but a connecting hierarchy where what seems paradoxical at one level could be resolved at a higher level.

Scholars from various fields seem to agree on the problematic nature of aspects of Western rationality. Prigogine (1996, pp. 1–7), for instance, spends the introduction to his book *The End of Certainty* on analyzing the problematic nature of determinism. To what extent can one claim that the future is open, or determined? With the theory of non-linearity and its relationship to negentropy, the "arrow of time" has again become of importance in scientific discourse and thinking (Kauffman, 1995; Prigogine, 1996, p. 3; Tyulenev, 2011a, pp. 133–134). He indicates how classical science focused on order and stability (and thus the reversibility of systems because they are mechanical), while the new rationality looks at "fluctuations, instability, multiple choices and limited predictability . . ." (Prigogine, 1996, p. 4). The new rationality he suggests views laws as expressing possibilities or probabilities. Before, science was about cause, not chance. Now it is about chance, possibility, and probability. In this new view, freedom and determinism also seem to hang together in a complex relationship, at the edge of chaos.

From the above, it is clear that the simplifying approach not only poses epistemological problems but also ethical problems. It not only problematizes the nature of our knowledge and the ethics of mutilating our objects of study, but it also poses serious questions as to our relationship towards the Other, that is, phenomena that do not fit into our schemata (also see Mbembe 2001, pp. 173–206). With these claims, Morin problematizes both knowledge and the organization of knowledge itself. As Arduini and Nergaard (2011, pp. 8–15) argue, it is the problem of what we know and how we know that poses a problem to current translation studies.

Having pointed out some problems with reductionist science, I have to concur with (Heylighen et al., 2007) that complexity science has actually, up to recently, been lacking a philosophical or, more particularly, an epistemological basis. As with the other scholars discussed earlier, he argues that complexity is a response to the limitations of the reductionistic, analytic bias in Western science, which is based on analysis, isolation, and the complete description of phenomena (see Heylighen et al. [2007] for a more detailed description of the premises of Newtonian science). However, what seems to be lacking is more systematic work on building a philosophy of complexity and on exploring the implications and problems thereof. As I am not a philosopher by trade, it is not in my current scope of ability to work out such a framework. I thus merely draw on the conceptualization of two scholars who have done some work in this regard, that is, Morin and Cilliers.

A philosophy of complexity starts from the assumption that reality may be both simple and complex, and it refuses to choose either as primary or dominating (Cohen & Stewart, 1994, pp. 396–443). It assumes that, in the case of all the typical binaries or conflicting concepts such as part and whole, mechanical and organical, universal and particular, culture and nature, both need to be conceptualized as constituting reality. None of these can be subsumed into their counter-concepts but need to be maintained in a paradoxical tension. Complexity is a philosophical stance that does not try to reduce either the one into the many or the many into the one. Rather it is a philosophy of paradox that maintains both one and many, universal and contingent, and, in the case of translation studies, source and target, self and other as constituent parts of reality. It is a philosophy that does not reduce messiness to some neat principle or law (Latour, 2007), but rather seeks to deal with both organization and disorganization (Morin, 2008, p. 6). This philosophy shuns idealism because it refuses to convey primacy on the power of ideas to dominate reality. A philosophy of complexity is also aware of the irrational nature of reality and does not claim to rationalize everything. In this sense, it is neither a radically constructive nor a radically deconstructive, nor a radically positivist stance.

A philosophy of complexity also tries to deal with determinism by conceptualizing the emergence of higher-order phenomena from lower-order phenomena. In this way, it frees scientific thinking from reductionism and the concomitant determinism that implies that "everything" has been given in the physical nature of reality. Out of the physical substratum, so complexity theory argues, much more than the physical is able to emerge (Holland, 1995). The process of the development or evolution of reality has not been determined solely by its physical substructure. It is realized every day through the emergence, from the physical, of new phenomena. The process of development is thus not deterministic but free, historical, probable (Heylighen et al., 2007). Simultaneously, one has to consider that development is not absolutely free but constrained by (even contingent) structure, history, and probability. Everything may be possible, but not everything is realized. Thus, freedom and determinism are also part of a binary structure that needs to be subsumed paradoxically in a philosophy of complexity. Structure and form are again fashionable terms in complexity theory, but this time they are the concomitants of local and historical processes, not timeless and universal ideas.

By means of the notion of emergence, built on a hierarchical worldview, complexity theory also seeks to overcome dualism. Mind is not something that is added to matter. Life is not something that is added to chemicals. Culture is not something that is added to nature. Rather, as the philosopher John Searle (1995, p. 227) says, culture is the form nature takes in certain cases. It is the particular organization, the particular relationships between natural phenomena that beget culture. This view of reality, which is neither monist, that is, everything is physical, nor dualist, that is, something has been added to the physical, is shared by complexity theorists. Yes, complexity theorists are physicalists in the sense that they agree that the physical is the basis of reality and that there is nothing "more" to reality than the physical. Life is not a substance added; mind is not a substance added. Life, mind, spirit, and culture are all real because they are the forms that the physical take in certain instances. Out of particular interactions between physical phenomena, emerge chemical phenomena. Particular relationships between the physical/chemical lead to the emergence of biological phenomena whereas relationships between the physical/chemical/biological lead to psychological phenomena. Out of the physical/chemical/biological/psychological relationships or interactions or connections emerge social phenomena. The advantage of this view is that one does not have to presuppose the addition of "extras" such as life, mind, and spirit. The particular configuration of the substrata leads to the new, the more, which emerges. In the next chapter, I go into emergence in much more detail.

A philosophy of complexity has strong links with complex systems theory in the sense that it is interested in wholes and parts, in how parts relate to one another to create wholes and in how wholes constrain parts (Van Kooten Niekerk & Buhl, 2004a, p. 4). This systems thinking operates at all levels of reality, even viewing humanity as part of the natural system (Morin, 2008, p. 8). However, not all systems theory is complex. Systems theory itself went through a development process, which has resulted in complex systems theory (Sawyer, 2005). Morin (2008, p. 10) argues that systems theory provides three philosophical advances by (1) conceptualizing of reality as a complex unity that cannot be reduced to the sum of its constituent parts, (2) conceiving of system not as a purely formal notion but as "an ambiguous, ghostly" notion, and (3) situating itself at the level of transdisciplinarity. In addition, a philosophy of complexity has links with actor-network theory, which is also based on a view of systems and on notions of complexity (Latour, 2007).

One of the subtexts of this chapter is to consider the implications of a philosophy or theory of complexity for the humanities, that is, looking wider than merely translation studies. Although I refer to him in more detail in the next chapter on emergence, the work of Van Huyssteen (2004) is an interesting example of an effort to think about the whole of reality from a complexity perspective. It obviously means that one needs to hold complex views on the relationship between nature and culture. Complexity has been considered in various natural sciences and some social sciences, that is, economic and studies on organization or management. What its implications are for the humanities, that is, anthropology, languages, history, art, and psychology, is not yet clear, though Latour's work, which I discuss in more detail later, could provide one avenue (also see Atkinson et al. 2008). My work in this book is yet another initial step in the direction of this ideal. Epstein and Axtell (1996, p. 19) seem to express the idea behind most of the work on complexity succinctly when they explain their aim as the following:

> The broad aim of this research is to *begin the development of a more unified social science, one that embeds evolutionary processes in a computational environment that simulates demographics, the transmission of culture, conflict, economics, disease, the emergence of groups, and agent coadaptation with an environment, all from the bottom up.* (Italics in original)

Discussing complexity is a complex endeavor itself. Complexity is not only a quantitative phenomenon. Of course, it is because of the size of certain systems that one could call them complex. However, phenomena could also be called complex because of their uncertainty, indetermination and randomness (Callon et al., 2011). Phenomena are complex because they are related to chance, precisely because they do not obey the laws of linear causality. This uncertainty relates to both the uncertainty in us, the limitations in our ability to comprehend and the uncertainty in the phenomena, because they are knowable to a limited extent only, and in the uncertainty in the interrelationships between phenomena, because they are complex. As Morin (2008, p. 20) puts it, complexity "concerns semi-random systems in which order is inseparable from the randomness that separates them". Complexity thus refers to the occurrence of both order and disorder in certain systems. Phenomena are complex because one is not able to get inside of them. This leads one to a philosophy of complexity which is able to deal with the insufficient and the fuzzy, with ambiguity in relationships, e.g. between subject/object and order/disorder.

A number of scholars draw a distinction between complicated and complex systems. Miller and Page (2007, p. 9) claim that complicated systems consist of elements or parts that remain relatively independent from one another. In contrast, complex systems have parts that have a high level of dependency on one another, that is, a high level of interrelatedness. In fact, it seems to me that one of the major insights of complexity theory is the view that reality is not only constituted by things but also by the relationship between things. In some cases, it is actually the relationships, the particular configurations (Latour, 2007), that constitute reality, not the things in themselves. This new kind of science, which is able to study both relationships and things, should thus also be able to synthesize and not only to analyze. It should be able to work across disciplinary boundaries. It should be much more of a network science than the silo type of science structures we currently have in the managerialist approaches to higher education.

Miller and Page (2007, pp. 6–7) argue that complexity is interested in an "in-between". In the main, complexity is interested in the "in-between" disciplines, in the "in-between" stasis and chaos, in the "in-between" control and anarchy, in the "in-between" continuous and discrete, and in the "in-between" particularity and universality. I should point out, however, that it is not only interested in the in-between as a place, a stasis, a concept. Complexity thinking is also interested in the in-between as an action, a verb, a movement (Latour, 2007). It is thus interested in the in-between and in the in-between-ing. Connecting this interest to current debates in translation studies, one could claim that complexity is interested in border, hybridity, and the effect of a reorganization of the same substrata. To this in-betweenness and in-between-ing, I shall return in Chapter 4.

To my mind, complexity is philosophically interested in what is usually called paradox. It not only attempts to add nonlinear logic to linear logic, but senses and tries to express this sense that reality holds insoluble paradoxes, thus adding paradox to logic if you wish. An excellent example of this insight is the work of the Old Testament scholar Walter Brueggemann (1997). In the mid-1990s, he published his monumental *Old Testament Theology* in which the underlying assumption was a logical break between the various voices in the Old Testament.[1] Until then, the assumption was that there had to be some theological unity to the Old Testament, most probably because God is one and because human logic dictates unity via reductionism. Brueggemann stepped out of this mould, claiming that the Old Testament represents two different perspectives on life, that is, witness and counter-witness. At the same time, I formulated a similar argument in my doctoral dissertation, claiming that trying to read the book of Judges in the Old Testament from a Western, unifying perspective is to mutilate the book—to use Morin's term—and to force a particular reading on the text (J. Marais, 1997). Rather, I claimed, Judges makes sense if the reader assumes perspectivism, juxtaposition, and paradox as the logical principles underlying its composition. Coming back to translation studies after this digression, it seems that complexity theory has, in its philosophical foundations, the assumption that one should look for other nuances in logic and causality than the linear, reductionist, unitarian logic currently dominating the Western scientific project.

Thus, to summarize, a philosophy of complexity holds a view of reality that is hierarchical, nonlinear, paradoxical, nonequilibrium and that views systems as open. This view could be characterized as ecological in that it sees the whole of reality as interrelated, having emerged from the physical. It is a philosophy that sees reality as historical, as a process of becoming. It sees its knowledge of this world as preliminary, probable, ever changing as reality is changing. An implication for the practice of translation studies is that a philosophy of complexity implies transdisciplinarity, precisely because it does not go along with the analytical simplification and managerialist division of reality. Translation studies, as a field of study interested in the in-betweenness and the in-between-ing, can thus not be a field of study on its own, but should be an in-between field of study.

4. COMPLEX ADAPTIVE SYSTEMS

In what follows, I attempt to outline some of the most salient concepts of complexity science. Here, once again, I am faced with difficulty. After the establishment of the Santa Fe Institute in the mid-1980s, many publications on complexity have been related to the Institute in some way or another. Some were written my members of the Institute, some by fellows, some by students, and some by converts. Much of my representation will thus be of the Santa Fe "brand" of complexity theory. My main criticism against this brand is that much of its thought is, to my mind, still reductionistic, although one could perhaps argue in mitigation that many of the Santa Fe scholars do much work in natural sciences where reductionism has proved useful to some extent. However, in the humanities and/or social sciences, I think there is much less room for reductionism and this is the reason why I started the discussion with Morin, Heylighen et al., and Latour. It is also the reason why I shall close again with their work. To my mind, complexity should not be conceptualized only to justify reductionism at a deep level. It should be a philosophical or at least epistemological frame of reference that takes as its point of departure the refusal to reduce that which cannot be reduced. However, in a debate on complexity, one cannot pretend that the Santa Fe phenomenon did not happen. Their ranks boast not only Nobel Prize winners such as Murray Gell-Mann, Ilya Prigogine, and Per Bak but influential names in a variety of fields of study such as John Holland, Stuart Kaufman, Melanie Mitchell, and Brian Arthur.

In the previous section, I focused on an epistemology of complexity; that is, I had a more philosophical intent. In this section, I move into more theoretical matters because most of what is called "complexity theory" is actually a form of systems theory. The epistemological or philosophical framework of the previous section does not need to be of a systems type, as Cilliers (1998) argued when he decided to connect complexity with notions of deconstruction or postmodernism. When applying complexity perspectives to fields of study such as biology or physics or economics, it is, however, mostly done within the ambit of systems theory. What follows is thus an exploration of complex systems theory, with a particular Santa Fe flavor. I do not pretend that I am able to draw a clear-cut distinction between what is epistemology and what is theory, because the two are complexly interrelated. However, I shall focus on the Santa Fe version of complex systems theory, which they call complex adaptive systems. The intention is, in Chapter 3, to conceptualize translation within the framework of complex adaptive systems.

Within the field of complex systems theory, the particular nomenclature used to refer to these systems differs. Mitchell (2009) spends an entire chapter on probable conceptualizations of complexity, concluding that a unified notion of complexity is not currently in existence. She considers complexity as size, entropy, algorithmic information content, logical depth, thermodynamic depth, statistics, fractal dimensions, and degree of hierarchy. Some complexity scholars refer to their field of interest as open systems, some prefer dynamic systems, and within the Santa Fe School, complex adaptive systems has become the preferred term (Miller & Page, 2007, p. xvii). I use complex adaptive systems, a term that focuses on both the complex nature of these systems as well as their historicity and their open, process-related nature. What the term *complex* in complex adaptive systems also adds to our understanding is that one does not have to assume that you can only describe a system as a whole once you understand each component, that is, each agent or actor in, for example, a social system (Miller & Page, 2007, p. xvii). This insight challenges the current focus in translation studies where, in case study after case study, attempts are made to argue for particular intentions at the level of the individual translator, without any argument as to how individual acts construe the whole or are constrained by the whole. I am not advocating a return to previous attempts at systems theory in translation studies such as that of Hermans (1999). What complex adaptive systems theory adds is a perspective on the complex, paradoxical relationship between agent and system, a perspective that contains benefits for translation studies (as I further argue in Chapter 3). Further, by calling these systems adaptive, one opens the conceptual space to theories of change and stability as it relates to these systems because you are thinking about these systems as open to influences from other systems or, as it is called in some theories, the environment.

Emmeche (2004, pp. 31–32) discusses, or rather lists, a number of features of complexity. I discuss them in this chapter but, for the sake of completeness, have presented them here in bullet form:

- Complex systems are hierarchical.
- Simple laws may generate complex behavior.
- Complex systems self organize.
- Open systems theory sees the introduction of history in hard science.
- Complex phenomena exhibit emergent properties.
- The behavior of complex systems is difficult to predict.
- Emergent properties exert downward causation of the parts from which they emerged.
- Complex phenomena can be simulated on a computer.
- Biological complex systems reflect the genotype-phenotype duality.
- Complexity is a historical phenomenon.
- In complex living systems, one finds relationships between natural selection, developmental constraints, and self-organization.
- Complexity occurs at the edge of chaos.
- Complex systems are characterized by self-organized criticality.
- Complex systems require explanations other than reductionist ones.

What follows is a discussion of the various features of a theory of complex adaptive systems.

4.1 Hierarchy

As indicated in the previous section, one of the aims of complexity theorists is to transcend the materialistic limitations of reductionism as reductionism usually assumes that all of life can be reduced to the physical part thereof (Coveny & Highfield, 1995, p. 14; Van Kooten Niekerk & Buhl, 2004a, p. 3). This kind of reductionism is not only limited to physicalism. One also finds it in cases in which the mind is reduced to chemistry or biology, society is reduced to individuals, and translation is reduced to language, literature, culture or some other constituent part. The way in which complexity scholars foresee solving the problem is by conceptualizing a hierarchical view of reality. In this view, reality is seen as consisting of "levels" of existence that emerge from one another; that is, the physical is given, and out of it emerges, in hierarchical order, the chemical, biological, psychological, and social. Complexity theorists do not believe that something new is added to form the next level; for example, that mind or spirit is added to the biological at the level of the psychological. What they do believe is that the next level is the form the previous level takes through particular new interactions amongst parts of the previous level or through particular new organizations between the parts. This means that, at the chemical level, there is nothing more than at the physical level. What accounts for the difference is the interrelationship or organization between the physical parts that has changed to create new phenomena. Paradoxically, there is more at the chemical level, but the more has not been added from the outside. The more is the new relationships, the new organization, and the new links and connections. Equally, nothing new has been added to the chemical level to achieve the biological level. The biological is the emergent result of particular interactions of chemicals, and so the psychological is the emergent result of particular interactions of biological phenomena. In this way, complexity theorists, in a complex, paradoxical way, maintain a monist view of reality as well as avoid a reductionist view. An example of this kind of complexity thinking is documented by Emmeche (2004, p. 33), who argues for a hybrid or complex position on complexity which he calls methodological reductionism. This view holds that reduction can be maintained as a valid tool in science without falling into the trap of what he calls constructionist reductionism, that is, the possibility of precise prediction and building up all higher-level phenomena from lower-level phenomena.

Stuart Kauffman works out the implications of this position in much more detail. What he (Kauffman, 1995, p. 302) does is reconceptualize humanity within the larger cosmos. Reality is not ours to control, to command. It is something we cannot control and something of which we stand in awe. This is contrary to the humanistic, constructivist position. Also, in translation studies, which is currently dominated by constructivist views, one has to reconsider the notion of human control over reality. I would rather suggest that one takes a complexity view in which humanity and its social creations are paradoxically material and nonmaterial, which implies that it is paradoxically constructed and constructing (see also Latour, 2007). In Chapter 2 and 3, I return to this point. For now, it will suffice to indicate that complexity theory implies quite a radical ecological perspective, which may contribute to Tymoczko's (2006) ideal of an international translation studies because it considers the constraints of various times and localities.

Apart from its questioning of strong forms of constructivism, the hierarchical conceptualization of reality also makes it possible to consider a phenomenon like translation both in its relationship to its substrata and its superstrata. Thus, translation could be conceptualized as emerging from the physical-chemical-biological-psychological substratum and playing a role in the emergence of various superstrata in social reality, for example, the economy, law, medicine, and architecture. One thus needs the substrata for translation to emerge, and one needs translation for the superstrata to emerge.

4.2 Complex Behavior from Simple Laws

In the words of Mitchell (2009, p. 4), the field of complex systems theory is "an interdisciplinary field of research that seeks to explain how large numbers of relatively simple entities organize themselves, without the benefit of any central controller, into a collective whole that creates patterns, uses information, and, in some cases, evolves and learns." Her conceptualization holds most of the salient features of complexity, that is, interdisciplinarity, self-organization, connectedness, part–whole relationships, open systems, life, and evolution.

However, her point of view also expresses one of the major problems with complexity theory, namely the reductive tendencies in some brands of complexity theory. I hope to clarify the point that a complexity perspective neither rejects nor accepts reductionism. Heylighen et al. (2007) argue that too much of complexity theory is still informed by a reductionist perspective, that is, seeking simplicity beneath the apparent complexity of reality. I agree and argue that a view of a complex reality undergirded by simple laws does not solve the problem. As Cohen and Stewart (1994, pp. 388–418) argue, one has to provide both for cases where simple reality is undergirded by complex laws, and cases where complex reality is undergirded by simple laws. Their notions of simplexity and complicity, though somewhat vague, do thus make some sense. In certain cases, it may be true that simple laws give rise to complex behavior, for example, Newtonian physics. The aim of a philosophy of complexity should not be to negate reductionism, but rather to include it in a larger frame of reference, that is, the complex. So, although it may be true that simple laws sometimes give rise to complex behavior, it quite often does not, and therefore, one cannot project onto everything the effectiveness of reductionism as an explanatory method. From a complexity perspective, simple laws may cause complex behavior, complex laws may cause simple behavior, simple laws may cause simple behavior, and complex laws may cause complex behavior. A complexity perspective is one that refuses to choose for a particular meta-frame of reference.

I suggest that one can conceptualize of translation as a complex phenomenon caused by complex, nonlinear laws. I shall work out over the next three chapters the implications of theorizing translation within a theory of complex adaptive systems. First, Tyulenev (2011a), building on the work of Hermans and others, has convincingly argued that one can conceptualize of translation as a system. The features of the systems theory put forward by complexity scholars will become clear in the rest of the chapter.

4.3 Self-Organization

In their definition, Coveny and Highfield (1995, p. 7) stress the collective nature of the behavior of certain phenomena which are of interest to complexity theorists whereas scholars such as Fischer (2009) provide a good overview on a variety of "swarm" phenomena. Their definition, "complexity is the study of the behavior of macroscopic collections of such units that are endowed with the potential to evolve in time," focuses attention on the fact that this new kind of philosophy or science is not interested in phenomena alone but in the relationships between phenomena (Coveny & Highfield, 1995, p. 7), as I have already claimed. In complexity approaches, one detects a sense that analysis has reached its explanatory potential. Having arrived at quarks and the like, we can virtually not cut reality up into smaller pieces. What we are now interested in is how these pieces relate to one another. In Chapter 3, I work out the implications of this point of view for translation studies in more detail. It will suffice to argue here that translation studies is fraught with examples of scholars trying to understand the "parts" of translation, that is, language, literature, pragmatics, culture, and ideology. It seems now to be the time to ask how these parts relate to one another. What we seem to be lacking is a conceptual space in which we are able to relate the parts of translation to the whole and the whole to the parts. Also, we need a conceptual space in which we can see translation as a whole as a part of larger social reality, that is, translation as a subsystem of social reality. To my mind, complex adaptive systems theory, with its notion of the global self-organized criticality that emerges from local interactions of agents, provides such a conceptual space.

The notion of self-organization holds that, in many kinds of complex systems, agents act locally, with no view of contributing to the whole. The whole emerges, through self-organization, from the local interactions. One of the most fascinating scholars of complexity is Stuart Kauffman. A biologist, Kauffman (1995) challenges Darwin's explanation that, through natural selection, life is accidental or coincidental. He argues that there is too much order in reality for it to be an accident. The fascinating feature of complex adaptive systems is not that they are accidental but that they are ordered (Kauffman, 1995, p. 15). Therefore, life is not an accident but to be expected. He thus poses self-organization as the guiding principle of life. This principle does not revoke natural selection and contingency, but rather augments it: Both self-organization and natural selection are principles underlying the self-organization of life (Kauffman, 1995, pp. 8–9). Kauffman is thus a complexity scholar in the sense that he does not reduce life to one cause.

If one asks about the definition of life, you cannot say that life is "in" something or is something added to reality. The same atoms that can be found in a dead stone, for example, iron, can also form part of a living system. According to Kauffman (1995, p. 24), therefore, the difference lies in the way in which particular parts interact. If they interact in a certain way, one has a dead system, in equilibrium. If they interact in another way, one has a living, nonequilibrium system. This argument has two implications. On one hand, certain features cannot be explained by reduction but by emergence. The "essence" of life is not found in the parts but in the interaction between parts; that is, it is an emergent property arising from the interaction or links among parts. This means that life is not to be explained by reductionism but by emergence. On the other hand, the interactions among parts of a phenomenon can explain the nature of that phenomenon.

Applying this insight to translation, I argue that translation cannot be explained by reducing it to any of its constituent parts, like language or literature or text. It can only be understood as the interaction of parts. Yes, it is language. Yes, it is literature. Yes, it is rewriting. Yes, it is culture. No, it is not language; otherwise, we would not have called it translation, but language. It is a particular configuration, a particular interaction of language, literature, culture, ideology, and sociology. It is from the particular interaction between these things that translation emerges.

If it is true that complex adaptive systems operate in a state of disequilibrium, at the edge of chaos, this holds major implications for a philosophy of translation. As has been previously argued (Even-Zohar, 2006; Toury, 1995; Venuti, 1995), translation is an activity that disturbs equilibrium. By connecting systems and by disrupting systems, it is then actually a prerequisite for the life and health of complex adaptive systems. Systems that are closed to change will not grow or develop. In this sense, development is the adaptation to the other—be that other times, other spaces, other ideas, other people. In complexity theory, scholars look for a view of reality that will include law-like properties as well as historical contingency. The translation itself, the process of translation and the systems from which they emerge and to which translation gives rise are systems in nonequilibrium, complexity constituted both orderly and chaotically, at the edge of chaos.

4.4 History and Hard Science

In the Newtonian worldview, three laws dominated: constant motion, inertial mass, and equal and opposite forces (Mitchell, 2009, p. 19). In this paradigm with its assumption of equilibrium and stability, time was not a factor. In closed systems, past and future are similar because systems will operate according to fixed laws, and there is nothing to disturb the operation of these laws (Marion, 1999, pp. 66–70). By knowing the current position of particles, for instance, and the laws operating on them, one would be able to reconstruct any position in the past and predict any position in future for those particles. However, once scientists realized that many phenomena in reality cannot be conceptualized as closed systems because these systems operate in states of disequilibrium and instability, the arrow of time became relevant, also, to hard science (Mitchell, 2009, pp. 20–21; Prigogine, 1996, pp. 1–7). It was realized that time does indeed matter in these kinds of systems. Open systems are governed not by the second law of thermodynamics, that is, entropy, but by negentropy. This means that they do not decay into chaos but maintain their organization by interacting with their environment. Whereas entropy tends toward dissipating the differences on which structure and order are built, negentropy tends to lead to the maintenance of difference (M. Taylor, 2001, pp. 119–121).

Negentropy is the reason why two people cannot produce the same translation. Human beings are not closed systems; thus, their thoughts and interpretations cannot be predicated based on initial conditions. Being open systems, the same stimuli, such as a text, could give rise to widely differing interpretations and thus translations because the initial conditions in two brains can never be the same. Translation is thus not a process of which one can predict the outcome; translational action can only produce probable outcomes. One cannot predict how two translators will translate or what effects a translation would have in a society. The laws of prediction have to be replaced by laws of probability. In this respect, a field such as translation studies has much to learn from the conceptualization of complexity theorists.

4.5 Emergent Properties

Another great scholar of complexity from the Santa Fe School is John Holland. In the next chapter on emergence, I refer to him in much more detail, with reference to his ideas on emergence. What is important to note at this stage is that he conceptualizes complexity studies as an attempt to understand "coherence in the face of change" or "the central question of coherence under change..." (Holland, 1995, p. 4). For him, complex adaptive systems are about the interactions between the parts of a whole rather than about the individual actions of parts. Also, these systems are able to adapt because they are able to learn. Thus, his ideas about complexity include three main features, that is, interactions, the aggregation of the diverse, and adaptation or learning (Holland, 1995, pp. 4, 9).

He discusses four properties and three mechanisms of complex adaptive systems (Holland, 1995, pp. 10–37). The first property is aggregation, that is, the ability to leave out irrelevant details, choose relevant details, and treat what you are left with as similar or equivalent. This strategy is used in the modeling of complex adaptive systems in order to make them simpler and more understandable. Holland (1995, p. 11) also identifies a second sense to aggregation, that is, the complex, large-scale behavior that emerges from the interactions of less complex agents. These emergent properties can act as agents at a higher level. This refers to the hierarchical conceptualization of reality by complexity theorists.

The second property is nonlinearity, which has been discussed in detail in Sections 1 through 3 of this chapter. The only point needed to be added here is that one should not confuse aggregation and averages. Holland (1995, p. 23) argues that aggregation is made complex by nonlinearity as one cannot predict the sum of a large number of nonlinear interactions by summing or averaging.

A third property of complex adaptive systems is flows. Holland (1995, p. 23) explains that all complex adaptive systems display patterns of flow of the type (node, connector, resource). The resource thus flows from node to node via a connector with the nodes acting as agents and the connectors as possible interactions. There seem to be some links between the notion of complex adaptive systems as espoused by Santa Fe scholars and the notion of actor-network theory as espoused by Latour. The detail of these links will have to be put aside for another day, however.

The last property that Holland discusses is diversity. In complex adaptive systems, one finds parts of different nature or agents of different nature. These depend on other parts, that is, a context, for their existence. The way in which agency is conceptualized in the theory of complex adaptive systems challenges translation studies scholars to rethink their notions of agency. First, the notion of nonlinearity questions the easy lines of causality drawn in many studies of agency in translation. Society is a phenomenon that emerges from a large number of nonlinear processes. Indicating one cause and effect relationship between, say, a translation/translator and a particular development in society, is thus highly questionable. Nonlinearity and the emergent nature of social reality challenge translation studies to rethink its conceptualization of causality.

Holland then discusses tagging, internal modeling, and building blocks as three mechanisms for complex adaptive systems. Tagging refers to naming, that is, grouping things together under a banner or flag. By tagging, complex adaptive systems manipulate symmetries, bringing together things that are the same. Internal modeling refers to the ability of complex adaptive systems to anticipate. Because they are able to model or form schemata, they can learn and adapt. Building blocks refer to the notion that phenomena can be broken down into parts and reassembled in different ways. This point seems to be seriously hampered by reductionist assumptions.

4.6 Prediction of Behavior

Considering prediction and complex adaptive systems, one should note that complexity theory is related to or has grown out of chaos theory but is not synonymous to it (Van Kooten Niekerk & Buhl, 2004a, p. 5). What chaos theory brings to the table is its focus on dynamic or nonlinear systems (Mitchell, 2009, pp. 15, 20). Mitchell (2009, p. 38) points to some of the most salient features of chaos:

- Deterministic complex systems can lead to seemingly random behavior without there being external sources to the randomness.
- Due to the sensitivity to initial conditions, the behavior of even simple, deterministic systems is sometimes impossible to predict, even in principle.
- Even chaotic systems show order.

Coveny and Highfield (1995, p. 9) further explains complexity as existing of two ingredients, that is, unidirectional time and nonlinearity. The first relates to the law of thermodynamics and the arrow of time that has already been discussed. The second refers to the disproportionate relationships between cause and effect. On this point, complexity theory displays a variety of perspectives. Some complexity theorists see the aim of complexity theory as explaining the complexity of reality by means of simple laws. Other complexity theorists want to explain the simplicity of reality by means of the complexity of laws. Yet others aim at explaining the complexity of reality by means of complex laws or patterns. Cohen and Stewart (1994) made the point that complexity theory does not pretend to replace reductionism in all cases. There might be cases in physics or chemistry where reductionism suffices as an explanatory tool. It thus seems that all three of the above options may be possible, depending on the situation. However, especially in the human and social sciences, I see, and support, a movement away from reductionism towards complexity.

Grounding her discussion in the history of the notion of change in philosophy, Mitchell argues that change can be viewed as either "constant" or nonlinear. Nonlinear change is the type of change that is said to be sensitive to initial conditions; that is, small changes in initial conditions may lead to large differences in the end results. Nonlinear change or nonlinear causality thus gives expression to the notion that similar causes need not lead to similar results. On one hand, minute differences in initial conditions, which are not calculable by human means, may exert major influences on the eventual results. On the other hand, seeing that all systems have histories, the historical influences on systems may differ with the result that end results differ. This approach thus differs from the classical mechanical view of reality in which motion or change was seen as constant. One of the most important implications of nonlinearity is that it makes prediction virtually impossible (see Mitchell [2009, pp. 20–27] for an overview of this argument), and it renders simple notions of causality problematic. The nonlinearity, the openness of social systems, and the sensitivity to initial conditions are three explanations for the non-replicability of development projects. Because one works with all these variables, a successful project cannot necessarily be replicated in a different context. Thus, what has been proved to work in "the Western world" may not work in developing contexts for this very reason. Similarly, one set of solutions to translation problems may not be applicable to a situation with different variables.

Kauffman's focus on disequilibrium has important implications for translation. It is precisely difference, potential, that underlies and drives complexity, which is reality (Kauffman, 1995, p. 19). Translation, as one instance where difference is negotiated, is thus an important driver in the maintenance of cultural disequilibrium, that is, cultural growth. Enlarging the current views on systems thinking in translation studies, in which one includes the complex relationship between agent and system, seems to be one of the conclusions implicit in Kauffman's work. This is done in detail in Chapter 3.

If presented with these kinds of disequilibrium systems, one cannot predict their behavior. Thus, Kauffman (1995, p. 22) argues that the shortest way to predicting their behavior is to watch them behave, which is basically also what Latour (2007) proposes. One cannot understand them deductively. The only way to understanding them is through observation. This relates to Tymoczko's (2007) argument in which she falls back on Wittgenstein. It is interesting that complexity has also been conceptualized as a concept with certain family resemblances, as Tymoczko tried to conceptualize translation (Emmeche, 2004, p. 33). For this type of phenomenon, observation and inductive reasoning is the only solution. This point is, once again, developed in Chapter 3. It follows that scholars in translation studies, such as Chesterman (2008), will have to reconsider their views on causality in light of these new findings on nonlinearity.

4.7 Downward Causation

This is one of the most hotly debated notions in complexity theory. Although many theorists still yield to the argument of upward causation or emergence, quite a number of them are skeptical about the notion of downward causation. In short, emergence, the topic of the next chapter, refers to the notion of much coming from little. Put differently, it is captured in the following slogan: The whole is more than the sum of the parts. The problem comes when one has to explain how the whole exerts causation on the parts. Especially for scholars who view wholes as epiphenomenal, that is, not really existing, it is difficult to conceptualize downward causation logically. You are welcome to jump to Chapter 2 now if you want to read a detailed discussion on emergence and these related issues. There, I further conceptualize translation as emergent.

4.8 Computer Simulation

Theories of complex systems all refer to the notion of information. The notion of information in complex systems refers to the fact that complex systems are viewed as self-organizational. This means that complex systems create order out of disorder by working against entropy. In fact, dynamic complex systems are viewed as working towards negentropy. In complex systems theory, entropy and information is linked (Mitchell, 2009, p. 45). Information transfer or communication is not limited to human systems, but is also viewed as central to natural systems as is evident from the second law of thermodynamics (Mitchell, 2009, p. 42). In this regard, Szilard was the first to link entropy and information by claiming that intellectual work, that is, ordering information, can be seen as work and as ordering work in particular (Mitchell, 2009, p. 45). Thus, the ordering of chaos through intellectual work contributes to negentropy.

In all books on complexity, one therefore finds reference to computation, as the technologically advanced way of dealing with (large volumes of) information. It seems that the development of computational abilities that came with the development of computers has made possible new views, vistas, and methodologies for studying complex phenomena (Coveny & Highfield, 1995, p. 15; also see their chapters 2 to 4 for a more detailed discussion).

One of the problems of complexity studies is that, if one accepts that scale is one of the causes of complexity, one has to come up with a methodology to study complexity at scale. It is precisely at this point when computation is claimed to make possible the study of complex phenomena, not only because computers are able to work on huge scales but also because they are able to compute in a nonlinear way (Epstein & Axtell, 1996, p. 1, as well as the rest of their book; also Miller & Page, 2007). Epstein and Axtell (1996, p. 16) base their computational work on a philosophical approach to sociology, that is, methodological individualism. This means that they study the interaction of individual humans in order to understand society as a whole. As explained by them (Epstein & Axtell, 1996, p. 33), they view this relationship between individual and society as one of emergence, a topic to which I return in more detail in Chapter 2. What is interesting, however, is that they claim that social structures emerge from the bottom up. They also hold that these structures, once emerged, have a downward causative effect on the individuals whose interaction caused the structure (see also the work of Giddens [1984] in this regard). This point of view seems to run through all discussions on complexity. The age-old tension between society and individual and between structure and action is viewed as a complex paradox that should not be resolved. Both are and both cause the other to be.

As my aim in this book in general and this chapter in particular is to open up a conceptual space for a complexity philosophy of translation, I shall not go into any detail concerning computational models. These will have to wait for another time or for a more mathematically minded scholar because to do justice to the debate, one has to become competent in computational matters. At this moment, pointing out the issue and requesting colleagues to assist in this regard, if they are convinced of its value, will have to suffice. It could be interesting to combine the computational models of complexity theory with corpus studies in translation studies. For instance, the notion of style, be it the style of the author or the translator, could be conceptualized as an emergent phenomenon based on a particular organization of phenomena such as words, phrases and sentences on the local level. How do these local choices result in a global pattern such as style?

4.9 Genotype–Phenotype Duality

In living beings, the distinction between genotype and phenotype relates to genes that cause particular phenomena. The genotype refers to the genetic makeup of an organism whereas the phenotype refers to the particular variations caused in the organism by the gene (e.g., Kauffman, 1995, p. 151). In complex adaptive systems theory, this duality is maintained in a paradoxical, complex relationship.

It becomes relevant for translation studies when one considers the notion of memes, conceptualized as "cultural genes" (M. Taylor, 2001, pp. 217–219), a concept that has been investigated in translation studies by Chesterman (1997). The theory entails that memes are cultural "ideas" that move from brain to brain and can inhabit the brain of a large number of people, causing a culture.

4.10 Historicity

One of the major contributions of systems theory is the notion of open systems. Open systems allow for the flow of information of various types; that is, it allows for life (Morin, 2008, p. 10). This means that these systems do not operate according to the laws of thermodynamics, a position that assumes equilibrium in systems. Systems theory has realized that equilibrium means death for any system. It is the apparent complexity or chaos that, together with simultaneous structure, makes life possible. Both structure and change are thus paradoxically a precondition for life.

An important implication of systems thinking is that systems are best explained by means of connections or relationships. On one hand, a system operates based on the interaction of its parts and, on the other, based on the operation of the system as a whole with other systems. As Morin (2008, p. 11) eloquently puts it: "Reality is thus therefore as much in the connection (relationship) as in the distinction between the open system and its environment". Furthermore, evolution or change (as in the case of translation) presupposes open systems that are able to interact with an environment (or other systems, which are the environment).

As I indicated in the previous paragraph, open systems need to interact with other systems for their survival. This interaction takes place by means of a movement of information, be that symbolical, chemical, biological, or any other kind of information. This information is organized within a system so that noise is diminished and negentropy is achieved. The interesting point that I wish to highlight here, and that I expand on later, is that this "inter-ness" or "inter-ing," this need for exchanging information between systems in order to keep them alive is the philosophical underpinning of translation. All systems need some kind of "inter-action." Thus, one could conceptualize of the action "inter" chemical systems, which translates or "carries over" chemical information, the action "inter" biological systems, which translates or "carries over" biological information in procreation. Then one could also conceptualize the action "inter" semiotic systems, which translations or "carries over" semiotic information. I worked on these concepts before having read Latour, but in having read his work, it seems that my line of thinking is in agreement with his. According to Latour (2007), the social, which is connected to the natural—if one has to make such a distinction—refers to links that change relationships continuously. It is a sociology of connections, but not static connections, rather connections that translate, that is, carry over or transfer, all the time. The social refers to moving relationships, in which carryings over, that is, translations, of various natures take place. Of these, linguistic carryings over are but one category of inter-ings or inter-actions.

Organization is thus needed, but not to the point of equilibrium, to sustain life. Yet another paradox is required. Organization, Morin argues (2008, p. 16), if not mechanistically viewed, and organism, if not viewed as carrying a vital mystery, could paradoxically be able to explain life. Seeing that one conceptualizes these systems as open, it follows logically that time flows unidirectionally in such systems and that history is an important factor. A translation performed forward and backward, that is, from source to target and from target to source, will not yield a copy of the first source, because of the unidirectionality of history.

4.11 Natural Selection, Developmental Constraints, and Self-Organization

Because I am not interested in the evolution of biological organisms, I limit the discussion in this section to a general explanation of the issue at hand. From a complexity perspective, evolution or the development of biological organisms is not explained by one cause only. The notions of natural selection, developmental constraints, and self-organization are all viewed as instrumental in the way in which biological organisms develop (Emmeche, 2004, p. 32).

4.12 The Edge of Chaos

One of the most well-known, and controversial, concepts to have come from complexity theory is "the edge of chaos." Although conceptualized slightly differently by different scholars, this concept is used to argue that complex adaptive systems are neither in a state of equilibrium nor in a state of chaos (Emmeche, 2004, p. 32; Kauffman, 1995; Miller & Page, 2007, pp. 129–140; Mitchell, 2009, pp. 284–286; M. Taylor, 2001, pp. 14–16). Complex adaptive systems are somewhere between, neither stable nor chaotic, yet definitely not in equilibrium. The edge of chaos perhaps best expresses the paradoxical or complex part of complexity theory. It reflects the refusal to choose between order and chaos, stability and change, universality and particularity. Some scholars would argue that complex adaptive systems do not exist anywhere on the continuum between order and chaos but at a precise spot: at the edge of chaos. For instance, Kauffman (1995, p. 58) argues that life exists at the edge of chaos, on the tightly balanced point between too much and too little order or chaos. It is chaotic enough not to be dead, and ordered enough not be all over the place. This means that one needs both structure and fluidity when thinking about a complex phenomenon. In fact, Kauffman (1995, p. 62) points out that life emerges as a "phase transition."

A phase transition is a notion from physics which indicates the point where, for instance, water as a fluid turns into a gas. For him, life exists at the point where there is exactly the right amount of order and chaos, where "dead" chemical phenomena turn into a different "phase" of existence.

Complexity theory then, to my mind, provides a philosophical framework for hybridity, actually claiming that hybridity is the nature of open systems because only closed systems can be pure. If complex adaptive systems exist near a phase transition, as Kauffman (1995, p. 26) argues, systems that are too stable will die and systems that are too chaotic will self-destruct. This betweenness, between order and chaos, is a prerequisite for life. Translation, as a border phenomenon, can be conceptualized both as at the edge of chaos itself and as a subsystem that functions at the "edge-of-chaos" nature of social systems. In the latter case, by continuously disturbing existing social systems with new information, translation prohibits them from settling into states of equilibrium. In the former case, translation is itself at the edge of chaos in a number of ways. It maintains the source and target parts of its existence at the edge of chaos. If it is too strongly biased toward the source, it becomes impossible to understand in the target context, whereas if it is too strongly biased in the direction of the target, it stops being a representation and becomes a new creation. Thus, the foreignization/indigenization (Venuti, 1995) or overt/covert (House, 1997) or instrumental/documentary (Nord, 2001) binaries should be conceptualized as being at the edge of chaos. They are aggregate positions, hybrid positions. Any translation is always both, paradoxically.

4.13 Self-Organized Criticality

One of the central concepts in complexity theory is the notion of self-organized criticality. Per Bak, a Nobel Prize winner, is one of the central figures in the development of this notion. He (Bak, 1996, p. 1) argues that "complex behavior in nature reflects the tendency of large systems with many components to evolve into a poised, 'critical' state, way out of balance, where minor disturbances may lead to events, called avalanches, of all sizes". Bak's idea is that systems organize themselves without a "hand of God". The way in which components of a system interact leads to its delicate state of imbalance, somewhere between order and chaos. Because the system is unstable, not in equilibrium, disturbances can cause changes of any size, and the size is not predictable. Bak proved this theory with his famous experiment with sand piles (see chapter 3 of his book).

Bak's theory is based on the argument that physical laws are complex, not simple. The laws are only able to provide for simple situations, such as considering two objects in relationship to one another. The moment one has to consider the relationship between three objects, reductionist laws do not suffice. In his definition, systems that show large variability are deemed to be complex (Bak, 1996, p. 5). Thus, his ideas about complexity relates to universality and individuality. The crucial point Bak (1996, p. 7) includes in scientific theory is that of time, an argument he shares with Prigogine (1996). History cannot be predicted, but it can be explained. Thus, he asks about the properties that history and biology have in common that make them sensitive to minor, accidental events (Bak, 1996, p. 9). Theories of complexity are, per definition, insufficient. They do not claim to explain everything or even to provide full explanations. Rather, their intention is to provide explanations of the complexity. According to Bak (1996, p. 10), a general theory of complexity needs to be abstract, statistical and probabilistic.

Bak's version of complexity constitutes systems that exhibit complex behavior, such as "large catastrophes, 1/f noise and fractals" (Bak, 1996, p. 28). All of these characteristics are based on either computational or mathematical principles. His point is that complex phenomena are neither linear nor in equilibrium, but contingent. He calls these kinds of phenomena punctuated equilibrium.

In his famous experiments on self-organized criticality, Bak and his team dropped sand grains on a plate to create a pile of sand. Once a pile was formed, the dropping of further grains of sand resulted in sand slides or avalanches of various sizes. Bak's revolutionary claim was that a sand pile is an open dynamic system that organizes itself to a point of criticality, on the edge of chaos. Once this point of criticality has been reached, there is no way to predict the influence of the next grain of sand. His experiments showed that the next grain of sand randomly caused minute, medium, or large avalanches. The local interaction of a grain of sand with a pile thus causes global responses that one cannot relate to one another in any linear way. Furthermore, the sand pile as a whole has become the functional unit, not the grains of sand. No matter how well one analyses each grain of sand, it will tell one nothing about the pile and its behavior. This pile is an emergent property of grains of sand. A further implication of Bak's theory is that, in nonlinear, complex systems, change happens by revolution. Change is not to be seen as taking place in equilibrium, happening at a constant rate, but as random, sometimes huge and sometimes minute. As Bak (1996, p. 61) says, "Self-organized criticality is nature's way of making enormous transformations over short time scales". Yet another implication of Bak's theory is that, regarding complex systems, prediction can only be made when everything is measured absolutely accurately everywhere, which is not possible.

What is of importance for translation is Bak's (1996, p. 61) claim that "the historical account does not provide much insight into what is going on, despite the fact that each step follows logically from the previous step". In other words, telling what happened historically does not yet explain causally what happened. The larger implications of this claim are a rethinking of causality; not that Bak claims that there is no causality in complex systems, but that determining causal links is a risky business. The problem with retelling, which one finds quite often in translation studies (Baker, 2006; Milton & Bandia, 2009b), is that an account of the things that happen does not necessarily prove or explain causality. In various ways, translation relates to local actions with global implications, as I consider further in Chapter 4, which means that we need a different way of looking at causality in translation studies. In this regard, I refer to Latour in Chapters 2 and 3.

4.14 Explanations Other than Reductionist

Miller and Page (2007, p. 14) claim that current social theory is driven by looking at average behavior that can be said to be representative of the whole. From a complexity perspective, this approach is limiting because, as they argue, "heterogeneity is often a key driving force in social worlds" (Miller & Page, 2007, p. 14). In its anti-reductionist stance, complexity theory shares the deconstructivist fight against binaries (Miller & Page, 2007, p. 21). However, where deconstruction wishes to dissolve the binaries, complexity theory maintains them. It assumes the existence of logical binaries and claims that one has to live with them.

In complex adaptive systems, it is exactly the interest in the interaction of differences, not generalizations, which drives the enquiry. Philosophically, this has major implications for translation. If one assumes a systems perspective, translation is one way in which systems interact, in which information from one system is transferred to another system, which is a prerequisite for keeping a system alive. In this sense, translation is a catalyst for keeping systems alive, making the interaction between various systems possible. For systems to be alive, they need to be at the edge of chaos, self-organized to the point of criticality. Theoretically, translation is thus one of the factors destabilizing stabilizing systems. In itself, translation is a system at the edge of chaos. As indicated earlier, if one considers the indigenization/foreignization debate from the perspective of complexity philosophy, a translation is a self-organized critical system at the edge of chaos. If it is too foreign, its load of information becomes too chaotic for the target system/reader to deal with. If it is too indigenized, it is too stable so that it either bores the reader or kills the target system. By being too familiar, it loses its edge, literally and figuratively.

Another interesting contribution to complexity theory is that of Axelrod. He asked the basic question: Under what conditions will cooperation emerge in a world of egoists without central authority (Axelrod, 1984, p. 3)? Although he does not explicitly work in the field of complexity theory, his question is typical of complexity theory. It relates to the emergence of global patterns from the interaction of local agents who are not governed by a central authority. In this case, his experiments with the Prisoner's Dilemma indicate that cooperation is the most successful means of human interaction. In this game, one assumes that two partners in crime are taken prisoner and are being interrogated by the police in different rooms. Each prisoner then has the option to remain loyal to the other or to defect. If both remain loyal and stick to their stories, they go free—which is first prize. If one defects on the assumption that the other will remain loyal, that one goes free and the other remains in jail, which is first prize for one and implies losing for the other. If both defect, both remain in jail, which means that both lose. In computerized versions of the game played by participants from all over the world in two competitions, the Tit for Tat strategy won both competitions. It was the simplest strategy of all, stating that one starts off by cooperating in the first move and that you then continue by doing what your opponent does, cooperating when he or she does and defecting when he or she does.

Axelrod's theory raises numerous questions for translation as the notion of cooperation has, per definition, been of interest in the field and as its conceptualization as an emergent phenomenon could shed light on the complex views that surround it. Not only has the notion of equivalence somehow always been about notions of cooperation, but even scholars such as Nord, who has moved away from equivalence, has found it necessary to devise the notion of loyalty because of their sensing that translation assumes some kind of cooperation. Especially in current agency theories of translation, where scholars like Baker rightfully question the cooperation model underlying translation on a sociological and ideological level, the emergence of cooperation as conceptualized by complexity theorists poses interesting questions to translation studies.

5. TOWARD A COMPLEXITY FRAMEWORK FOR TRANSLATION

In Chapter 3, I work out the implications of the philosophical and theoretical conceptualization of Chapters 1 and 2. For now, I wish to close this chapter by drawing some parameters for conceptualizing translation from a complexity perspective.

The first implication of holding a complexity perspective seems, to me, to be that translation studies should conceptualize of its binaries, such as source and target and indigenization and foreignization as constitutive parts of nonequilibrium systems. Thus, source and target both constitute the reality of translation and, from a complexity perspective, are related to one another "at the edge of chaos." My point here is that source and target stands in an insurmountable, nonequilibrium tension. The moment either source or target dominates, a system in equilibrium is obtained, which does not create a living translation. Philosophically, one does not have to try to dissolve this tension, which translation scholars sometimes seem to feel needs doing. This means that the eager efforts during the past decade or three to untie the umbilical cord between source and target in translation studies are philosophically a waste of time. Just like metaphors, one needs to conceptualize translation as a paradoxical juxtaposition of two fields. This does not mean that their relationship will be balanced or that one always needs to look for some kind of equilibrium between them. On the contrary, the relationship will always be one of nonequilibrium, even at the edge of chaos.

Second, translation studies should revise its notion of systems. In this regard, translation studies may find it beneficial if it considers translation in terms of complex adaptive systems or actor-network links. Here, translation studies should not only consider literary systems as complex adaptive systems (Even-Zohar, 2006), but they should also think of the systems of media translation, political translation, historical translation, pharmaceutical translation, engineering translation, and so on. All of these form complex adaptive systems in which translation plays a particular role. Within these kinds of system, the tension between agent and system is maintained, and it provides one with the conceptual space to consider the intricate relationship that has been lacking in translation studies (Sawyer, 2005). The way in which agent and system are conceptualized as opposites or binaries in translation studies does not help the theorization of the field. In a complex way, translation studies need to conceptualize its interests as both agent and system, giving priority to neither.

Third, translation studies would, in my view, do well to reconsider its reductionist philosophical underpinnings. To my mind, all kinds of conceptualizations of translation "as" something else are reductionist. Efforts to conceptualize translation as culture, as reported speech, as rewriting, as ideology, or as anthropology are all subject to reductionist tendencies. Also, the plethora of turns in the field with their claims of exclusivity or of now having gotten to the core of the problem seems to indicate such a reductionist tendency. A complexity perspective would hold that, once one has conceptualized translation, you could hold complex perspectives on fields of study that could contribute to your understanding. Or you could conceptualize translation as a complex phenomenon in itself. Philosophically, translation is a complex phenomenon. It has many parts, and as a whole, it forms part of many other wholes. Thus, translation is language, and literature, and culture, and pragmatics, and ideology. No, it is none of these. Translation is translation, which is a phenomenon constituted by language, text, literature, culture, ideology, history, politics, and psychology. Furthermore, translation is translation, which forms part of the emergence of political reality, scientific reality, legal reality, literary reality, cultural reality, medical reality, and the media reality. Conceptualized in the terminology of complex adaptive systems theory, translation is both a complex adaptive system constituted by complex adaptive subsystems and a complex adaptive subsystem that co-constitutes a number of complex adaptive systems, or social reality as a complex adaptive supra-system.

Translation studies scholars will need to look in much greater detail into the computational work done in other fields. I am not here referring to work done on machine translation and efforts to compute natural language. Rather, I am suggesting that translation studies scholars look at the computational models used to study systems at the edge of chaos such as the weather, traffic or disease. In this direction, the possibilities seem to be huge.

In order to make these arguments in more detail in Chapter 3, I now first need to argue the nature of emergence, that is, the relationship between part and whole, in Chapter 2.

2   Emergent Semiotics

1. INTRODUCTION

I argued in the previous chapter that a philosophy or epistemology of complexity and/or a theory of complex adaptive systems represent an advance in scientific thinking because, as an epistemological point of departure, they both include as well as supersede reductionism. As an epistemology, complexity thinking tries to hold on to both parts of what have traditionally been thought of as paradoxical or logically exclusive positions, such as local and global, individual and society, particular and general. It is, in my view, providing a meta-epistemology, trying to step back one more level, to see if scholars cannot reconcile the hitherto logically irreconcilable. In this sense, it is a shift in perspective, a shift in standpoint, and a shift exercising the human ability to recursive thinking (Hofstadter, 1979, pp. 103–152). In this moving up one level, it argues that some paradoxes cannot be solved and cannot be dissolved. We have to live with them, and we should stop trying to get rid of them but rather should include them in our thinking. By questioning and trying to supersede the anti-paradoxical nature of scholarly thought itself, an epistemology of complexity stretches our understanding of reality further than has previously been done. It tries to deal with the recognition that rationality needs to categorize. However, this categorization causes problems because reality is more complex than rational categories allow, and categorization deconstructs the unity of reality (Hofstadter, 1979, pp. 246–272). In fact, as Morin (2008) argues, rational categories could do violence to the intricate complexity of reality. One could thus perhaps claim that complexity thinking takes the complexity of reality as its point of departure, and it does not try to simplify reality by its conceptual work but rather allows for this complexity. Put simply, it asks the question, How can one think, be rational, while maintaining the complexity of reality?

What I have only hinted at and what I wish to discuss in more detail in this chapter is how complexity thinking proposes to deal with the anti-reductionist stance it takes. As I argue, one of the central notions in superseding reductionism is emergence. In this chapter, I first conceptualize emergence, thinking about it particularly from a complexity perspective. Second, I discuss social reality as an emergent phenomenon. Thereafter, I conceptualize the role of language in the emergence of society by focusing in particular on the linguistic philosophy of John Searle as one way of conceptualizing the emergence of society through semiotic interaction. Last, I conceptualize the emergence of social reality as it relates to semiotics. The chapter closes by drawing certain conclusions for the study of translation.

2. CONCEPTUALIZING EMERGENCE

Miller and Page (2007, p. 9) have pointed out that a philosophy of complexity usually argues for a hierarchical view of reality in which the various levels of reality are said to be related to one another by means of a process that is called emergence. Although emergence is sometimes viewed as either too vague to be of scholarly use or a cop-out for natural processes that scholars do not yet understand (see, for instance, Holland, 1998, p. 5), it is used widely and, for now, I make use of it. I am also aware of the work of Latour, which is similar and yet different to the notions of complexity and emergence that I have presented in the previous and this chapter. I shall leave a detailed comparative discussion of the Santa Fe brand of systems thinking and Latour's actor-network theory for another day. However, in the next section, I attend to the implications of Latour's work for my ideas on the construction of the social, and in the next chapter, I reflect on his use of translation for my widened conceptualization of translation.

Emergence is thus a concept used to think about reality without reducing it to any of its constituent parts, or to think about systems without reducing them to any of their constituent parts. It wants to conceptualize wholes and parts in an anti-reductionist fashion. In particular, I refer to Agassi (2007, p. 158), who indicates that traditional metaphysical systems of thought, for example, religions, have argued that humans do indeed have an answer to the issue of particularity and universality, whereas traditional positivism has argued that we have no answer to this issue. The solution of the former being irrational and the latter rational, both these biases cannot be overcome by ignoring them but by engaging with them, criticizing them and trying to develop them in what was conceptualized in the previous chapter as an epistemology of complexity. Note that the irrational tendencies in postmodernism run parallel to the traditional religious view on the problem. The notion of emergence thus relates closely to both philosophical and even religious notions, as well as mathematical and statistical notions (Cohen & Stewart, 1994; Hofstadter, 1979; Kauffman, 1995; Van Huyssteen, 2004; Waldrop, 1992). It is a scientific, philosophical concept, but it definitely also contains metaphysical (Agassi, 2007, p. 158) or even quasi-religious or religious connotations (Hofstadter, 1979, pp. 246–272) as complexity scholars try to think about reality without reducing it to matter—or something else.

Emergence was not first used by those who are now termed complexity scholars. With its roots in the late nineteenth century, it received substantial attention in the early decades of the previous century from British emergentists such as Mead (1969) and C. Morgan (1923) who endeavored to think in terms of process and relationship rather than essence and entity (also see Sawyer, 2005, p. 20). These scholars were particularly interested in the relationship between wholes and parts, giving prominence to wholes, for example, Smuts's (1926) theory of holism. Although not always using the term *emergence*, the notion has been at the center of sociological debates ever since. In the natural sciences, it was first the chaos scholars and then the complexity scholars, in particular the Santa Fe brand thereof, and in particular John Holland (1998), who revisited emergence. However, many scholars have since used, abused, reused, and crucified the notion (for an overview of the history of social emergence, see Sawyer, 2005, pp. 27–44; also for an overview in the natural sciences, see Holland, 1998).

Thus, emergence—much coming from little (Holland, 1998, p. 1)—has become a way of explaining the "development" or "evolution" of higher or more complex or new or different—if one does not want to attach a value to the levels—levels of reality from lower levels. Emergence is not only interested in the evolution of high-level phenomena, such as life or mind, but also of everyday phenomena such as the way in which a cell turns into an organism, for example, a seed turning into a tree with roots, trunk, branches, twigs, leaves, flowers, all on the right places at the right time, or in the way in which thousands of ants turn into a colony (Hofstadter, 1979, pp. 311–356). Emergence is interested in how things become, in the interrelationships between parts that, though in many cases not understandable, lead to phenomena—be they simple or complex—that owe their existence to new constellations of interrelationships. Emergence is an epistemological position that assumes one world while rejecting reductionism. It holds that the physical is the basis of all reality without reducing all of reality to the physical.

As argued earlier, explaining the way in which levels of reality emerge from lower levels, acquiring qualitatively new properties, is the task of emergence theory (see, for instance, work on this as early as C. Morgan, 1923, pp. 2–20). This holds equally for the emergence of biological phenomena from chemical phenomena, for the emergence of living organisms from molecules and for the emergence of mind from the material brain. Complexity theorists would thus typically argue that the most basic level of reality is the physical, out of which emerges the chemical, out of which emerges the biological, out of which emerges the psychological or mind, out of which emerges the social, and, some would argue, out of which emerge the religious. Graves (2009, p. 503) indicates that the physical, biological, psychological, and social are usually regarded as the basic levels of existence, but one also finds that some scholars conceptualize the chemical in between the physical and biological and, some others, the spiritual beyond the social.

In reductionist science, scholars try to understand each level by reducing it to the constituent parts in the previous level (Emmeche, 2004, p. 22). For instance, a reductionist approach would try to explain the mind as "nothing but" biology or chemistry. According to this line of argument, if you understand the chemical reactions in the brain, it follows that you understand the mind and humanity. In a similar fashion, translation is sometimes described as "actually" language or reported speech or rewriting or text or literature or culture. I contend that the prevalence of a number of "translation as" approaches can be explained by an underlying reductionist epistemology which permeates the field (see, for instance, Lefevere's [1990, p. 3] comment on positivism in translation studies). What is needed is an epistemology that frees us from reductionism so that we can conceptualize translation as translation.

As indicated earlier, in complexity science, scholars attempt to understand the relationships between the levels of reality, the ways in which, for instance, chemicals obtain the quality of "life" in a particular configuration manifesting in what we know as a rabbit, or the way in which life obtains the quality of "intelligent" in a particular configuration called humanity. Life is one of the forms material reality takes, just as culture or society is one of the forms that material reality takes or as culture is the form biology takes (Searle, 1995, p. 227). In this way, the project of emergence entails explaining reality as one, without reducing it to one constituent element or one level of reality. It is a way of conceptualizing both the individual phenomenon and the complex phenomenon. To my mind, emergence is one particularly interesting way in which to solve the age-old problem of equilibrium and change, particular and universal, individual and society. It relates to the different organizations of materiality on different levels, which give rise to new phenomena.

One of the most fascinating examples of emergence is mind, which constitutes one of the subjects in which emergence was initiated (C. Morgan, 1923). How, so the question goes, can one explain mind from its physical, chemical, biological substratum? How can a few billion unfeeling cells have feeling or emotions or logic? How can it love? Revere? Hate? Scholars of emergence will argue that it is in the particular organization of the physical, chemical, and biological that mind emerges. Contrary to certain religious and dualist philosophical views, nothing has been added to the physical, chemical, and biological, nothing but a particular organization. Thus, mind is an emergent phenomenon.

In this regard, scholars operating from a physicalist perspective assume that causality only occurs within the natural or physical world, which means that emergent properties, such as mind, cannot have any downward causation (Bickhard, 2009, p. 551; Lavassa, 2009). This argument entails that the physical can cause or influence the psychological but not vice versa. In contrast, scholarship that is built on emergence argues that it is not substance but process or organization, and the process of interrelationships at that, which results in new forms of reality and which requires explanation (Bickhard, 2009, p. 553; Seibt, 2009, pp. 481–486). Although not physical, the emerged mind is as real as the biological brain, and it can effect downward causation. Emergence thus represents an epistemological shift from studying substance or stability to studying relationships, process, or change based on substance or the complex relationship between them. As Crutchfield (2009) argues, pattern discovery has been the point of focus in science in the twenty-first century. In support of this argument, Bickhard (2009, p. 553) explains three features of emergent phenomena. First, processes do not have fixed boundaries, and therefore, boundaries should be explained, not assumed. Second, the causal power of processes is located in their organization, which means that one does not have to postulate a metaphysical block to the levels and meta-levels of emergent power. Last, if emergence is a metaphysical phenomenon, it implies that mind and normativity are also emergent. In the elegant words of Beinhocker (2010, p. 1), "Complexity theory states that critically interacting components self-organize to form potentially evolving structures exhibiting a *hierarchy of emergent system properties*" (italics mine). MacKenzie (2010, p. 81) argues that persons are "organized, temporally extended systems of mental and physical events characterized by dense causal and functional interconnectedness, including complex physical and psychological feedback loops." Furthermore, one has to think of emergent phenomena as ensembles or networks, which self-organize spontaneously from local interactions that have been constrained globally. An emergent property thus does not belong to a single part or element. Hofstadter (1979, pp. 369–390) has a similar notion of mind or consciousness being the emergent property of local physical, chemical, and biological processes in the brain that leads to a global phenomenon such as consciousness or intelligence. The determination of causation in emergent processes is thus bidirectional or complex, from the local to the global and from the global to the local, that is, upward and downward causation. Thus, the local and the global hang together in a complex, insoluble relationship in which the global constrains and makes possible the local and in which the global emerges or is the result of the interactions of the local, for which MacKenzie uses the term dynamic co-emergence (MacKenzie, 2010, p. 86).

It is clear from the preceding discussion that complexity theory assumes levels of existence and hierarchical levels at that. Whether these levels are ontological or epistemological in nature is a matter of debate among philosophers (Heard, 2006; Holland, 1998). For the sake of the current debate, I am not sure whether it matters that much, and therefore, I shall reserve judgment on the matter. Whether "real" or "only a matter of epistemology," reality is conceived as emerging from simple forms of reality into more complex forms of reality. The relationships between the simple and the complex are still a topic of heated debate, for example, whether the lower levels cease to exist when higher levels emerge and how little can become much. The bottom-up causation or relationships are thus called emergence, and the top-down causation or relationships are called supervenience. It thus follows that a phenomenon can, at one level, be emergent, and, at the next, part of the substructure from which another phenomenon emerges. In this way, the biological emerges from the physical but simultaneously forms part of the substructure of the psychological, which, having emerged from the biological, in its turn forms part of the substructure of the social.

This notion of supervenience is highly contested in emergence debates. For epiphenomenalists, emergent properties do not really exist, and therefore, they find it difficult to acknowledge that these properties can have downward causative power. To my mind, one does not need to solve the issue of the reality of emergent phenomena before you can make use of the concept. Let us use yet another example. In the Ant Fugue in his phenomenal book *Gödel, Escher, Bach*, Hofstadter (1979, pp. 311–336) has the anteater telling Achilles and the Tortoise how he is a friend to the ant colony, Aunt Hilary, while simultaneously being an enemy to individual ants. Aside from the complexity assumptions to this statement, Hofstadter argues that the behavior of the ant colony is an emergent phenomenon that cannot be explained through the behavior of individual ants. For instance, no ant wants to be eaten by the anteater, but for the colony, it is good that some ants be eaten because it forces the renewal of the population. Furthermore, the emergent phenomenon, the colony, while emerging from the behavior of individual ants, constrains and co-determines the behavior of those very ants. To me, this is supervenient behavior or downward causation. The colony does not cause the ants to come into existence, obviously, but, in a sense, it causes them to behave in certain ways because it constrains and makes their behavior possible. So, if the properties of the whole were wholly determined by the properties of the parts, one would not have emergence. In this case, the whole has properties that the collection of parts does not.

In order to conceptualize emergence, one has to be able to think paradoxically, nonlinearly (Deguet et al., 2006, p. 30). The emergent phenomenon supervenes on the substratum in the sense that the substratum does not disappear, but what emerges is more and/or different from the parts. What is this more or this difference? To my mind, it is the interaction or organization of the parts. As Szliard already argued in the early part of the previous century, intelligence or interaction or information can be a nonmaterial change factor that influences the nature of material phenomena (Mitchell, 2009, pp. 43–47). Who organizes the parts? Kauffman (1995) claims that they self-organize. Somewhere between order and chaos, conglomerations of parts tend to self-organize into states that are more/different from the states than if those parts had remained unorganized. Through this organization, phenomena with new properties emerge. To this, one should add, as Francescotti (2007, p. 51) points out, that emergence means that something cannot be explained sufficiently from a materialist point of view. Supervenience thus also means that the properties emerging from the interactions between parts of a whole have causal power in the sense that these powers are distinct from the powers of the parts (Francescotti, 2007, p. 60).

In this view of emergence, one moves away from a study of phenomena only to a study that includes relationships or relationality. Many phenomena cannot be explained by analysis, that is, by cutting them up and understanding their parts. One can only understand them by synthesis, that is, by understanding how the relationships between parts lead to the properties of the phenomenon. Thus, I concur with Francescotti (2007, p. 58), who claims that consciousness is emergent (Mead, 1969; Searle, 1995). This means, as I shall argue below, that language is also to be viewed as an emergent phenomenon, as Queiros and El-Hani (2006) have argued (also see Jäger & Van Rooij, 2007). To conceptualize the cultural or social level of existence, one has to conceptualize more than one organism (Graves, 2009, p. 506). It is this interaction between organisms, the semiotic or symbolic interaction, which leads to the emergence of social reality, as is argued in greater detail in the next section.

As indicated previously, reductionism is one way of explaining reality, and it explains a large part of reality. However, the moment a phenomenon functions as a system, in particular as an open system, reductionist explanations fail (Morrison, 2006, p. 878). Thus, one cannot study mind by means of chemical laws; the phenomenon that emerges requires a new way of studying the phenomenon because it is a new phenomenon, not just a version of the subvenient parts (Morrison, 2006, p. 878). In particular, the moment one moves to a higher level, for example, moving from particle physics to mental states, what Morrison (2006, p. 878) calls "the catastrophe of dimension" kicks in (on swarm behavior, see also Fischer, 2009). Finding the right dimension at which to study a phenomenon seems crucial. As a theory of everything, reductionism goes as far as claiming that everything we know is matter. In this extreme form of materialism or naturalism, the human being is nothing more than matter, explainable in terms of the laws of physics. The evolution of "higher" forms of reality is thus explained in terms of the lower forms and in actual fact reduced to the lower forms. It is the type of argument characterized by "nothing but" arguments; for example, the human being is "nothing but" matter, or love is "nothing but" chemistry (see, for instance, Morrison, 2006).

In contrast, the theory of emergence was developed to claim the unique nature of new forms of development, that is, new phenomena that develop (out of existing ones). It operates on the principles of levels, or as Klapwijk (2008, pp. 106–138) calls it "ontological stratification." The point is that, in terms of a theory of emergence, the higher level is not reducible to the lower level. On each level, novel forms of being develop. Klapwijk (2008, pp. 120, 138) calls these new forms idionomic forms of being. Thus, the substratum of matter can explain much about the chemical superstratum, but it cannot explain all of it. Some of what is chemical can only be explained on the level of the chemical itself. In this sense, emergence stands in contrast to reductionism. Similarly, consciousness can to an extent be explained as a biological and even a chemical phenomenon, but it cannot fully be explained as biological or chemical. Some of it has to be explained on a new level of being, that is, that of the level of consciousness. Emergence theorists thus claim that self-consciousness emerged out of the substrata of matter, chemistry, and biology to form a new form of being. This new form of being is both novel and irreducible to its substrata.

Klapwijk (2008), for one, has already argued for phenomena of human culture to be called emergent. So have Cohen and Stewart (1994, pp. 349–351). My argument is thus that human culture in its entirety emerges out of the physical, chemical, and biological substrata on which it rests. The next step is to indicate how this happens. However, the phenomena of human culture could also be understood as emerging, not only out of the material, chemical, and biological substrata but also out of human consciousness. In line with Jousse (2000; see also Marais, 2010), I would thus argue that bodily human interaction is the basis from which to consider communication; that is, communication emerges out of the human body. Arguing further, literature, as a cultural phenomenon, emerges out of language and is constructed by new relationships between the parts of language, but cannot be reduced to language. Thus, one cultural phenomenon could be conceptualized as emerging from other cultural phenomena. To my mind, this is a way of explaining the "construction" of new cultural phenomena and the relationship between these phenomena. It opens up the possibility of thinking in non-reductionist terms about cultural phenomena.

If one says that emergence is concerned with "much from little," one has to ask what this "much" consist of, or as Francescotti (2007, p. 48) puts it: In what sense are emergent entities novel? He argues that one should distinguish between the resultant and emergent properties of phenomena. For instance, if you put five bricks into a bag, each with a mass of one kilogram, you know that the resultant mass will be five kilograms without even weighing the bricks. Total mass is thus a resultant property of the constituent parts of a phenomenon. It also means that one uses reductionist principles to understand the notion of mass and that one can predict the property of the whole by knowledge about the properties of the parts. However, when you have a few billion brain cells together in a brain, knowing the nature of each cell will not explain or predict the nature of intelligence or consciousness (Francescotti, 2007, p. 50). Thus, consciousness is not a resultant phenomenon but an emergent phenomenon.

The physicality of emergent properties has also been hotly debated. For instance, Yates (2009, p. 112) claims that only properties are emergent; there are no emergent substances. However, some would argue that a common substance such as water or salt is an emergent phenomenon because water has none of the properties of either oxygen or hydrogen, nor is it possible to predict the properties of water from the knowledge of either oxygen or hydrogen, or both oxygen and hydrogen. The same holds for salt, sodium, and chloride. What does seem true, however, is that emergence seems to imply a metaphysical thesis, namely that emergent, non-physical properties are determined by physical properties (Yates, 2009, p. 112; see this same reference for some of the problems with downward causation, or see Toner [2008] for some philosophical problems) or as Searle (1995) says, culture is the form matter takes in certain cases. Morrison (2006, p. 883) makes the important observation that it is not the parts that disappear when a new phenomenon emerges but the emergent phenomenon that disintegrates when the whole is taken apart. Thus, not studying an emergent phenomenon at the level of the emergent phenomenon, but at the level of some part, means studying something else, which is a meaningless endeavor. Similarly, Heard (2006, p. 56) thus argues that emergent predicates predicate only whole systems, not parts.

One of the possible dangers of emergence theory is that one has to be careful of using terminology from evolution theory and concomitant notions of development when discussing cultural phenomena. To my mind, emergence does not necessarily have the troublesome underlying evolutionist notions that assume some cultural artifacts or practices as "higher" or "further developed" than others (Sturge, 2007, pp. 35–55). What it does explain, however, is the relationship between cultural phenomena as both "emerging from" and "non-reducible to." It explains the relationship between language and literature, for example, by arguing that literature "emerges" out of language; that is, literature is based on language and cannot be conceptualized without recourse to language, but literature cannot be reduced to language. Literature is "something more" than language, but it is "constructed" by using language; that is, it emerges out of language. Similarly, I would argue that translation emerges out of language, but it cannot be reduced to language.

Having created a conceptual space for thinking about emergence in general, I now turn to social emergence.

3. SOCIAL EMERGENCE

The particular aspect of emergence that concerns me in this section is that of social emergence. Although the entire pattern of emergence is important because, as I argued in Chapter 1, it allows one to conceptualize translation within an ecological framework, I am concerned with conceptualizing the ways in which social reality emerges out of the physical, chemical, biological, and psychological substrata and how it is related to these substrata. In this conceptualization, I provide an overview of social emergence, which to a large extent is also related to the basic theories of sociology. Once again, I am not attempting to provide a critical analysis of the notion of social emergence; I am instead creating a conceptual space to employ later on to talk about the role of the semiotic in the emergence of social reality.

3.1 The Social as Problem

As indicated in the previous section, emergence is a way of conceptualizing, from a complexity perspective, the relationship between part and whole. When one then considers social reality, emergence pertains to the question concerning the relationship between individual and social phenomena and between the "natural" and the "social." Put differently, it concerns the way in which a social system's global behavior emerges from the local interactions of its parts, that is, human agents (Mead, 1969; Sawyer, 2005, p. 2). Emergence is somehow related to a view that values both part and whole, that refuses to let go of either in its thinking. So, how can one conceptualize the emergence of social reality? In the history of sociology, scholars have suggested various approaches to solve this problem. Sawyer (2005) provides a detailed overview of various conceptions in this regard. For the purposes of this chapter, I limit my discussion to the notion of methodological individualism. The question in sociology is how to study multiple levels of analysis (Sawyer, 2005, p. 58), in other words, how to study society as a whole and as parts and how to relate the individuals to the whole. This goes hand in hand with the question whether social phenomena "really" exist. In this debate, two extreme positions have crystallized, that is, social realism and ontological individualism (Sawyer, 2005, pp. 63–99). Social realism argues that social reality is as real as the material world, it is a thing, and it is both logically and ontologically prior to individuals. Ontological individualism argues the contrary, that is, that social reality does not exist; only individuals do. Social reality is only an aggregate of individual interactions. Recent developments in sociological thinking tried to correct the extremes of the above polarity, but one still finds scholars accusing one another of tending to be of either persuasion.

A middle position is what is called methodological individualism. It argues that both social reality and individuals exist, though they would claim that this existence differs in modality. In its analysis, methodological individualism takes its point of departure as the individual, hence "methodological" individualism, but ontologically it does not give primacy to either individual or society. It thus argues that social reality emerges out of the interactions of individuals, without claiming ontological priority for individuals. In this view, symbolic interaction is the way in which social reality arises (Sawyer, 2005, p. 93). Individuals interact by means of their symbolic systems of interaction, and this interaction gives rise to social phenomena. Thus, two people may interact by talking to one another, and out of this interaction may emerge a stable relationship recognized as dating, which, in certain societies, may lead to engagement or marriage or living together or civil union. The latter are social phenomena that have emerged out of social interactions. Once social phenomena exist, for example, marriage, these constrain and make certain actions by the individuals possible; for example, having sex with someone other than the marriage partner is seen as destroying the marriage. In other words, social structure emerges out of individual interaction and then assumes, as it were, a life of its own as a social phenomenon and can exert downward causation on individuals while, simultaneously and paradoxically, being maintained or ended or changed by the interactions of individuals.

The view described earlier openly rejects reductionism in social science. It does not reduce social reality to individuals, but explains how social reality emerges from individual interactions and then supervenes on individuals. Also, it does not subsume individuals in social reality by providing social reality with logical or ontological primacy. To quote Sawyer (2005, p. 94):

> Perhaps the solution lies in a wise combination of lower- and higher-level explanation in developing a complete scientific explanation. To return to the argument of the previous chapter, this combinatory approach is exactly what complexity thinking is about and where emergence finds its function.

So, if one does not want to use reduction as a method, how do you go about thinking about social reality? Sawyer (2005, pp. 95–97) argues that irreducibility has four features: non-aggregativity, near decomposability, localization, and complexity of interaction. Aggregative properties refer to a position that holds that the properties of a system are not a product of the way in which the system is organized. Let us again look at our example of the mass of a bag of bricks. Whether the bricks are neatly stacked or randomly thrown into the bag, their mass is the same. The organization does not change the properties of mass. In contrast, whether you have two hydrogen atoms and an oxygen atom randomly floating around or organized into a molecule makes a huge difference to what is constituted. Cooperative or inhibitive interactions between the bricks exert no influence on the mass. In emergent systems, properties cannot be seen as an aggregate. The particular interactions play a role in the outcome. It is as if bricks organized in a line would weigh more than bricks organized in a circle. Second, the properties of components of decomposable systems can be determined in isolation from other properties of the system despite the fact that the components interact. Thus, by weighing each brick and adding the masses of all the bricks, one gets to the total mass without ever having to weigh all of the bricks together. Social systems are not decomposable in this way because their nature emerges from the interaction between their components, not from the nature of the individual components. Their very nature is determined by relationships, by connections, and by organization, not by the properties of the parts. If you decompose them, they stop existing. As far as localizability is concerned, a system is localizable if the functional decomposition of the system corresponds to its physical decomposition and if one can identify each property of a system with a single part or subsystem of the system (Sawyer, 2005, p. 96). If one cannot identify the properties of a system with the parts, that is, if the properties are distributed over many parts, the system is not localizable. Last, complex, that is, nonlinear, interactions are non-reducible. The reason for this is that if there is no linear relationship between cause and effect, you cannot reduce a system to its parts because the effects of the interaction of the parts add up to more than, or at least something different from, the interaction of the parts. Thus, the conceptualization of the social proposed here holds both the emergence of the social from the individual and the downward causation from the social to the individual (Sawyer, 2005, p. 100).

The features of complex systems, as discussed in Chapter 1, apply to social systems. Emergent systems, that is, social systems, are complex dynamic systems that display global behavior that one cannot predict from understanding the parts even if one were able to come to a full and/or complete understanding of those parts, which you usually are not. The reason for this is that the nature of complex social systems are determined by the interactions of their parts, and these interactions are per definition nonlinear; that is, the systems are sensitive to initial conditions. This position on social reality can be described as non-reductive materialism, which argues that reality is material in its base but that all of reality cannot be reduced to the material. The "more" that is added to the material is located in the interactions and organization between material parts that take forms or have effects that are not material. This view thus argues for process ontology. The material is real. Many other features of reality, that is, biological psychological and social reality are a product of the patterns or processes of interaction of the material. These entities, structures and patterns are ephemeral and dynamic, and they are reconstituted quite often; that is, they are not stable and in equilibrium. Thus, one cannot separate individual and society. Society is forever in the process of becoming or being made or emerging.

One more feature of emergent social systems needs to be considered. These systems are not necessarily designed. For instance, in economics, Adam Smith argued long ago that economics is not organized by "the hand of God"; it emerges from the interaction of local actors without them having a global goal in mind. Similarly, many social features, for example, patterns of traffic or sports preferences, have not been designed by anybody. They have emerged out of local actions or choices and have resulted in global patterns. Sawyer's (2005, p. 189) claim that emergence only focuses on undesigned results is perhaps too strong, because, as will be seen in the next section, human interaction may also be intentional in nature. However, complexity theory has argued that the intentions going into the creation of a society are usually local, or partial. What emerges is usually more than what was intended. An example could be the South African constitution. Although all parties in the negotiations concerning the new constitution had an idea of what they wanted for "South Africa," they were also constrained by their constituencies and partisanships. They wanted to see that their own, local interests be covered in the constitution. Out of that process emerged a constitution that cannot be reduced to the interests of the individual political parties or could not have been predicted from the local interests. Local actions have led to a global result.

In the conceptualization of social emergence I am proposing, one has to conceptualize of humans as the parts of social reality or the various social institutions (Giddens, 1984; Searle, 2010) as the whole. In this sense, one uses an analogy which is used in all systems thinking, for example, to think about atoms as parts and molecules as wholes, to think about molecules as parts and cells as wholes, to think about cells as parts and organisms as wholes, and to think about organisms as parts and society as a whole. A whole in one system can thus be a part in another. In this way, one conceptualizes the whole of reality as interrelated, in some way connected, in some way constructed by its connectedness. The notion of emergence thus holds that "relatively simple higher-level order 'emerges' from relatively complex lower-level process" (Sawyer, 2005, p. 3). These complex systems may have laws and properties at the global level that are not reducible to the lower level and, by implication, to the lower-level sciences. One usually conceptualizes of emergence as appearing where many parts interact with one another in networks that are themselves densely connected (Sawyer, 2005, p. 2). In other words, the global system cannot be broken down into its subsystems, or rather, if the global system is broken down, it ceases to exist. The parts provide little or no information about the properties of the whole. Once again, this leads to a focus on the interaction between parts as well as between systems. The properties of systems are a function of the interrelationships of the parts, and seeing that systems can be subsystems of other systems, they form part of the interrelationships of larger wholes.

What Sawyer points out is that sociological theories have been looking for a conceptualization that will balance individual and society, part and whole. This was to a large extent achieved through the notion of symbolic interactionism or semiotic interactionism, which holds that social phenomena emerge from the symbolic or semiotic interaction of human agents. Human relationships are built and maintained by means of symbolic interactions. However, these theories, according to Sawyer (2005, p. 35), do not explain in enough detail the way in which social phenomena emerge from individual interactions. To fill this gap, he proposes a theory of social emergence in which the levels of individual agency and social structure emerge in phases. Individuals start interacting by means of discourse, collaboration and negotiations and these interactions form certain patterns. From these patterns of interaction emerge what Sawyer calls "ephemeral emergents", that is, topics, contexts, interactional frames, and so on of a relatively passing nature. These lead to stable emergents, that is, subcultures in groups, slang, and other sociolinguistic phenomena. These kinds of stable emergents then lead to social structures, that is, laws, cultural norms and material and infrastructure (Sawyer, 2005, p. 220; see also Latour's [2007] argument that the social is continually being constructed by means of local links). To my mind, this framework helps us to better describe the emergence of social reality. By recourse to semiotic phenomena, and sociolinguistics in particular, Sawyer has provided us with a clearer framework within which to conceptualize the emergence of social reality. In the next section, I fill the picture in with even more detail when I investigate the philosophy of language acts.

When one considers a sociological theory, the challenge seems to be to maintain both materialism and individualism without giving in to the pressures of reductionism (Sawyer, 2005, p. 57). With emergence, one can maintain the position that "nothing has been added" to reality; that is, life was not added to chemicals, and spirit was not added to life. An emergent view of reality maintains one world that is material but that takes different forms as higher levels of existence emerge from the material. How, then, does one maintain the relationship between individual and society? Sawyer (2005, p. 92) uses the following argument. Social causation is a lawful relationship between social properties and individual properties; that is, the one causes the other or is caused by the other. In a paradoxical way, social reality, that is, law, simultaneously constrains individual interactions and is supervenient on individual interactions; that is, the law emerges from social interaction.

3.2 Actor-Network Theory

In recent years, actor-network theory has been proposed as a conceptual tool with which to think about the assembling of the social. I am particularly interested in actor-network theory because of its proponents' use of the term *translation* in their theory. Also, much of what has been suggested in actor-network theory seems to be similar in approach to the complex adaptive systems theory of the complexity approach that has been suggested above. In this section, I provide a brief overview of actor-network theory, and in Chapter 3, I explore the implications of its notion of translation in more detail.

In my interpretation, Latour's aim with actor-network theory is to change sociology's conception of its field of study from a substance or from stasis or from equilibrium to a process or movement or connection. His approach is radically anti-reductionistic (Latour, 2007, p. 256). For him, the social is a network of connections between nodes, and these networks are of various number, strength, and duration. Also, and extremely important, these networks are not stable and fixed. They are, rather, in movement, being forged and reforged all the time (also see Akrich et al., 2002a; 2002b). Thus, the social never is (a stasis) and never is done. It is a process of connecting and reconnecting and maintaining existing connections. The more connections or links that a node has to other links, the stronger its influence or causality.

If one conceptualizes the social as thus, it means that sociology is not a science of the social but a science that traces the connections, the associations, the movements by which the social is assembled (Latour, 1987, 2000,

2007, p. 5). It is through being able to account for these associations that sociologists are able to understand and explain "the social." Latour's is thus clearly a sociology of process, of movement, and of becoming, and in this sense, he has much in common with the complexity thinking that I have explained in the previous chapter.

Sociology, for Latour, should, as a rule of thumb, focus its attention on five sources of uncertainty because controversies are the source of the making of the social. Latour (2007, pp. 21–25) criticizes the sociologist of the social for studying the social as something that exists, that is there, not as something that is becoming, that is being assembled. In his view, studying controversies and contestations provides one with a much better understanding of the processes of creating the social. The uncertainties to which he refers are the following:

- No groups, only group formation: His focus on process and construction is further enhanced by his notion that sociology should not study groups, but group formation. Because groups never are, but are always being made or maintained, they should be studied as a process, in particular, as a process of making and maintaining and contesting the links or associations between people (Latour, 2007, pp. 27–42; see also Akrich et al., 2002a, 2002b).
- Action is overtaken: Latour problematizes the traditional sociological views on agency. He distinguishes between intermediaries, which are passive connectors in already established links between nodes, and mediators, which are active actors making someone do something (Latour, 2007, p. 58), claiming that the latter is where sociologists should focus. He works with nonlinear logic in his explanations of causality and agency and makes it clear that sociology has only a very vague view, if any, about what it means to make someone do something, that is, of agency.
- Objects too have agency: In a move that resembles the arguments for a unified ontology that I made previously, Latour includes the material world in his sociology, arguing that one cannot think of the social without thinking of materiality. For him, the social has to do with the symbolic, the semiotic, and the translation of the material into symbol, and he argues that "there exists many shades of metaphysic between full causality and sheer inexistence" (Latour, 2007, p. 72).
- Matters of fact vs. matters of concern: His next source of uncertainty is that sociology too often confuses matters of fact with matters of concern, or, rather, moves too quickly from matters of concern to matters of fact. For him (Latour, 2007, pp. 87–120), the social is forged in the contestation of turning concerns into facts.
- Writing down risky accounts: For Latour (2007, pp. 121–140), the laboratory of the social sciences, where facts are constructed, is the writing of texts. Facts are not to be found; rather they are to be created

by testing them under disciplined and controlled circumstances. For social sciences, this entails giving an account, writing a text in which the social is constructed.

Latour also suggests three moves by which to reassemble the social, which are the following:

- Localizing the global: In typical complexity fashion, he (Latour, 2007, pp. 173–190) points out that the global does not exist as a substance but as the links between nodes, as associations that are continuously being created and maintained. Thinking global cannot happen without recourse to thinking local. Thus, "context" is not something out there or behind the local. Rather, it is found in the links between local sites.
- Redistributing the local: Similarly, the local is never purely local, it is always already linked, and these links are what is meant by global or social (Latour, 2007, pp. 191–218). No site or node is thus purely local, but local sites are always already connected to other local sites, which is the global. An unconnected site does not exist in the network—it is the gap between the strings of the net.
- Connecting sites: The social is thus the process or action of connecting sites. For him, the social is being socialized, psychology is psychologized and, in my case, translation is being translationized. (Latour, 2007, pp. 219–246, 257)

As I have indicated, Latour's ideas have much in common with complex adaptive systems theory. His advantage is that he has worked out the implications of systems thinking for social science by focusing on the connections between actors or sites. He uses the concept of translation, suggesting that his sociology should be called a sociology of translation to refer to the continuous change, negotiation and movement that is needed to maintain social associations. In Chapter 3, I work out the implications of his notion of translation for my theory in more detail.

3.3 Translation and the Social

So what is of interest here, and which I hope to explore in much more detail in the next chapter, is "inter-ness" or "inter-ing." I use the term to refer to what happens between systems or what happens between the parts of a system. Much is known about phenomena or systems, but we do not know enough about "inter-ness" or "inter-ing," that is, what happens between parts or systems and how the inter-relationships between parts constitute wholes. If one operates with process ontology and especially if you think in terms of systems, your interest shifts from entities to relationships between entities, that is, inter-ness and inter-ing. How entities relate, what the interrelations between them are, or how they are organized into new constellations with new properties, rather than what they are, becomes the focus of interest, as pointed out by Latour. I argue in the next chapter that translation is exactly an instance of the larger category of "inter-ness" or "inter-ing." I use both the noun and the gerund as I wish to maintain the complexity thinking that chooses neither, but maintains them in a complex paradox, also pointed out by Latour (2007). When one then considers social emergence, one has to consider the interactions between individual humans, and even individual subsystems, from which social phenomena emerge but to which they are not reducible (Sawyer, 2005, p. 8). These social interactions between humans logically imply the use of language and any semiotic system through which humans interact. Thus, the notion of emergence focuses the attention not on essence but on relationships, relatedness. It focuses the attention on process rather than ontology, without discarding the latter. In social reality, it focuses on that which makes the relationships possible, that is, the semiotic.

I think Sawyer's and Latour's arguments hold two important implications for translation studies. The first is that the emergence of social reality is a complex phenomenon. Theories of agency in translation, to my mind, assume very simple arguments concerning intentions and actions when they argue for the ways in which translators are agents of the creation of culture. The more detailed conceptualization of the role of symbolic interaction provided by Latour can fill this gap. Second, the theory opens up the space to talk about the role of semiotics, and language in particular, in the emergence of social reality.[1] Theoretically, it opens conceptual space for a philosophy of semiotics to underlie social reality. This is not to reduce social reality to semiosis, yet again. It is to realize that the kind of social reality that humans have created is not possible without the constitutive role played by semiotics, and as a logical extension, translation as mediating human interaction in multilingual contexts.

4. THE SEMIOTIC SUBSTRATUM FOR THE EMERGENCE OF SOCIAL REALITY

In the previous chapter and the first sections of this chapter, I have prepared the ground for arguing for the constitutive role of the semiotic, and language as one particular semiotic subsystem, in the emergence of social reality. I have done this by arguing for the central position of symbolic interaction in social emergence. Though with different emphases, all theories concerning the emergence of social reality seem to agree that various semiotic interactions by individual human agents constitute the substratum of social reality (Tyulenev, 2011a; also see the work of Griffin, 2002; Griffin & Stacey, 2005a, 2005b). In this section, I delve deeper into this phenomenon. I do this by exploring John Searle's linguistic philosophy of speech acts. Once again, by using Searle's ideas on emergence and language, I do not claim to support all of his philosophy (see for instance the difference in opinion between Searle and deconstructionists in Cilliers, 2005). Although Searle is a prolific author, I limit my discussion of his work to three books which deal specifically with the emergence of social reality through language, that is, *The Construction of Social Reality* (1995); *Mind, Language and Society* (1998); and *Making the Social World: The Structure of Human Civilization* (2010). Because my aim is not to discuss Searle for the sake of philosophical analysis, I thought these works to be representative of his thought and accessible to nonspecialists in philosophy (such as myself). Also, because my interest is in his views on emergence and the role language plays in the emergence of social reality, I do not attend to other matters that he addresses in his books, such as free will, human rights, and power. I do not claim that Searle's is the only way of conceptualizing the role of language in social emergence. For the sake of my argument in this chapter, I do believe his argument to be cogent enough to illustrate the point I want to make. As a strategic choice, once again because I am not interested in a historical development of his thoughts, I take his last work as a point of departure, referring to earlier works only when necessary. I present Searle's work under the following subheadings, which seem relevant to my argument: social ontology, intentionality, language and emergence, and, last, social institutions and language.

4.1 Social Ontology

Philosophically, Searle (2010, p. 3; 1995, pp. 1–2) is interested in understanding the relationship between physical and social reality without reducing the latter to the former. His aim (Searle, 2010, p. 4) is to explain the world as one, not having to resort to dualism or trialism to describe notions such as mind or society. How is it, he asks, that we have a world existing of physical and chemical phenomena, and in that same world, we have mental, psychological, and social phenomena (Searle, 1995, pp. 5–7; 1998, pp. 1–6). To put it simply, where does the mental come from, or how does the physical become social? It should immediately be clear that he addresses the same issues as those addressed by scholars of emergence, although he (Searle, 2010, p. 4) explicitly avoids the notion of "reduction" and other notions such as "supervenience" because of them being sources of confusion, the reasons for which he does not discuss. He is adamant that one should not answer these questions by avoiding what he (2010, p. 4) calls "the basic structure of the universe," that is, the facts of sciences such as physics, chemistry, and biology. He thus explores the nature of the essence or existence of social reality or, philosophically speaking, social ontology.

The particular problem is that social phenomena have no physical properties, and yet we talk about them as if they do exist. In what sense, then, can they be said to exist. Also, he takes as his point of departure the observation that many social phenomena find their "being" in the fact that people agree on them being what they are (Searle, 1995, p. xi). For instance, a note of money is a physical thing, but its function as money bears no relation to its physical features, except perhaps for what has been printed on it. Rather, this particular collection of molecules that we call money constitutes money because humans agree to call it money and because humans agreed to have it function as money. It is clear that what we have here is a semiotic movement or translation: A paper is taken as money in the formula of all semiotics; that is, *a* is taken as *b*. This basic working is a representation of what underlies the way in which semiotic objects function. What Searle then explores is this process through which human beings create social reality by calling things into being, literally. So what is the conceptual framework behind this ability?

Underlying the creation of social reality is the use of language acts to create it. To quote Searle (2010, p. 13),

> The claim . . . is that all of human institutional reality is created and maintained in existence by (representations that have the same logical form as) SF Declarations, including the cases that are not speech acts in the explicit form of declarations.

For Searle (2010, p. 7), the distinctive feature of human social reality is the ability of humans to impose functions on objects and other people by declaring it thus. This is what he refers to as status function (SF) declarations in the preceding quote. Furthermore, humans are collectively able to recognize the status afforded to an object or person, which Searle (2010, p. 8) calls collective intentionality. A third feature of Searle's (2010, p. 9) framework is that status functions carry deontic powers; that is, it imposes rights, duties, and obligations, among others, on people. Searle (2010, p. 9) then links the deontic nature to humans' ability to act independent of their own desires; in other words, they can act on the basis of the attributed deontic features, not only on the basis of their own desires. The preceding features lead to the creation of constitutive rules, which both constrain and make possible the creation of social reality (Searle, 2010, p. 10). They create what Searle (2010, p. 10) calls "institutional facts", that is, facts which are facts because human institutions created them, such as the money note with Nelson Mandela's face thereon, which was created by the institution of the South African fiscal system. These he contrasts with brute facts, which are facts of nature and which would have existed even though no humans were there to observe them or to call them into being. As Searle (2010, p. 10) says, "[a]n institution is a system of constitutive rules, and such a system automatically creates the possibility of institutional facts".

How do these status functions come to be? They are declared by human beings through speech acts. I assume that most readers of this book will at least be familiar with the notion of speech acts, and therefore, these are not discussed in detail. At this point, it will suffice to indicate that Searle did not imply representative speech acts but instead declarative speech acts, that is, the kind that does not make the statement fit the world but makes the world fit the statement (Searle, 2010, pp. 11–13). These kinds of statements actually create "world," that is, new phenomena, new social phenomena, new reality. They change the world or create new world by "declaring that a state of affairs exists and thus bringing that state of affairs into existence" (Searle, 2010, p. 12). Thus, Searle concludes that all of institutional reality, except language itself, is created by acts of speech. These acts do not have to be language only. Any kind of symbolic representation could do the same trick (Searle, 2010, p. 14), which means that social reality could be created multimodally. For Searle (2010, p. 17), then, social phenomena are dependent on the attitudes of human beings and he thus terms them "intentionality relative," which means that they depend on human intention to exist.

In his conceptualization, Searle thus posits the semiotic as an intermediary between mental or psychological and social reality. This very basic insight does two things, philosophically. First, it constitutes the semiotic as a pervasive inter-ness or inter-ing system throughout social reality. It makes it possible to see the semiotic in all of social reality and study the way in which it contributes to the emergence of social reality. In particular, it opens the conceptual space to discuss the role of semiotics, and language in particular, in the development of societies, which is the theme of the second part of this book. Second, it provides a conceptual space on which to base the notion of translation as constitutive in the emergence of social reality, either in societies that speak more than one language or in global contexts where societies, with different semiotic universes, are in continuous interaction.

4.2 Intentionality

The next question is thus: What is the nature of intentionality? If it is true that social reality is created by human minds agreeing on it being so, we need to understand the working of the human mind. In this section, I am not going into neuro-scientific explanations of mind, which will require a whole book to do it justice (see, for instance, Hofstadter, 1979; Tymoczko, 2013). For now, I choose to remain with philosophy of language, relying on Searle's insights into intentionality, but I can foresee that with the development of the neurosciences, this will become a major field of interest for translation studies because we know relatively little about the working of the brain and the emergence of mind from it. Searle (2010, p. 25) explains intentionality as "that capacity of the mind by which it is directed at, or about, objects and states of affairs in the world, typically independent of itself". Intentionality thus refers to a state of mind, of being conscious of what that state of mind is about. Typical intentional states of mind would be belief, desire, or hope. They refer to the attitude toward something. Searle (2010, p. 26) points out that there are also non-intentional states of mind where you feel or experience without feeling or experiencing about anything, for example, nervousness. Also, you could have conscious or unconscious intentions. Thus, one could have conscious intentional, conscious non-intentional, unconscious intentional and unconscious non-intentional states of mind (Searle, 2010, p. 26).

Searle (2010, p. 27) identifies the structure of intentional states as consisting of the state of mind and its content. When I believe that it is raining, the intentional state is thus "believing" whereas the content is the proposition that it is raining. So I could have a number of different intentional states about the same propositional content. I could wish that it was raining; I could hate that it is raining; I could hope that it is raining; I could know that it is raining. Searle (2010, p. 27) argues that the intentional state is usually not directed at the proposition but at objects and states of affairs in reality. I am, once again, aware of the contentious nature of this claim, but, though I may not necessarily agree with Searle on all details, I do want to put forward a more realist position on ontology (Latour, 2007; Van Huyssteen, 1986). I believe, and argue in more detail in the next chapter, that strong versions of constructivism represent an epistemological position that is not only unecological but suited to Western conceptualizations because it is related to powerful societies where people have the power to construct their reality. In a postcolonial context, it is an open question whether people have that power. Furthermore, I believe that much of constructivist power is an attempt to opiate the masses with the illusion of personal freedom and power, not allowing them to realize the extent to which they are constrained by both physical and social reality. It functions on the illusion that humanity is at the center of the universe and the illusion that humanity is in control of reality, thus rendering it a dominating epistemological position.

To get back to intentionality, Searle draws the important distinction between speech acts that represent states of affairs, that is, when the proposition has to fit the world, and speech acts that propose the world to be as the speaker would like to see it, that is, when the world has to fit the proposition. If two people say, "Let's get married", they are not representing a state of affairs in reality, but how they would like reality to be, that is, their being married. It is this last category of speech acts that is of interest. For these propositions to be true, they have to fulfill the conditions that they want to achieve. "Let's get married" can only be true once we are married. Thus, as Searle (2010, p. 29) states, these kinds of intentional states represent their conditions of satisfaction. They say how they would like reality to be and the things that should happen for reality to be that way.

Searle draws a further distinction. In his opinion, there is a difference between the intentions one has prior to acting and those that are held while acting (Searle, 2010, p. 33). He calls these prior intentions and intentions-in-action. Prior intentions are what are usually called plans or decisions. The prior intention is thus a state of mind while the intention-in-action is a physical event (Searle, 2010, p. 33). The intentions-in-action are usually called trying, such as "I am trying to lift my hand or fasten my shoe laces." For both prior intentions and intentions-in-action to be satisfied, they have to function in a causal relationship towards the production of an action. This means that the intention has to lead to the action, and provably so.

Searle also expands the notion of intentionality to include collective intentionality. To explain social reality as the result of human intention, one has to explain how humans, together, are intentional. This means that one should be able to explain we-intentionality as we have explained I-intentionality earlier. This we-intentionality arises from cooperation, which Searle (1998, pp. 23–26) defines as the existence of shared intentionality between agents. In other words, the mere fact that two people are knowingly doing the same thing, that is, driving to Cape Town to watch a soccer match, does not lead to collective intentionality. Their intentionality has to be shared and of the form "we intend", not "I intend and know that you intend and know that I intend". Thus, for Searle, we-intentionality cannot be reduced to I-intentionality.

Social reality is thus constructed from intentional states of mind of human beings, in particular by states of mind of the kind that does not fit reality but causes reality to fit it, that is, states of minds that create social reality.

4.3 Language and Intentionality

The way in which Searle conceptualizes language as the catalyst in the emergence of social reality from physical reality is the main reason why I am using his philosophy in my argument. He calls his philosophy of language "naturalistic" in the sense that it views language as both a biological and a social phenomenon (Searle, 1998, pp. 39–65; 2010, p. 61; also see the work of Jousse, 2000). This view of reality as a hierarchy of ontological levels (Searle, 2010, p. 61) with each higher level emerging from a lower level and exerting downward causation on it (Searle, 2010, p. 63), which is typical of complexity thinking, seems to fit neatly into the scheme into which I would like to conceptualize translation. Apart from being naturalistic, his philosophy also conceptualizes language as a constitutive factor in the emergence of social reality. As Searle (2010, p. 61) succinctly states, he is interested in moving "from intentionality to language and then from language to social institutions" (see also the work of British emergentists such as Mead, 1969, p. 124). Semiotics, conceptualized in this naturalistic way, is thus the factor that causes or makes possible or constrains the emergence of the social from the physical. For conceptualizing translation as a factor in the development of societies, one needs to be able to make the link between semiotics and society, one that is ignored by most scholars in the social sciences.

What is important in Searle's argument is that he does not preclude the downward causative power of semiotics. In other words, not only does physical reality give rise to semiosis, through the biology of the brain from which mind emerges, but through mind, semiosis is also able to exert downward causative power on reality, changing reality, creating new forms of reality. This is achieved semiotically by the performative nature of declarative linguistic statements (Searle, 2010, p. 69). Declarative speech acts have the ability to create social facts, social reality, as has been discussed above.

Once one has determined the world-creating power of semiosis, one needs to consider the fact that the symbolic interactions among humans, out of which social reality is created, assumes deontics. What Searle (2010, p. 80) means by this is that one cannot communicate in social settings without somehow being committed to the truth of what you are saying. Inherent in the social nature of human interaction stands this commitment. The declarative language act that creates a status function thus creates social reality. Let me quote Searle (2010, p. 84–85):

> If you have the capacity to say "He is our leader", "He is my man", "She is my woman", "This is my house", then you have the capacity to do something more than represent pre-existing states of affairs. You have the capacity to create states of affairs with a new deontology: you have the capacity to create rights, duties, and obligations by performing and getting other people to accept certain sorts of speech acts.

In cases such as these, the linguistic representations do not reflect states of affairs in reality; they create these states by referring to them.

4.4 Social Institutions and Semiosis

I think one can state it as a truism that much of reality around us consists of institutional facts, such as economic institutions, religious institutions, educational institutions, governmental institutions and the institution of translation (Halverson, 2004, 2008). That they exist is not the problem. What seems to be the problem is that we are so used to them that we experience them as virtually invisible. They are the world we live in. Just as we do not see the oxygen we breathe, we do not see the institutions that constitute our social reality. And what is more, Searle (2010, p. 90) argues, is that we see even less the semiosis through which this reality emerges. It is especially the workings of semiosis in this emerging process that is difficult to perceive and for which to account. To my mind, this state of affairs constitutes a serious problem in our understanding of social reality. I see a similar argument here to the one Derrida (1973) used for interpretation, claiming that, because we view language as immaterial and invisible, we do not see that the materiality of language constrains, if not renders impossible, our efforts at interpreting. Semiosis is not a window through which we obtain a clear view of reality; rather, it is a broken mirror that complicates our understanding. Similarly, semiosis is not an invisible "hand of God" through which we create our human reality. We have become so used to semiosis that we do not see that it is a material tool with which we shape our social reality. Understanding social problems and, if you want to be an optimist, solving social problems should thus logically include an understanding of semiosis and a conceptualization of the emergent role of semiosis in the construction of social reality. In this particular case, it should include an understanding of the problems of constructing social reality in multilingual contexts in which not only semiosis but also different semiotic systems are a factor.

Searle (2010, p. 93) makes it clear that, though social reality is constituted by semiotics, it is more than semiotics. This is the typical language of emergence: much coming from little. What Searle seems to be claiming is that the very social phenomena that are constituted by semiotic or semantic or symbolic acts obtain "a life of their own". They become real. Created by a status function declaration such as "We are imposing the status function A on an object B in a context C", this new phenomenon is as real as any physical object. A judge telling you that you are guilty changes your whole existence, especially if he or she sentences you to life in prison or death. It is the institution of the law and the declaration of having been found guilty that causes this change in physical reality—obviously with a physical substructure to support it.

Searle (2010, p. 94–100) discusses three examples of the creation of institutional facts by means of declaring status functions. The first is a case of collective recognition; that is, we all agree that A is the case. The second is an example of constituting new institutional facts by the formula "A counts as B in C"; for example, this piece of paper counts as money in South Africa. The third is an example of constituting a complex new institution such as a corporation, which is performed through an agreement that "the performance of these written speech acts—'executing and filing articles of incorporation'—counts as the creation of the corporation" (Searle, 2010, p. 98).

As indicated at the beginning, with this discussion, I never had the intention of providing any deep analysis of Searle's work or the development of his thought, or a comparison with other philosophers. My aim was much more modest. I wanted to establish the point that semiosis is one of the points of connection between materiality and society that has been hinted at in the previous chapter. This now opens up the conceptual space for considering translation as a factor in the development of society, as well as translation as constrained by the development of society.

5. THE ROLE OF SEMIOTICS IN THE EMERGENT SOCIAL

In the above, I have argued for a complex conceptualization of reality that is neither reductionist nor monist, neither dualist nor trialist. In particular, I have pointed to the role of semiosis in the emergence of social reality. Whereas I have argued for the value of Searle's insights in this regard, I do believe that his theory has a limitation. This limitation is that he focuses on the linguistic only. In what follows, I propose that one expands his theory by incorporating his notions about language within a larger framework, that is, the semiotic. For the social ontology that he proposes, one needs some kind of intentionality, as he has argued. What I would like to do is to expand the next point in his argument, that is, that this intentionality is expressed through language. I do not contest his notion that speech acts are constituents of social reality. What I do contest, is that his basic underlying conceptualization of the construction of social reality, that is, taking *a as b*, is particular to linguistic acts. Taking *a as b* is not particular to language, but to all semiotic phenomena. It is the basis on which semiotics, of which language is but one subsystem, operates. One can distinguish this semiotic operation, that is, *a as b*, from the logical one, that is, *a is b*. The second instance defines thought or logic, the first the semiotic, that is, the ability to consider absence and presence in a juxtaposed paradox, not to be resolved.

If one were thus to expand Searle's view on the construction of social reality to include all semiotic processes and/or phenomena, you gain by providing a much broader explanation for the emergence of social reality. (Here I understand social in the sense that Searle does, including all phenomena based on the semiotic interaction of humans, that s, society, but also culture, aesthetics, morals and ethics, religion, or, as Latour does, as the associations between people and things.) In this regard, I differ somewhat from Halverson (2004, 2008), who also uses Searle's work in her conceptualization of translation, in that I am not so much interested in translation as a social institution but in language and interlinguistic transfer as the substructure that makes the construction of social reality possible (Searle, 2010, pp. 109–115). In this sense, I am trying to provide an all-encompassing conceptualization of the role that semiotic phenomena or inter-ings play in the emergence of social reality. For instance, if limited to linguistic intentional acts, you cannot explain the construction of a social reality such as a park. How is it that this particular configuration of trees, shrubs, grass, and flowers has the social function of a place of relaxation, even spirituality in some cases. This is so because humans are able to bridge the "gap" between nature and culture through semiotics, taking this configuration of trees as a park, that is, as a place of relaxation, taking *a as b*. The fact that humans can construct meaning, value, and deontics, including social meaning, entails more than language; it entails the whole semiotic enterprise.

I am arguing here, then, that the semiotic provides the link between the material and the social. Note that I am not reducing the social to the semiotic. My argument is not one that claims that everything can be simplified to signs. I am not arguing that you can only understand economics if you understand semiotics or that law is nothing but semiotics. I am also not claiming that one should view religion "as" semiotics. What I am arguing is that social reality is co-constructed by means of semiotic activities. I am arguing that semiotics permeates and makes possible social reality, but social reality is not reducible to semiotics. I am arguing that, without semiotics, social reality would not have emerged, but this does not mean that one can reduce all of social reality to semiotics. I am arguing that semiotics is crucial in forging and maintaining the links among nodes in a network or system that is designated as social. Understanding the role that semiotic interactions play in the emergence of social reality will assist us to better understand some aspects of social reality, not everything.

In short, what I am suggesting is that reality is physical. From a complexity perspective, there is nothing more than the physical; that is, nothing has been added to the physical, and simultaneously, there is much more than the physical that is not physical but that is always also physical. The chemical, the biological, the psychological, and the social are physical yet more than physical. In terms of the discussion earlier, these phenomena of reality emerged out of the physical reality, having a physical substratum yet being "more than" or "other than" or "different from" the physical. This "more than" or difference is what I call emergence. The implication is that the levels of reality build on one another, presuppose one another. Thus, one cannot have chemical reality without physical reality, as one cannot have biological reality without chemical reality, as one cannot have psychological reality without biological reality. Similarly, one cannot have social reality without psychological reality, while, and this is crucial, the social is not reducible to the psychological. The social is something different, "more", emergent.

So, how then does the social emerge from its complex substrata, in particular the psychological, which is the individual? If I read philosophers like Searle and sociologists like Sawyer and Latour, it seems clear to me that semiotics is the key to unlocking the emergence of social reality. The human ability to represent, to take *a as b*, to create semiotic systems or associations of various nature underlies social reality. I am, once again, not claiming that social reality should be reduced to semiotics, far from it. What I am suggesting is that semiotics should form the emergent link between the physical-chemical-biological-psychological and the social. What I am suggesting is that the "boundary" or "border" between the psychological and the social, permeable as it is, is the semiotic. The semiotic is like a Janus figure, having roots in the physical-chemical-biological-psychological but simultaneously transcending it, translating it. It is rooted in the brain, one can even say in the psychological, which emerges from the brain, and it is simultaneously, paradoxically, part of the social where more than one physical brain interacts. It is in itself a boundary phenomenon. This means that one does not have to pose a typical constructivist divide between the first, nature, and the second, culture. Nature and culture are one because semiosis is both physical-chemical-biological-psychological and social.

Seeing that the semiotic is involved in the emergence of all aspects of social reality, this implies, as far as the field of translation studies is concerned, an inter- or even transdisciplinary link between translation studies and other fields of study, that is, anthropology, history, economics, mathematics, law, and religion. Because all of these are social phenomena, by my conceptualization, they all emerged from semiotic interactions between actors, and therefore, one can study their semiotic substratum and the role that this semiotic substratum, particularly language, plays in the emergence or development of these social phenomena.

I hope that by this time, the implications for translation studies, which I work out in detail in the next chapter, are starting to become clear. If my argument holds, that is, that social reality emerges by means of a semiotic substratum or by semiotic associations, cases in which some kind of semiotic inter-ing (which I explain in the next chapter) among the subsystems of social reality takes place constitute exactly where translation comes into play. Also, because of their semiotic substratum, any inter-ing between social systems per definition contains a semiotic aspect.

Another advantage of conceptualizing translation within a framework of emergent semiotics is that one is able to conceptualize the agency role of translation more complexly. To this, I devote a whole section of the next chapter. For the present moment, it will suffice to indicate that agency, which is one of the current hot topics in translation studies, is in need of a solid philosophical and theoretical underpinning.

6. CONCLUSION

In this chapter, I built on the conceptual foundation laid out in Chapter 1. I conceptualized emergence as the mechanism underlying the complexity philosophy of reality. If one is to reject reductionism, on one hand, and monism, dualism or trialism, on the other, emergence offers you a conceptual tool for doing so. It explains how lower hierarchical levels of existence give rise to higher levels. Paradoxically, it maintains the materiality or physicality of all social phenomena without reducing those phenomena to their parts. Zooming in further toward the topic of the book, that is, translation and development, the emergent philosophy of semiotics suggested in the preceding discussion provides the philosophical space and tools to talk about the role of translation in society. Up to now, even sociological theories of translation have largely assumed this relationship without exploring it philosophically and theoretically (someone such as Tyulenev [2011a] is an exception to this deplorable state of affairs).

In the next chapter, I discuss translation both as an emergent phenomenon and as a factor in the emergence of social reality. Simultaneously, I conceptualize translation to supervene on its substructure and to be supervened on by its superstructure. Translation is thus both emerging from and supervening on its substructure and part of the substructure of social reality and is being supervened on by social reality.

What remains to be done in my efforts to develop the concept of translation is, in the next chapter, to work out the implications of the philosophical and epistemological framework of these two chapters by bringing the framework into dialogue with current epistemological views in translation studies. In particular, efforts over the last two or three decades to define or conceptualize translation studies as a field of study are my point of focus.

3 Developing Translation Studies

1. INTRODUCTION

The history of (Western) thought has been characterized by a never-ending swing of the pendulum between a number of basic concepts that have been regarded as mutually exclusive. The most basic of these, I suggest, are change/stability, universal/particular, knowable/unknowable, finite/infinite, singular/plural, necessary/contingent. Thus, the Greeks were already divided on whether reality is changing or unchanging; whether, at its base, it is one or many; whether reality is knowable or unknowable; whether knowledge is universal or particular, finite, or infinite; and whether phenomena are necessary or contingent (Cronin, 2006, p. 11; Stumpf, 1975, pp. 3–113). As far as the current epistemological situation is concerned, what is known as the "modernist" paradigm is usually characterized, roughly, as a system of thought that is biased towards the permanent, universal, knowable, finite, singular, and necessity pole of the binary set. Problems with this kind of thinking have been pointed out and attacked by what has become known as "postmodernism". In contrast, what is known as the "postmodernist" paradigm is usually characterized, roughly, as being biased toward the changing, individual, unknowable, infinite, plural, and contingency pole of the set of paradoxes. Both of these paradigms are currently being questioned by what could be called a complexity approach.

The relevance of this excursion into philosophy for translation is the following: I contend that one of the problems with conceptualizing translation and translation studies is that it is not done with due consideration of epistemology and the epistemological and/or philosophical assumptions prevalent in thought in translation studies. What I mean is that not enough consideration is given to underlying assumptions about how we know and how the things we study and the knowledge we have about them relate to other things in reality and our knowledge about them; that is, there is not enough of a meta-disciplinary discourse in translation studies. Even James Holmes's (2002) map does not relate translation studies philosophically to the "larger scheme of things", except for references to the sciences from which translation studies emerged. Most discussions on translation and translation studies, notably the discussions on the turns in translation studies, seem to have been conducted from within the field, that is, by means of theoretical considerations, trying to explain translation in terms of yet another of its constituent parts. The ideas have obviously been borrowed from other fields of study, so in that sense, they are not from "inside" the field. What I mean is that translation scholars rarely take a meta-stance or philosophical perspective on their work.

As I understand the philosophy of science (Strauss, 1978, pp. 5–7), the moment you ask the question, "What is science x?" you are no longer engaged in a theoretical discussion within the field of study, but find yourself in a meta-theoretical question concerning what you are doing. You have stepped outside of the boundaries of your field of study, asking meta-questions, which are per definition epistemological or philosophy of science questions. Thus, the question, "What is a square root?" is a mathematical question whereas the question, "What is mathematics?" is not a mathematical question but a philosophy of mathematics question. In the same vein, the question, "What is translation?" or "What is translation studies?" cannot be answered by translation theories, but by meta-theoretical conceptualizations. Let me make clear that I am not looking for neutral ground or a God's-eye view from which to think about translation. That there are no neutral spaces, I take for granted. However, meta-conceptual thinking is possible (Hofstadter, 1979), and this is where I am heading. Perhaps then, I am not asking, "What is translation?" which could be construed as looking for a typical necessary and sufficient definition. Rather, I am asking how the phenomenon of translation relates to other phenomena in reality and what the implication of this is for translation studies as a scholarly enterprise. I am asking, "What is the relationship of translation with other things?" This chapter aims to conceptualize translation and translation studies meta-theoretically.

This leads to the second problem, namely, that a whole number of philosophical or epistemological assumptions are at work in the efforts to conceptualize translation and translation studies, assumptions that have not, to my knowledge, formerly been analyzed and discussed. One could therefore say that a number of underlying philosophical or epistemological forces that are at work in translation studies shape the way in which the field is developing without the scholars that are involved in these developments reflecting on their own conceptual roots. In terms of the basic paradoxes discussed above, I argue in the following that current approaches in conceptualizing translation studies can quite clearly be located in the postmodernist paradigm and that this bias in conceptualizing translation studies needs to be put on the table for discussion (Simeoni, 2007). I then try to provide a complexity perspective on this bias, suggesting a complexity conceptualization of translation and translation studies that takes serious both constituents of the paradoxes mentioned earlier without dissolving either.

A third problem in conceptualizing translation and/or translation studies is that theorists are attempting to define the object of study. Once again, my understanding of conducting science is that a field of study is not, in the first place, defined by the object of its study but by the angle of its view, its perspective (Strauss, 1978, p. 3; see also the way Latour [2007, p. 257] conceptualizes different fields of study). The reason for this assumption is that its contrary leads to essentialism. If one were able to point out objects of study that were "only" translations or only mathematics or only history, you would end up with a world full of "essential" things, that is, mathematical or translation or historical things. In other words, there are no "pure" translations or translational phenomena in reality. There is reality, from which translation scholars have to decide which aspect they will be considering. This consideration is arrived at by a twofold activity, that is, identifying and distinguishing (Strauss, 1978, pp. 3–4). By this time in the history of science, I assume it general knowledge that reality does not consist of essences but of multifaceted phenomena, that is, phenomena that partake holistically in all of reality. Thus, a common kitchen table is physical, chemical, biological, mathematical, semiotic, historic, and so on. To put it more elegantly, any object in reality takes part in the whole of reality and can therefore be analyzed from a variety of perspectives. Thus, to use the example of mathematics again, mathematicians are not embroiled in a discussion on which phenomena in reality are mathematical phenomena. They study all of reality, but their focus falls on the mathematical qualities of all of reality; that is, they study reality from a mathematical perspective. A particular science can be likened to a pair of glasses that you put on and that determine what you see. So the question will never be, "Is a tree mathematical?" or "Can mathematicians study cars?" The question is, "What is mathematical about trees or cars?" In this vein, I further develop the notion of translation studies by discussing the particular angle from which scholars approach reality in translation studies. I shall thus ask, "What is translational about reality and how could one conceptualize a perspective that will assist you in studying the translation-ness of all aspects of reality?"

In this chapter, I thus intend discussing the question, "How is one to think about translation in a scholarly way?" and "From which perspective does translation studies as a scholarly activity look at reality?" This discussion is part of a very long thread of discussions on the nature of translation and the nature of the field of translation studies, to which I am obviously indebted. It is meant as part of an ongoing discussion in which, to my mind, we are still looking for the right questions to ask. I shall structure the discussion as follows. I start with a discussion in which I analyze the current philosophical underpinnings of translation studies, as I see it. Then I put forward a complexity perspective on translation in which I conceptualize translation in its relationship to other aspects of reality, claiming that translation is an instance of inter-systemic relationships. In particular, I suggest a theory of emergent semiotics as a framework for thinking about translation. The word *instance* is important here. I am not conceptualizing of translation "as" semiotics. I am rather arguing that translation is an emergent semiotic phenomenon that underlies, in part, the emergence of social reality. Also, I do not try to "define" translation or translation studies but rather consider the conceptual spaces necessary to consider translation or translation studies.

2. AN ANALYSIS OF PHILOSOPHICAL UNDERPINNINGS IN TRANSLATION STUDIES

As indicated previously, this section provides an analysis of recent efforts to conceptualize translation and translation studies. By recent, I mean the recent history of translation studies as a field of study that started with the Second World War (Tymoczko, 2007) and that was conceptualized by Holmes's famous map in the early 1970s. In my analysis, I attend to the seemingly never-ending series of turns in translation studies, which I read as consecutive efforts at conceptualizing both the object and perspective of translation studies in a reductionist fashion. Second, I turn to the use of metaphor and a number of "translation as" conceptualizations in which I explore further efforts to talk about the object and perspective of translation studies. Third, I turn to Tymoczko's work as the first effort, to my mind, to propose a meta-theoretical conceptualization of translation. Last, I consider recent conceptualizations of agency in translation studies as another strand of thought in the efforts to conceptualize translation and translation studies. My argument is that all of these efforts, despite their very strong postmodernist epistemological assumptions, turn out to have reductionist tendencies, reducing the complex notion of translation to one of its constituent parts.

2.1 Turns in Translation Studies

The motivation for analyzing the philosophical and epistemological underpinnings of translation studies arises, in my opinion, from the current state of affairs in the discipline (Arduini & Nergaard, 2011). In this regard, one could firstly refer to what has generally been termed the turns in translation studies, which have seemingly come to an end. Each turn represents not only a different, and mostly valid, perspective on translation but also a (epistemological) conceptualization of what translation and translation studies is or should be. In these turns, scholars have conceptualized translation in terms of other disciplinary perspectives, for example, linguistics (Nida, 2004), comparative literature (Gentzler, 2008), pragmatics (Hatim, 1997; Hatim & Mason, 1990); culture studies (Bassnett & Lefevere, 1990), sociology (Tyulenev, 2011a, 2011b), ideology studies (Baker, 2006), postcolonial studies (Bassnett & Trivedi, 1990), or history (Simon, 1990). These turns usually meet with one common criticism: They reduce the complexity of the phenomenon of translation to the particular point of interest of the turn. This has given rise to a situation in which the next scholar to enter the debate needs to proclaim a next turn because he or she is considering an aspect of translation which the previous scholar did not. Referring back to the discussion on a philosophy of complexity in Chapter 2, I do not want to contest any of the turns and the value that they have added to the field. Translation can indeed be studied from the perspective of language or culture or society, and translation scholars have contributed to the understanding of the field as a whole by considering the various parts thereof. Translation is indeed rewriting or indirect speech or representation. Translation can indeed be metaphorically conceptualized as acting, smuggling or cross-acting. What I hope to add is a conceptual space in which to relate these perspectives to one another and within which one could understand why these avenues are taken in the attempts to conceptualize translation. This conceptual space should, to my mind, not only focus on either difference or similarity, as all of the above-mentioned efforts have done. Rather, it should be a conceptualization that continually identifies (similarity) *and* distinguishes (difference); that is, it maintains a conceptual paradox between aspects of translation. Understanding the interrelationships between the various aspects of translation could assist in creating an understanding of the phenomena with which we are working. It could also assist with the approaches we take in studying them.

If one analyses the turns in translation studies from a philosophical perspective, you find that they all assume a particular perspective from which to study translation phenomena. Now, on one hand, this is the nature of Western science, it cuts off or opens a part of reality and then focuses its attention on that part only (Tyulenev, 2011a, pp. 6–12). However, the problem in translation studies is that, as in most other Western-informed sciences, scholars do not seem to have clarity as to the relationship between the parts under analysis. In other words, one part of scientific work could rightfully be to analyze phenomena, but the other part should be to synthesize the findings, to consider how the parts relate to one another and to the whole. One part of science could constitute the taking apart of the whole and studying the parts, but the next part of science should be to ask about the relationship between parts, the organization of parts into wholes, the links between parts that makes them into a particular whole. Furthermore, philosophically, translation studies scholars seem not to know about or to reflect on how these perspectives relate to one another. What is it that keeps these different perspectives together in one field of study? Why is it possible to study translation from so many different perspectives? It is true that the object of study is multifaceted, but it is also true that the field of study is one. So the one and the many should be kept in paradoxical juxtaposition in a complex conceptualization because choosing the one above the other implies a mutilation of reality (Morin, 2008). The field of translation studies has clearly brought the diversity of the field to the fore. It seems time now to relate that diversity to unity without sacrificing either or lending primacy to one or the other. This is attempted in Section 3 of this chapter.

2.2 Metaphors

Metaphorical thinking has become part and parcel of the efforts to conceptualize translation. The drive in this approach is motivated by two arguments. The first is, based on Lakoff's work, to argue for the conceptualizing power of metaphors (St. André, 2010a, 2010b, pp. 1–8). In this kind of argument, metaphors constitute the way human beings think and create new knowledge, sometimes going so far as to claim that it is the only way. The second argument is that, in the history of science, one finds sufficient examples of metaphors having been used to conceptualize new developments in various fields of study. Examples from physics, chemistry, and biology are usually provided as proof for this argument.

Underlying the search for metaphors in the conceptualization of translation seems to be the agreement amongst translation scholars that a sufficient and necessary definition of translation is neither possible nor necessary. Based on this argument, these scholars seem content to conceptualize translation metaphorically. For example, Hermans (2007) views translation "as" indirect speech, as does Gutt (2000). Tymoczko (2007) herself views translation "as" representation, transmission, and transculturation, or to be more precise, she frames translation as these three things. Bandia (2008) views translation "as" reparation, and Bassnett and Lefevere (1990) as well as Bassnett and Bush (2006) conceptualize it "as" writing or rewriting.

In a recent attempt to explore the role of metaphors in translation, St. André (2010a) brought together a number of thought-provoking articles in which translation scholars have attempted to "think through translation with metaphors". According to him, metaphors are commonly used in the development of a field of study and to conceptualize new theories (St. André, 2010a, p. 7). The question is, however, whether the use of metaphor can be maintained in the conceptualization of a theoretical or meta-theoretical discourse without developing a theory with which to conceptualize it (Tyulenev, 2010). In all other fields of study, the metaphor actually acts as some kind of trigger in the conceptualization process, but then the metaphor, or actually the insight mediated by means of the metaphor, is theorized. In the case of translation studies, it seems to me that many scholars expect of the metaphor to become the theory. Thus, Van Wyke (2010) conceptualizes translation as clothing, a cover that allows the invisible body behind it to be best appreciated. Benshalom (2010, p. 48) conceptualizes translation as acting, as someone speaking what someone else has written. St. André (2010b) himself conceptualizes translation as cross-action, pretending to be something that you are not. Heniuk (2010) explores the metaphor of translation as squeezing a jellyfish, and Tyulenev (2010) conceptualizes translation as smuggling. Although it is true that one could conceptualize of translation as any of the preceding, the questions are, Why? What makes it possible? Is it not a fact that all of these different conceptualizations have something in common? On what basis do all these different metaphors make sense? Returning to the introduction, is the varying nature of metaphorical conceptualizations not based on the sameness of something that is common to all of them? In postmodernist fashion, these metaphors keep on deferring the meaning of the notion of translation, relating it to some other notion. While the logic of difference has been made clear, at times one needs to draw boundaries, though contingent and temporary, to these deferral processes because you have to act (Cilliers, 2005, pp. 263–264). So, although this deferring process is legitimate and can continue, it is equally necessary to come to some tentative understanding of what we are talking about. This tension—between deferring and settling—I argue, exists at the edge of chaos, not in some kind of equilibrium.

The preceding conceptualizations also raise another question: Why is language never conceptualized as acting, that is, the other way round? And it raises a further question: Why is acting never conceptualized as language? In other words, why the need in translation studies to think of it in terms of something else? And what makes it possible? And why not go straight to the problem to ask, "What is translation?" One reason, among a legion others, could be that translation studies has tried and is trying to define the object of study rather than the perspective of the field of study. I suggest in the following that both should be performed.

Another problem here seems to be that using metaphor to conceptualize translation is becoming a self-fulfilling prophecy. Scholars with an interest in drama will inevitably conceptualize translation as acting; that is, it is an easy and uncritical (and also reductionist) assertion of similarity. Why does nobody in translation studies ask about the difference between translation and rewriting or acting or smuggling? Defenders of the position may argue that everybody knows that there is a difference. Fine, but by continuing, book after book and article after article, to conceptualize translation as similar to basically anything in reality is constitutes only one half of what our task involves. We also have to ask what is different, that is, unique based on similarities, about translation.

Tyulenev (2010) and Guldin (2010) thus both argue along the lines I am indicating here, that the metaphors in themselves cannot be regarded as theories but have to be theorized. Guldin (2010, p. 168) rightly indicates that any use of metaphor to conceptualize a new theory is reductionist in nature as there is usually only one point of comparison which is developed. In particular, he (Guldin, 2010, p. 176) theorizes translation as the simultaneous co-presence of both sides, the source and the target—similar to metaphor. Thus, one has to conceptualize a theoretical space in which the complexity and variety of metaphors can be accommodated. As with translation, metaphor deals with change based on stability, foreignness based on similarity (Guldin, 2010, p. 174). This means that both metaphor and translation embody a paradoxical logic, both deal with relating systems, with boundaries, with crossing borders, and with inter-ness. If one considers all the metaphors explored in St. André's collection and the other metaphors discussed previously, it appears that two aspects emerge on a theoretical level. The first is the ability to relate two things to one another in a paradoxical way that creates new meaning, be that two words or two texts and be that in the same language or in two different languages. Conceptualizing this idea systemically, one could argue that the nature of semiotic phenomenon is that they "inter" between two systems, paradoxically holding to both systems. These are the metaphors of clothing and smuggling and cross-acting. It is the carryover idea; that is, something changes and something remains stable. The second is the idea of being able to represent what has been said in numerous ways. This is reported speech, representation, and acting. It also relates to the metaphors of translation as reported speech, rewriting, and representation. Once again, something changes and something remains stable.

I contend here that these metaphors all refer to aspects of the nature of semiotics. First, whether we like it or not, form and meaning can be distinguished, though not separated, contrary to both modernism and postmodernism. From a complexity perspective, this is yet another of the famous binaries of Western thought. Let us assume, as the complexity theorists suggest, that form and meaning exist in a nonequilibrium system at the edge of chaos. This means that the exact relationship between the two cannot be predicted and can be explained with laws of probability only. Claiming, as modernity does, that form and meaning are clearly separable and that meaning can be "extracted" from form without much ado and claiming, as postmodernity does, that meaning cannot be divulged from form at all are both reductionist enterprises. Somehow, some aspect of meaning can change in form and, by some means, can retain a resemblance of itself. Note the repeated use of "some". Somehow, you can say something and I can tell someone else what you have said, using other words, and the two utterances still bear a resemblance to one another. This is the nature, not of translation, but of semiotics. It is similarity based on change and, paradoxically, change based on similarity. It is presence based on absence and absence based on presence.

Another problem with the use of metaphors in translation studies is of a methodological nature. Martín De León (2010), Heniuk (2010), Guldin (2010), and Monti (2010) all seem to employ an ethnographic methodology by looking at how translators and the public conceptualize translation. The same impetus underlies Tymoczko's (2006, 2007) attempts to explore words used for translation in general language and in various cultures in order to come to a better understanding of translation. Note again, that ethnographic studies focus on the local and difference, which forms part of the epistemological paradigm currently dominant in translation studies. Although the approach itself is valid, the way in which it is used in translation studies poses at least two problems. The first is that the scholars conducting ethnographic studies on notions of translation usually commit the first sin in the ethnographic table of commandments; that is, they criticize the layperson for having a particular point of view, or they present a different view of translation (see in particular Heniuk, 2010, p. 145; also Latour, 2007). This is similar to early anthropologists calling the people on which they were reporting "barbaric". To my mind, if one wants to use an ethnographic methodology in translation studies, you cannot use it in the service of your own ideological stance, that is, to "de-Westernize" or "de-modernize" concepts of translation. You have to regard the local in terms of its own values. I cannot see the use of doing ethnographic work if one is not to take serious the local views or if you merely study ethnographically concepts that strengthen your own theoretical point of view. I am therefore not sure whether lay views on translation can be used to conceptualize the field of study. Ethnography is aimed at understanding what the other thinks and does in a particular context. Turning those local conceptualizations into an international theory seems be an extreme case of "translating" the other into the self, as Sturge (2007) has argued.

The second problem with these ethnographic approaches seems to me that at least some of them perform the etymological fallacy. They look at the "original" meaning of words without taking the history of its evolution into account. No word can be said forever to have had the same meaning. This fallacy was committed quite often in New Testament studies when the so-called original meaning of New Testament words was excavated from the classical Greek, ignoring the fact that meaning in Koine Greek, a later version, differed from that in classical Greek. In the case of translation studies, can one claim that the meaning lies in the word or is the meaning in the practice, whichever word was chosen for it? To quote Shakespeare, if we called translation anything else, would we do it differently? Tymoczko (2007), for instance, argues, based on the meaning of Igbo words, that translation is conceptualized as narration. The question is, however, not what the Igbo chose as their word for translation but how they translate, or more importantly, how they translated? This immediately brings history into play. In Setswana, a South African Bantu language, the word for translation is the same word that is used for turning something over (Molefe, 2011), and in Xitsonga, another South African Bantu language, the word used also includes explanation (Mapengo, 2011). This does not mean that Setswana-speaking or Xitsonga-speaking translators currently translate differently to English-speaking translators because they use a different word for the action of translating. It may just be that they have been confronted with a new phenomenon, written translation, and chose a word that carried the intended meaning—changing something while keeping it the same. Claiming more than merely this seems overkill to me logically, etymologically, and historically. What would render valuable insight is if one could consider the historical development of translation practices (and for that matter terminology) in a particular culture, as Quoc Loc (2011) did in the case of Vietnamese. It is the only way in which one could argue for or against the influence of Western-dominated practices in translation.

Theorizing these notions, one thus has to move to the meta-question: What do all these metaphorical perspectives have in common? To my mind, they share the commonality that they all refer to features of semiotics. As indicated in Chapter 3, semiotics is the human ability to represent one thing as another, that is, *a as b*. It is the human ability to conceptualize change based on similarity and similarity based on change. To be able to function semiotically, one has to be able to see difference based on similarity, and you have to be able to hold this paradox and not dissolve it. To be able to function semiotically, the thing you are representing, which is usually absent, has to be related to something different, which is put in the place of the first, and based on this ability, you have to be able to relate the absent and the present. You do it based on being able to see similarity and difference. You know that the sign is not the thing and the thing is not the sign, but you simultaneously know that they are related, you set up ties or links between them without claiming identity. They only work if you can hold on to the paradox of similarity and difference. This similarity/difference can relate to semiotic medium (i.e., language to film), or to space (i.e., from here to there), or to time (i.e., from now to then) or for any other conceivable category.

As a comment aside, one then has to acknowledge that other fields of study may find translation helpful as a metaphor. The typical lamentations in this regard, that is, that "it is diluting *our* field"[1], cannot hold in the face of the way in which translation studies itself makes use of metaphors.

I conclude by pointing out that, to my view, the efforts at conceptualizing translation through metaphor constitute yet another one-sided, postmodernist epistemological effort. Metaphors are preferred because they valorize the local (Tymoczko, 2010, p. 112), which falls within the postmodernist biases of my initial philosophical analysis. It focuses one-sidedly on the local, the contingent, the irrational or unknowable (continually deferring the fixing of meaning) by using the very individuality of metaphor formation to theories translation. What is epistemologically interesting, however, is that it maintains the modernist undercurrent of reductionism, by thinking about translation in terms of its constituent parts and not in terms of the relationship between the parts.

If one asks the question as to why turns and metaphors and "translation as" definitions are possible and popular, the theory I am espousing explains it because of the semiotic nature that all these features share. Translation can be such as language, or literature, or metaphor (Heniuk, 2010, p. 168) because all of these phenomena share the fact that they are semiotic phenomena. The one mistake would thus be to reduce translation to any of these because then you would only focus on similar characteristics, ignoring the differences between them. For instance, it may be true that translation is like cross-acting, but it is also not. Thus, a metaphorical conceptualization of translation needs to theorize both the similarities and the dissimilarities of the comparison.

Put simply, why can we not view translation "as translation", or what would it take to come to such a view? Do we ever consider the point that philosophy does not use other disciplines to define itself? Or that nobody would claim that sociology is actually "just" a form of philosophy? Philosophers would claim that philosophy is philosophy, full stop! Do we ever consider the fact that, philosophically speaking, we have a unique phenomenon to study, a phenomenon that emerges out of other phenomena but is not reducible to any one or all of those phenomena? Translation scholars seem nonplussed by the fact that they borrow conceptual material from nearly all other fields of the humanities, for example, anthropology, sociology, linguistics, literary theory, critical theory, and pragmatics. They seem to be comfortable with the fact that the use of these differing fields of study is done without theorizing on the implications thereof. Is it just a matter of "plurality goes", or is translation a phenomenon of such a nature that it has to be explained by a multitude of substrata, that is, by way of complexity theory? I am not questioning the fact that translation scholars use other fields of study but rather the fact that they do not conceptualize this use.

To my mind, what makes translation difficult to define is not only its cultural multiplicity or fracturedness, although that does play a role. To my mind, translation is difficult to define because it is a complex phenomenon. Why is it possible for translation scholars to write chapters and books about translation as culture, as diplomacy, as politics, as language, as indirect speech, as ecology, as literature, as history, and/or as system? I argue that these are possible because translation is all these things, because language is all these things or, rather, because semiotics as a subsystem of social reality makes possible all these phenomena and constitutes them. Social reality is construed by means of symbolic interaction, that is, semiotic interaction, and thus, politics has a semiotic substratum, law has a semiotic substratum, history has a semiotic substratum, and so on. If one does not want to go the route of reductionism, you then have to conceptualize a framework within which you can think about translation as the multi-semiotic vehicle for all these phenomena. In this sense, it is an inter-phenomenon, which operates on the process of the creation of social phenomena. It does so by inter-ing between systems, be that vertically between the biopsychological and the social, or horizontally between, say, legal and economic systems (see the discussion and the figures presented in Section 3.1 of this chapter).

2.3 Cluster Concept

To my mind, Tymoczko (2002, 2006, 2007, 2010, 2013) has gone the furthest in her efforts to conceptualize translation. In the process, she has tried, particularly, to engage the positivist and reductionist assumptions underlying translation studies. I first discuss her seminal insights and then argue that one could go even further, both conceptually and epistemologically.

Let me first point out that, to my mind, Tymoczko is an excellent example of the postmodern strand of thinking to which I pointed at the beginning of the chapter. I am not trying to label or box her in, but I am trying to engage with the epistemological assumptions at work in the conceptualization of translation. Early on in her book (Tymoczko, 2007, p. 16), she starts by claiming that scholars are trying to understand and gain knowledge of life, with life conceptualized as "lived and experienced in a multi-centered manner". The reference to "multi-centered" indicates her deep belief in particularity, multiplicity, and contingency as founding concepts for understanding reality. In line with her assumptions, she then proceeds by showing how linguistic, literary and cultural efforts have been made at a definition of translation (Tymoczko, 2007, p. 52). What her approach gains on earlier approaches, and where she comes close to the complexity perspective which I am proposing here, is that she holds together complex paradoxes in her argument that translation is an interdiscipline. She proposes a dialogic and multi-perspective position on translation (Tymoczko, 2007, p. 53). In her estimation, the complex nature of the concept of translation causes the complex nature of the field of study (Tymoczko, 2007, p. 53). Although I do agree on the complexity of translational phenomena, I do not agree with her efforts at conceptualizing a field of study on the basis of an object of investigation only. As I have indicated, fields of study are primarily conceptualized in terms of the perspective they hold on reality. For instance, a translated text also has physical and chemical properties that the physicist and the chemist will study, not the translation scholar. Looking for something in reality that can be called "translation" seems to me only part of what we need to be doing. What we also need to do is what, for instance, the founders of literary science did. As they tried to conceptualize literariness, translation scholars need to try to conceptualize translation-ness. The same holds true for the founders of sociology: They tried to conceptualize social-ness (Tyulenev, 2011a). In the same vein, I suggest that translation studies will not progress toward a conceptualization of the field unless it asks, "What is translation-ness?" Once it has asked that question, it could go Tymoczko's route toward an inductive conceptualization of features of translational objects. This is discussed further later in this section.

In an effort to "enlarge translation", that is, to open up a conceptual space within which to theorize translation wider than is currently the case, Tymoczko points out a number of problems with the current efforts at defining translation. She (Tymoczko, 2007, p. 78) argues that the typical reductionist way of defining a concept, that is, by finding necessary and sufficient conditions that would cover all instances of a phenomenon, does not suffice in the case of translation. The reason why reductionist definitions are not adequate in all instances is the complexity of social or cultural concepts. She argues convincingly that culture acts as a fragmentary factor to fragment the practices and products of translation to such an extent that one is unable to define it, and therefore, she proposes, one should conceptualize of translation as a cross-cultural concept (Tymoczko, 2007, p. 79). She asks, "Is it possible to conceptualize translation without retreating to a culturally chauvinistic and limited point of departure for theory or to a prescriptive stance for practice, both of which reject the cultural production of other peoples" (Tymoczko, 2007, p. 83)? Although she rightfully points to the fragmented nature of translational processes and products, I think she is biased toward the contingent in a way that fragments reality more than is necessary. I am thus asking whether reality is as fragmented as she portrays it and whether her assumptions presuppose this fragmentation.

To solve her problem with defining translation, she turns to concept formation to try to understand how one could think about complex concepts such as translation (Tymoczko, 2007, p. 84). According to her, the concept "translation" is related to the category of translations and the category of activities that produce translations. Where she decidedly moves toward a complexity perspective is when she claims that nonlinearity underlies the inconsistent and contradictory practices of translation phenomena (Tymoczko, 2007, p. 84). She suggests that one should turn to relational thinking rather than essentialist thinking when considering complex cultural concepts, something to which complexity scholars would only agree, but not only for cultural phenomena—for all complex phenomena. She claims that translation cannot be defined reductively, that is, in terms of features or parts that predict the whole. Although translation is based on language (Tymoczko, 2007, p. 85), one finds partial and overlapping similarities between translation phenomena that relate to differences in time and place. Note again her emphasis on difference.

Tymoczko bases her work on that of Wittgenstein (1958), who argued that notions such as language or game do not have one feature in common in all instances. Rather, all instances of the notion are somehow related (Tymoczko, 2007, p. 84). She (Tymoczko, 2007, pp. 84–85) then uses the term *cluster concept*, i.e. concepts that do not lend themselves to definition in a reductionist fashion or concepts that are conceptualized by viewing them as a family. The way to conceptualize these phenomena, for example, game, tool, translation, is to describe the resemblances between them, just as one would do with a family. (Note, as an aside, that Wittgenstein formed his notion of family resemblances before the availability of detailed genetic knowledge, which may, these days, indeed lead to the ability to provide a necessary and sufficient definition of a family, or at least some families and family relationships.) Cluster concepts, as Tymoczko calls them, would thus show similarities or resemblances without certain features necessarily occurring in all instances, i.e. being necessary and sufficient. These similarities sometimes lie in the detail and sometimes in the overall structure and cannot be defined a priori, but can only be described a posteriori. One can thus not define translation; one can only describe the similarities or relationships between translation phenomena. Note the preference for the bias towards unknowability and change/difference; that is, each instance is different.

From Wittgenstein, Tymoczko borrows the notion of game as a cluster concept or a concept the instances of which are related by family resemblances (Tymoczko, 2007, p. 85). As Wittgenstein (1958) argued, these concepts can be conceptualized not by deductive definition but by pointing to phenomena and saying, "This and all things like it are x." She also explores the notion of emergence, without calling it that, in the example of fiber which seems to be one thing but which is actually made up of a number of thinner fibers (Tymoczko, 2007, p. 85). The aim in this kind of concept formation is not to look at something that these phenomena have in common, but at some similarities between them or at the relationships that obtain between them. Membership of clusters is not a matter of logic (note the preference for irrationality) but of practice and use, emerging, to use complexity nomenclature, out of the practice of social interaction. In her argument, Tymoczko poses an empirical approach, that is, Wittgenstein's "do not think, look" over against a theoretical or deductive approach. Does one detect a measure of empiricism in her argument? I do think so, because it suits her focus on difference, the particular and the contingent. Thus, translation can only be conceptualized a posteriori and not in an a priori way.

To my mind, Tymoczko (2007, p. 84) then takes a huge leap forward by arguing that translation is a "complex cross-cultural concept". Tymoczko does not clarify the notion of complexity, but I suggest that her notion of a cluster concept is related to what is seen as a complex concept in complexity theory. In other words, it is a concept that is explained by nonlinear logic, that is, sensitivity to original conditions and nonlinear causal relationships between input and output. This means that translation is a complex phenomenon, emerging out of substrata, and knowledge of which cannot assist in explaining or predicting the whole. She does, however, make use of the concept of categories, calling translation a category that includes all the translations found around the world. She does not attempt to conceptualize the category, which is what I hope to do in Section 3. She further argues that one finds a category of activities that produces translations. With this move, she avoids a reductionist definition and opts for a pragmatic definition, not "thought" but "seen". In her view, translation is a pragmatic quality and is to be defined pragmatically. She further grounds translation in cultural practice, which she also argues is a family type of phenomenon. It has similarities with other cultural phenomena but, being cultural, is contingent.

I see the seeds of emergence as already sown in Tymoczko's work. I thus first want to argue how her views are emergent, and then I want to build on her argument for a more adequate theory of emergence. First, Tymoczko claims that one finds a category of activities all over the world that "produce" translations. Various, that is, a complexity of, activities thus result in a (relatively) simple phenomenon, recognized as translation all over. Second, she argues that translation is based on language. This is the typical language of emergence. In fact, I argue that translation emerges out of a number of substrata, which are each culturally contingent. The notion of cluster concept itself presupposes an emergent way of thinking. It refers to a concept with a complexity of underlying forms and practices resulting in one phenomenon. Lastly, Tymoczko refers to cluster concepts that are not based on fixed features, that is, essences, but on holistically structured activities. In emergence theory, the superstrata subsume the substrata in a holistic way.

Tymoczko's work holds a number of implications for my project. She has opened the possibility for moving away from reductionist definitions of translation. She has opened the space for meta-theoretical conceptualizations about translation as a complex phenomenon, which she calls "a puzzling philosophical matter" (Tymoczko, 2007, p. 88). Again, this is the point at which I would like to take up the baton and enter into a dialogue with her about un-puzzling the issue philosophically or meta-conceptually. Lastly, she has opened up the space for conceptualizing translation in terms of emergence because she conceptualizes it as arising out of "practice and usage". I do not claim that she was thinking about emergence, but I argue that the implication of the way in which she conceptualizes translation, in fact, assumes some notion of emergence.

In analyzing Tymoczko's move toward conceptualizing translation studies as a cluster concept, I contend that it is no accident that she bases her work on Wittgenstein. He is a very interesting philosophical figure. On one hand, he has strong rationalistic tendencies, but he is not a universalist. One would be able to call him an individualist rationalist, which is what makes him a precursor to postmodern thought. Thus, he fits Tymoczko's program like a glove, having enough rationality to be scientific and enough individualism to be postmodern. In this sense, one could argue that it is not translation that is necessarily thus defined, but Tymoczko's conceptual framework. She cannot but define translation the way she has done, not because that is the nature of the phenomenon, but because that is the scope that her conceptual frame of reference allows her. In the end, valuable as her insights are, they are skewed toward the particular, the infinite, the many, the unknowable, the changing, the contingent, and difference, that is, the postmodern. To come to a less-skewed understanding of translation, one has to juxtapose her conceptual framework with the "other side", that is, a more deductive approach, in a complex way to be able to deal with the full array of complexities concerning translation.

The second problem with her conceptualization is that she is not able to relate translation to the rest of reality in a philosophical way. Although she rightfully argues in favor of interdisciplinarity, she conceptualizes how translation relates to other phenomena in reality and how one would conceptualize it as a field of study. This relates to a third problem in her thought. She may be able to indicate phenomena that are part of the family of translational things in reality. However, this does not yet allow her to conceptualize the field of translation studies in a logical way. Unless one is able to motivate the perspective of your field of study, i.e. the lens through which you look at reality, I contend that you have not yet conceptualized a field of study.

What I shall thus attempt in Section 3 is to propose a deductive way of conceptualizing translation and translation studies with a focus on the general, the finite, the one, the knowable, the stable, the necessary, and similarity. My argument is that, to conceptualize the field of study, that is, the perspective taken in translation studies, my conceptualization is sufficient. Paradoxically, to conceptualize the object of study, Tymoczko's conceptualization suffices. Together, in a complex paradox, our views present a framework for thinking about, researching, and teaching translation and translation studies.

2.4 Agency

The newest developments in translation studies globally have one thing in common: the agency of translations/translators (Cronin, 2007). Testimony to this is the work of leading scholars such as Pym (1998) on translation history, Bandia (2008) on translation as reparation in the African context, Baker (2006) on the narrative nature of translation in contested situations, Hermans (2007) on translation as reported speech, Tymoczko (2007) on the conceptualization of translation studies and the agency of translators, and Gentzler (2008) on translation as an agent in the creation of identities. One also finds edited collections such as that of Baker (2010); Bührig et al. (2009); Milton and Bandia (2009); Munday (2007, 2012); St. André (2010a); St-Pierre (2007); and St-Pierre and Kar (2007). The reader can also refer to Singh (2007) and Trivedi (2007) for contrary views. In this section, I intend analyzing this development in translation studies as part of the problem of conceptualizing translation and translation studies, arguing with Tyulenev (2011a) that translation studies needs to think deeper about agency and its relationship to the social.

When one talks about agency in translation, you are, to my mind, talking about the relationship between translation and the social or cultural (Dasgupta, 2007; Latour, 2007). (I follow Searle [2010] here in my use of the terms social or social reality or social phenomenon here without any distinction between social and cultural—which are contested anyway.) When you talk about agency, you are asking how individual actions cause other individual or social actions, which is a question concerning the influence of the agent on social reality, that is, on other agents (Milton & Bandia, 2009b, pp. 1–16). Obviously, one has two phenomena to deal with here, that is, the individual and the social. Although it is true that one could study agency from the perspective of the individual psyche or individual ethics (see volume 5, issue 1 of the journal *The Interpreter and Translator Trainer*), once you ask questions about the cause and effect of agency, you are into the realm of the social. In keeping with the complexity stance I have taken in Chapters 1 and 2, individual agency and the social cannot be separated. In what follows, I analyze the ways in which translation scholars currently conceptualize this intricate relationship between the individual and the social. My argument is that translation studies assumes rather than argues a causal link between individual action and social system and that the field can benefit from conceptualizing agency from a complexity perspective. Second, I argue that translation studies, because of its individualistic and critical studies bias, is not able to theorize translational action in which there is no clear intent towards agency. In other words, I do not think that translation studies scholars have thought deeply enough about agency, that is, how to get someone to do something (Latour, 2007, p. 58).

Wolf (2011) claims that the background of a sociological turn in translation is the changing production background, that is, globalization. This is also the view of Cronin (2006), who conceptualizes the role of translation in identity formation against the background of the forces of globalization (see also Heilbron, 2010). Schäffner (2010) argues that, with globalization, the world media is a point of interface for the languages of the world and thus a rich point to study to understand translation. These scholars are thus interested in the relationship between translatorial action and social systems, and their interest goes both ways, that is, how the agent influences the system and how the system influences the agent (Chesterman, 2006; Pym, 2006, pp. 24–25). Milton and Bandia (2009a) conceptualize agency in terms of innovation and change, that is, the process of modernization. Although they offer a number of case studies in support of their claim for the agency of translators, their theorization is not all that extensive (see Tyulenev, 2011a, p. 3). Except for reference to Bourdieu, and that through a secondary source, I find no theorization of the data in terms of sociological theory. These scholars may argue that it is not necessary, because they look instead at theories of patronage and power (Milton & Bandia, 2009b, p. 2–8). The problem is that the claims of authors in the collection all relate to sociopolitical change. How can one make valid claims concerning these phenomena if you do not theorize your data from the perspective of social and/or political theory? For instance, in most of the case studies presented in the book, influential agents or influential texts are chosen as data for the case studies. This does not solve the question as to how to account for the large number of texts translated everyday by anonymous "agents of translation" who may have very little intention concerning agency beyond earning a living. As long as the agency theories of translation studies cannot account for the latter, we still have a biased field of study.

Susam-Sarajeva (2006) considers the travel of ideas and the influence this exerts on the development of a society. What makes her work so valuable is that she theorizes the data in terms of sociological theory. She uses travel theory to explain what happens when ideas travel (Susam-Sarajeva, 2006, p. 7–12). The gain of her insights is that one does not have to study a particular translator and that one does not have to assume particular intentions on her part to argue for a causal relationship between translations and social effects, that is, the travel of ideas. Combining her ideas with theories on memes in complexity theory (which explain the transfer of social information by means of memes analogously) to the transfer of biological information by means of genes should render new insights in the role of translation in the travel of ideas.

Bandia (2008) offers another example of a scholar who theorizes his conceptualization of agency (reparation) theoretically, that is, in literary theory. Although one-sided in the sense that he does not consider nonliterary translation, he deals with the complexities and hybridity of African literary writing in European languages. One of the contributions of his study, which has not really been taken up, is the "internal translation" he assumes in the psyche of the author who translates from the home language into a foreign language before he writes. What is even more far-reaching is the notion that turning African oral rhetoric into Western novels can be seen as a form of translation. This is inter-semiotic translation par excellence, and it theorizes the agency of the translator in crossing borders, not only of language but also of other semiotic systems.

Baker's (2006) work on translation and conflict has become somewhat of a classic in the field. Contesting the conventional notion that translation bridges gaps and mediates, she argues that translation is used to reconfirm the own narrative, that is, the self. Using narrative theory, she argues that the world is one great conflict, with no neutral ground and no way to understand the other (Baker, 2006, p. 1; see, for instance, Spivak's [2007] argument for listening in translation to transcend the divide between self and other). Perhaps the most important point Baker raises is that translation could have an inherently conservative drive. Looking back at the history of apartheid in South Africa, in particular at the founding of the South African Translator's Institute that followed, in 1956, on the rise to power of the National Party, Baker's fears of translation as self-justificatory action are not unfounded. It could be an action that is meant to keep people safely in their own comfort zone (as I shall argue again in Chapter 5). Although she certainly has a point concerning the possible conservative nature of translation (Baker, 2006, pp. 162–163), her work raises a number of important epistemological questions for translation scholars to consider. First, I contend that her conceptualization of narrative is that of a closed system, which is immune to influence from outside and which therefore makes cooperation impossible (Axelrod, 1984; Lewis, 2007). In her view, there is no room for growth in social reality because everybody lives securely in their own narrative. There is only room for conflict and no mediation. Self-legitimization is the only function of translation. Although claiming a postmodern epistemology, Baker seems to be stuck in a reductionist frame of thought by reducing translation to one of its aspects, that is, maintaining conflict. Although she senses the problem, she is not able in the last chapter of her book to provide a perspective on the reductionist stance she has taken. Yes, she is correct in arguing that even reason is already value laden (Baker, 2006, p. 142), but why should one even consider the opposite? By this time in the history of thought, we should all know that there is no safe space. The issue is not whether there is some value-free rationality out there, but how we move forward in a world in which there is only ideology (Barnett, 2003).

This is where complexity theory asks us to consider more than one perspective. First, humans are not only caught up in their own narratives, but they also have the ability to meta-narrative thinking or self-reflexivity (Axelrod, 1984; Hofstadter, 1979; Simon, 2007). A complex conceptualization should thus consider the human condition as both caught up in narratives and able to transcend narratives, at least in principle. An example to show that people are able to transcend their own narratives may be found in the choices of Nelson Mandela in the South African transition to a democratic system. Second, Baker's position could be described as one of strong constructivism. The consequences of her thoughts are exactly that of strong constructivism. If there is no shared reality outside of my consciousness and/or culture and/or narrative, then, yes, we have only conflict. In my explanation of complexity theory, I have, however, indicated that we live in one world, a physical-chemical-biological-psychological-social world. If one separates the psychological world from the social or physical world, it becomes easy to think in terms of constructivism. However, if the atoms in your body and in mine are kept together by the same physical forces, if we share the same chemical substances, if we share 99 percent of the same genes, is it so easy to claim that we each construct our own world? Do we not have to take cognizance of the fact that we are also constructed? As I understand it, this is the claim of sociologists, that is, that social reality constrains (constructs?) human possibilities just as physical reality does it. Also, if we consider the social and its constraints on our being, are we not also socially constructed? Furthermore, is constructivism not a particularly Western philosophy, and does it not arise from an ideological stance where people think that they have conquered nature? Are people living in abject poverty or extreme heat or cold able to hold to constructivist theories? I am well aware that constructivism is, in part, a response to essentialist tendencies in social thought. In this case, apartheid was one of the results of such essentialist thought. However, denouncing essentialism or natural determinism in social relationships does not have to lead to the other extreme, strong constructivism. I am thus questioning the radical forms of constructivism that are currently rife in translation studies. A more ecologically sensitive model, such as the one that I have suggested in Chapters 1 and 2, is more tuned to the complexity of the human condition.

In Muñoz-Calvo and Buesa-Gómez's (2010) collected volume, Schäffner (2010) and Toury (2010) both consider the agency of translators, the former arguing that media in a globalizing world provides agents with an opportunity to have an ideological voice (Schäffner 2010, p. 122). Toury (2010, p. 167) argues that the entire field of translation studies has "sold out to socio-political struggle and is not science anymore", a view that

Latour (2007, p. 236) shares regarding sociology. Although Toury obviously responds to the internal academic politics within translation studies that is not directly related to my study, I must say that he seems to have a point in questioning the preponderance of notions of agency in current translation studies. On one hand, the cultural, power and social turns in translation explain the interest, and makes it relevant. On the other hand, it seems like a Western bias again, in particular a bias rooted in critical thought. If you consider the typical binary distinctions in critical thought, you always have good and bad pitched against each other (as an example, see Steiner, 2009). In this simplified worldview, it is the task of the scholar to be against the bad. This is, for instance, why Tymoczko (2007) opts for translation as activism rather than as resistance. The entire translation activity is framed within a "good–bad" conceptualization and everybody is zealously required to join the fight of good over bad—which was once the job of religion, which these same critical scholars have disbanded for its ideological problems. Activism has thus become science—and religion. Although I immediately agree that no science is neutral, I do not think we gain much by equating science with activism. Changing a problem is something different from understanding a problem. To my mind, it remains the primary task of scholarly work to understand, and through understanding to change or to provide others with the arguments to change. I thus think that one has, from a complexity perspective, to juxtapose the functions of understanding and activism. I also suggest that there is more to translation than joining on one side of the fight between good and bad and that a complexity view on translation should be able to think more complexly about the field. Complexly spoken, it could be precisely scholars' role of understanding that could render an activist service in a world in which people commonly act before they consider. Bringing some kind of understanding to social reality could thus, in itself, function as ethical antidote for a world in which action and taking sides have become ideologies unto themselves.

One of the fields in the social sciences in which complexity theory and emergence theory have been considered is organizational theory. The Complexity and Management Centre at the Business School of the University of Hertfordshire in England has developed a theory of complexity with which to conceptualize social phenomena as emergent concepts. Not all of what they have said is relevant to translation studies, but in the context of the current relevance of agency in translation studies, I briefly consider their argument and its implications for translation studies.

In a series of books, some by Griffin (2002) and some edited by Griffin and Stacey (Griffin & Stacey, 2005a; Stacey & Griffin, 2005; Stacey & Griffin, 2006), they outline a theory of human agency that problematizes traditional systems theory. They start by asking whether systems are "real" phenomena. Based on an analysis of Kant's philosophy, they claim that systems theory has been guilty of thinking of social phenomena not "as if" they were real, but as real (see also Latour's [2007] criticism on sociologists taking the social as already constructed). In their analysis, this has led to a situation in which individuals are no longer seen as responsible for their actions and are in fact left passive because "the system" is seen as dominant and unchangeable. The moment the system is deemed real, it overrides the individual. In their view, this type of argument holds negative consequences for ethics because people can abdicate responsibility to the system.

Their argument is that systems theory has gone wrong in ignoring the paradox of universality and individuality in favor of universality. Proponents of systems theory usually argue that both the universal and the individual exist; that is, systems are real things independent from individuals. The eventual consequence is that either the system or the individual is accorded primacy. Furthermore, human beings could as rational beings experience or observe these systems from the outside. Here the implication is that systems are rationally changeable by input from leaders.

In place of this view, Griffin and Stacey (2005a) propose a theory of complex responsive processes. In this argument, they propose a paradoxical relationship between individual and system, but in their theory, the system does not exist prior to symbolic interaction between individuals. A system is an emergent phenomenon that emerges out of the relationships between individuals. Their theory is thus more a theory of process than a theory of system. Society is not a stable thing but a process of human interaction within historical and geographical contexts. They focus on Kant's notion of a system "as if" it were real, but it is not real. In this theory, society emerges out of the bodily interactions or relationships between human beings. They define the nature of complex responsive processes of relating as first being complex. They understand complexity to entail paradoxes, that is, stable and unstable, predictable and unpredictable, known and unknown, certain and uncertain—and they stress that all these hold simultaneously (Griffin & Stacey, 2006, p. 8). Furthermore, complex responsive processes are self-organizing, which they explain as the interaction of local agents according to their own organizing principles. Last, complex responsive processes are evolving.

The implications for translation studies are, at least, twofold. First, this theory provides a theory of agency that has seriously been lacking in translation studies writings on agency. In even extremely influential works such as that of Milton and Bandia (2009a), some notion of agency has been assumed, but agency itself has not been theorized in this development. Also, notions of systems are rife in translation studies, to which this theory may bring sobering insights.

Secondly, Griffin and Stacey make use of Mead's philosophy, which claims that the bodily interactions between humans are what constitute society. This claim resonates with arguments I have made concerning translation based on Jousse's (2000) linguistic anthropology (J. Marais, 2010) and with claims Tymoczko has made based on Wittgenstein's theory of family resemblances. It is through the interactions, the gestes between humans, which can include mechanical or vocal gestures, that a society emerges. This means that semiotics plays an important role in the emergence of a society. As far as translation is concerned, this theory provides a conceptual space within which to consider the implications of semiotic, including interlingual, interaction between human agents, that is, forms of translation action. In a globalizing world, interlingual interaction is one of the most important ways in which a large part of society emerges (Cronin, 2006).

Griffin and Stacey's theory of complex responsive processes offers interesting vistas in conceptualizing the relationship between semiotics and different aspects of society. It has to be worked out in much more detail than what is possible here, but it is clearly a theory of agency which will take into account both aspects of the turn advocated by Gentzler (2008): social and psychological. The theory also opens up space to consider agency both at the informal level, that is, informal economies, workplaces, socializing, and the formal level, that is, the choices professional translators make when they translate and the way in which they actively or by default play an agentive role.

My reference to Griffin and Stacey's work aims, first, to show how complexity theory and emergence can be applicable to social and human sciences. Second, it provides us with a conceptualization of the presumably binary nature of agency/social system. It also points out a number of problems with current theories of agency in translation:

- They are prescriptive by expecting all translators to fit into the straightjacket of a critical analysis of reality.
- They assume agency rather than problematizing or theorizing it.
- They cannot prove a causal link between the individual and the social.
- They cannot explain self-organization or unintended consequences.
- They cannot theorize the majority of translation activity in which the translator has no particular intent, other than making money of having to do a job.

I now turn to proposing a complexity conceptualization of translation and translation studies.

3. TOWARD A PHILOSOPHY OF TRANSLATION

I argued earlier that translation studies is currently biased toward a postmodern epistemology that I argued to be, at best, one-sided and, at worst, reductionist. I also indicated that this epistemological bias has a bearing on issues such as the conceptualization of translation and the conceptualization of translation studies as a field of study. In this section, I espouse a conceptualization of translation with a view to addressing the bias by incorporating it into a complexity perspective. Note yet again that my aim is not a classical definition, that is, a necessary and sufficient definition, but a (meta-)conceptual framework within which to conceptualize translation and translation studies.

3.1 Inter-ing

Searle (2010, p. 3) expresses my quest in this section elegantly: "Our task is to give an account of how we live in exactly one world, and how all of these different phenomena, from quarks and gravitational attraction to cocktail parties and governments, are part of that one world" (see Figure 3.1).

Based on my conceptualization of complex adaptive systems in Chapter 1 and the emergent semiotics in Chapter 2, I conceptualize translation in this section in terms of the relationship between complex adaptive systems (see also Tyulenev 2011a, p. 133–157). Put differently, semiotics is one particular instance of the category of inter-systemic phenomena in reality, whereas translation is one particular instance of the category of inter-systemic semiotic phenomena in reality. In this section, I hope to explain the detail of this approach. At its most basic, translation is a phenomenon of inter-systemic relationality.

At this point, I wish to link my argument with that of Latour (1987, 2000, 2007; Akrich et al., 2002a, 2002b; Lewis & Mosse, 2006), who set out to devise a "sociology of translation". By this, he does not mean what translation studies scholars mean, that is, the role of translation proper in society or a sociological perspective on translation proper. Rather, what

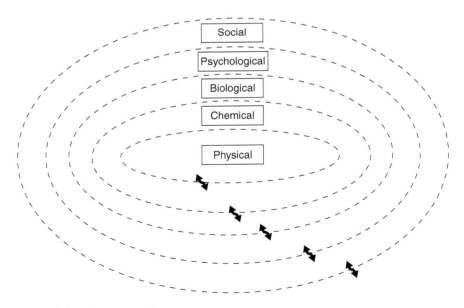

Figure 3.1 Emergent reality

he indicates is that the type of sociology he advocates is a translation-type sociology. Translation thus becomes an adjective describing sociology. The social is a phenomenon of the translation type, being constructed by translations between actors/nodes/systems (Latour, 1987, pp. 108, 208–209; Latour, 2007, pp. 64–65).

The reason why Latour takes this line of thought is that he is arguing that the social does not exist but is continually constructed and maintained by means of the connections between actors, hence actor-network theory (Latour, 2007, p. 7). He views the work of sociology as accounting for the connections between actors. To my mind, this conceptualization is very close to the work on complex adaptive systems and especially that of Kaufmann (1995), who similarly works on the creation of networks by means of connections between nodes. Latour (2007, p. 184) applies this kind of thinking to the social, claiming that the social is a process of the construction or assembly of links. This construction is a process of change, connection, movement or, as he calls it, translation.

In my understanding of Latour, he uses translation in the sense of connecting sites or actors, as changing the relationship between sites or actors, of linking sites and actors and maintaining those links. He is thus in agreement with complexity theorists who do not view reality as being in equilibrium but at the edge of chaos, always in the process of becoming. In a sense, Latour sees translation as change, the inter-action between actors and/or systems; it is the construction of systems.

Latour seems lately to have stepped down from the term *sociology of translation*, but he still uses the term translation in his latest works. To my mind, his work has conceptualized from the perspective of sociology what I have been trying to do here. He has searched for a theory of social process or what the complexity theorists call inter-systemic relationships. He has rejected the idea of looking at the social as a substance, a thing. Rather, the social is an assemblage of connections that are continually translated. What I am trying to argue is that one should expand this thinking to free it from the subject-specific claims of either sociology or translation studies. The scientific project as a whole needs to study relationships (links, connections) and the processes that establish, destroy, and maintain those relationships between systems. All disciplines could contribute their understanding of inter-systemic relationship and its maintenance and construction (inter-systemic-ness and inter-systemic-ing) to this debate, and they could learn from the ways in which this phenomenon occurs in various fields of study. Translation studies thus becomes a field of study that studies all of reality from the perspective of inter-systemic relationships, and it could have subfields of study where inter-systemic semiotic relationships (in particular) and inter-lingual semiotic transfer (even more specifically), and its role in the development of the social are studied.

In a manner typical of complexity approaches, the ontology in Figure 3.1 posits aspects of reality, here conceptualized as complex adaptive systems, which are all inter-related, hence the dotted lines, and in inter-systemic relationship to one another, hence the double-headed arrows on the dotted lines. Although they do have boundaries between them, these boundaries are paradoxically what make the relationship between them possible, thus the boundaries both delimit and connect (for a discussion of the notion of frontier in history, see Legassick, 2010; also see Kauffman, 1995). From a complexity perspective, one has to consider the boundary as a paradoxical phenomenon of stability/change and delimitation/connection. I call these paradoxical points of connection (spatially conceptualized) or relationships of connection (systemically conceptualized) or acts of connection (conceptualized in term of process) "inters" because they are the inter-relationships between systems. The exact nature of all these different kinds of inters are not within my purview at this stage, but comparing the differences and similarities of various instances of inter-ness or inter-ing could assist in understanding the broader category in itself. In terms of complexity theory, it is these inters that make the connection between open systems possible, which accounts for life and growth and health in systems and which accounts for the self-organization of systems "on the edge of chaos" (Kauffman, 1995, pp. 26–29).

In particular, the semiotic inter is based on the nature of semiotics, that is, taking *a as b*. The semiotic process cannot be reduced to something more basic than the taking of one thing as another, that is, *a as b*. It differs from a more basic process, which is logic, that is, *a is b*. Logic would be something that animals have in common with humans, for instance, a zebra is food, grass is food, and this smell (a lion) is danger. Logic entails a process of identity. The semiotic, in contrast, entails a paradoxical process of *a as b*, in which there is both similarity and difference in the process itself (for a similar discussion, yet from a different angle, see also Tyulenev, 2011a). This process of substitution, of seeing similarity based on difference and difference based on similarity, makes complex human thought possible because it entails the symbolic, though some animals have been shown to have limited abilities in this regard (Yule, 1996, pp. 30–39). Thus, in symbolic thinking, one does not only take things as they are, but you also can creatively relate them to other things. Note that the detail of these issues has been discussed in depth by eminent semioticians such as Eco (2001; see also Andrews, 2005; Torop, 2002; Toury, 1986).

The particular nature of inter- and intrasemiotic relationships (or inter or translation), on which much work has already been done (e.g., Sebeok [1986] will have to wait for another day). Here, I wish to establish, against the background of my exposition of complexity theory and emergence, a basic conceptualization of translation as a phenomenon of relationship between systems.

Questions are surely to be raised concerning my use of the notion of inter. For many, it may perpetuate the Western metaphor underlying translation studies, that is, the metaphor assuming transfer between two spaces. This particular metaphor has come under fire because of its supposed assumption of fixedness in the source and target and its assumption of the ability of transfer as a neutral process. Although I agree that these assumptions are problematic, I contend that the assumptions underlying notions of translation in other cultures cannot be assumed to be without this kind of problem. Further, I agree that inter, on its face, seems to presuppose a spatial conceptualization. However, a closer look at conceptualizations of inter in the Oxford Dictionary (Oxford Dictionary, n.d.) indicates two semantic fields related to inter. The first could, indeed, be seen as a spatial conceptualization, that is, inter as between. However, it also has other meanings related to spatiality such as "among, amid, in between, in the midst". In particular, it lists meanings such as "between or among other things or persons; between the parts of, in the intervals of, or in the midst of, something; together with". The latter examples do not necessarily relate that strongly to the metaphor of transfer used traditionally in translation studies. The second semantic field, however, includes the notion of mutuality or reciprocity, for instance, interactive. Collins (2006) gives as the second semantic field "together, mutually, or reciprocally" and lists "interdependent" as an example of the latter. I thus use inter in a complex semantic manner as indicating relationships of various natures between systems. I do not specify the relationship, which could have many different characteristics. It could be spatial, it could include transfer, but it need not. It could include process or relationship, but it need not be limited to either. In this way, I suggest that one conceptualizes the field in such a way that it provides space for both supposedly Western, that is, transfer, and supposedly non-Western notions of translation (although I have indicated previously that I find some of the arguments around the distinction unconvincing). Furthermore, I do not specify the nature of the (at least) two phenomena or systems related in the relationship. I am merely positing them, and I cannot see that by merely positing them, anyone could construe my intention as attaching a particular content to either the relationship or the related systems/phenomena. I also need to point out again that my conceptualization of system is in terms of complex adaptive systems that are conceived of in terms of nonlinear logic and openness. This means that systems depend on other systems for their survival, which is a way of conceiving the systemic inter-related nature of reality and phenomena like translation.

It is my contention that, considering translation from all the angles from which it has been studied up to now, one could call it a phenomenon that is characterized by the philosophical notion of change based on stability. Philosophically speaking, reality is constituted by both stability and change. Phenomena change based on their stability and are stable based on change. I want to posit translation as a phenomenon of, primarily, change based on stability, that is, stability based on change. Whichever way one looks at it, in translation you have a (relatively stable) something that is viewed as being changed into a (again relatively stable) something else. This holds true irrespective of the theoretical perspective one takes, for example, linguistic, pragmatic, functional, cultural, descriptive, sociological, or ideological. It also holds true for all the metaphors used for translation, for all historical periods, and for all culturally different practices. In its broadest sense, one thus has a category of phenomena in reality that is characterized by the notion of change based on stability. In physics, we encounter energies changing into other energies as determined by the law on the conservation of energy. In chemistry, we see the process of catalysis through which chemical substances change form. In biology, osmosis sees a process where information moves into and out of cells. Conceptualized systemically, all systems have borders. The border both contains and connects the system. Any contact between the system and another system assumes some kind of inter-relationship between the two systems. At this stage, I call these phenomena inter-phenomena or inter-ness, from which I obtain the verb *inter-ing*. I have chosen to remain with these relatively abstract notions because I do not want to define the nature of the inter-ness. Inter-ness itself is the larger category of which one may have various instances.

Thus, one may have physical, chemical, biological, psychological, and/ or social inter-phenomena. In particular then, in the field of semiotics, which I have indicated to form part of the substratum from which social reality emerges, one would find semiotic inter-ness or semiotic forms of inter-ing. They partake in the characteristics of all other forms of inter-ness and may benefit from studying these kinds of inter-ness. However, they are also specific forms of inter-ness, that is, semiotic forms of inter-ness or inter-ing. Through this kind of complexity conceptualization, I intend to maintain both similarity and difference, two fundamental philosophical conditions.

Note that I have conceptualized, following Tyulenev (2011a, pp. 146–157), the semiotic system as an inter-phenomenon in itself. Its function is, amongst others, to make inter-ing between psychological phenomena possible. From this inter-ing between psychological phenomena, social reality emerges. The semiotic itself is also a translation process where material reality is assembled into the social (Latour, 2007, p. 71). As Figures 3.2 and 3.3 try to make clear, the semiotic (the bold boundary line) constitutes the border between the psychological and the social and is, as such, an inter-phenomenon similar to many other inter-phenomena in reality. I aim to zoom into this boundary line, this border, and turn it into the focus of my further conceptualization.

If it is true that one has a category of phenomena that you can call semiotic inter-ness or inter-ing, you are at Jakobson's (2004) definition of translation (see also Eco, 2001; Toury, 1986). What Jakobson thus did was to think in binary terms to categorize semiotics. He rightly saw that all semiotic actions entail a movement, a change, a relationship, that is, *a as b*. Thus, understanding means understanding *a as b*, that is, a house as a place where people live. The semiotic works by relationships—of the nature *a as b*.

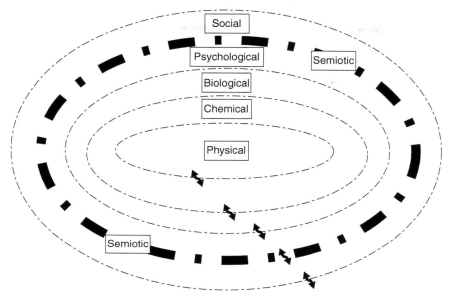

Figure 3.2 A schematic representation of inter-ness

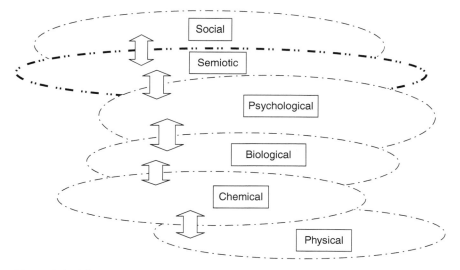

Figure 3.3 The emergent semiotic

Jakobson then considered whether this relationship takes part between parts of a system or between systems. In this way, he arrived at the well-known distinction between intra-linguistic, inter-linguistic, and intra-semiotic translation. As indicated earlier, my intention here is not to go into the categories

102 *Translation Theory and Development Studies*

of semiotics. My intention is to conceptualize an ontology in terms of which translation scholars can think about translation. In particular, my focus is to conceptualize the lens through which translation studies look at reality. In this respect, Jakobson poses two problems. First, if one takes his argument to its logical conclusion, all semiotic activities are translations. This leads to the question, What is the difference between semiosis and translation if all semiosis is translation? Second, he does not take account of the fact that inter- at one level could be intra- at another level.

Conceptualized in terms of complex adaptive systems, the semiotic seems to me to be a nonlinear, open, nonequilibrium system, and it is in various relationships with other systems (see Figure 3.4). However, the semiotic is simultaneously a system with subsystems that are in relationship to one

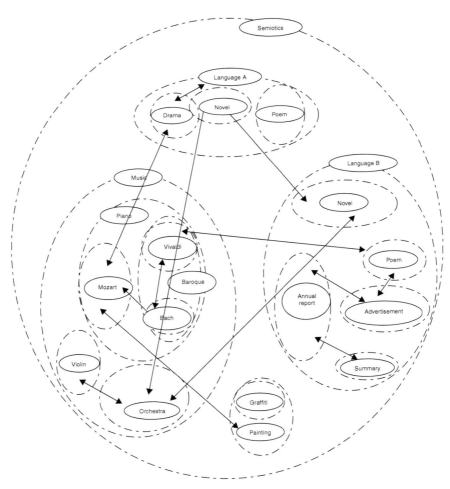

Figure 3.4 The complexity of inter- and intra-semiosis

another, and sub-subsystems that are in relationship to one another, and sub-sub-subsystems that are in relationship to one another, theoretically ad infinitum. Also, there are relationships among the different levels of semiosis. My point is that the distinction between inter- and intra- is a fluid, complex one, depending on the level of analysis. Let me illustrate the point by considering Jakobson's example itself. On the level of language, explaining one word by using other words is an intra-systemic phenomenon because it operates within the system of the same language. However, on the level of morphology, this would be an inter-systemic phenomenon. Let me further clarify by considering the often-used notion of translation as rewriting. If you take the linguistic system as your level of analysis, rewriting (if you assume it takes place within the same language) is an intra-systemic phenomenon. However, at the level of text it is an inter-systemic phenomenon. The semiotic thus consists of an endless set of inter- and intra-relationships between its subsystems that cannot be fixed into the neat categories conceptualized by Jakobson. If one conceptualizes culture as a semiotic system, you could even consider the inter-cultural relationship a translation. If you consider semiotic media as semiotic systems (see Basamalah, 2007, p. 118; Nouss, 2007), you could consider the relationship between a book and a film a translation, as well as the writing down of an oral narrative. Thus, on the level of language, reported speech would be an intra-systemic phenomenon, whereas on the level of individual speech acts, it is an inter-systemic phenomenon.

This complex of relationships, to my mind, further explains why one could conceptualize of translation "as" a number of other things. Semiotic phenomena share their "semioticness", which makes them similar. Figure 3.4 shows the complexity of the notions of inter-ness and intra-ness. Thus, between language A and language B, the translation of a novel would be an inter-phenomenon, relating two systems at the same level. Turning that same novel in language A into a drama in language A would be an intra-phenomenon within the linguistic system but an inter-phenomenon on the level of literary genre.

Setting the novel from language A to a score for orchestra in the music subsystem would be an inter-semiotic activity on the level of semiotic systems. Summarizing an annual report in language B would, on the level of linguistic systems, be an intra-systemic act, while on the level of type of communicative text it would be an inter-systemic act. Within the system of music, one could even have sub-subsystems. For instance, you could have Mozart rework a piece of Baroque piano music for piano in his time, which would be intra-systemic on the level of instruments and inter-systemic on the level of musical style. Or you could have Bach rework a theme by Vivaldi, which remains an intra-systemic semiotic act if you consider the Baroque style as a system, but an inter-systemic act if you consider Bach and Vivaldi as two musical systems because of their different styles.

The question, however, remains: How does translation differ from other semiotic phenomena? As indicated earlier, Tymoczko has given up the search for a logical answer to this question. She follows Wittgenstein who advises us not to "think" but to "look". And yes, taking the route of inductive reasoning with an emphasis on practice and cultural difference does help our understanding of translation. However, starting from the other end of the logical spectrum, that is, deductive reasoning, I do think it possible to conceptualize of translation as an inter-systemic semiotic phenomenon. Furthermore, I can see that conceptualizing of translation in terms of inter-systemic relationships could assist our understanding of translation. Going further than that, it seems to me, will go against the grain of my complexity assumptions. It seems that, between Tymoczko and me, we have now arrived at the meeting point between the orderly (my deductive reasoning) and the chaotic (her inductive reasoning). Fine-tuning this meeting point and its implications is a task for another day. I thus conceptualize of translation in terms of the inter-relationship between various complex adaptive systems. Translation always has an inter-systemic nature, but it partakes in many other features of reality, for example, intra-systemicness. Translations are thus a category of phenomena of reality (Tymoczko, 2007) that share the characteristic of inter-systemicness, whichever way that may be realized in every particular case. The focus or lens of the field of translation studies is thus that of inter-systemic relationships. If need be, one could narrow this down to a subfield of interest that would study semiotic inter-systemic relationships, and if needed, one could narrow it down to inter-systemic linguistic relationships, which brings you to the definition of translation proper.

One thus remains with the problem: Which phenomena in reality do we call translations? If it was easy to distinguish between intra- and inter-systemic relationships, one could easily have called all inter-systemic semiotic phenomena translations. The problem remains that what is inter-systemic at one level is intra-systemic on the next. Also, complexity theory has taught us that reality constitutes complex phenomena partaking in more than one of our categories. My idea is thus to try to get out of "category thinking" into relationship and systemic thinking.

Current suggestions for using the term translation are at two opposite poles of thinking. On one hand, there are scholars who propagate the use of the word translation for "translation proper"; that is, phenomena characterized by an inter-linguistic relationship (Trivedi, 2007). On the other hand, you have scholars who wish to expand the notion of translation to include all inter-phenomena in reality, also the physical, chemical, and biological inter-phenomena (Tyulenev, 2011a). Theoretically, both seem to be possible. Both also pose their own problems. With the first, you exclude so many phenomena of a hybrid inter- and intra-systemic nature that the field of translation studies is narrowed down to only the linguistic instances of inter-semiotic relationships. With the second, the term could be diluted because it includes virtually all of reality. At the same time, this so-called dilution could be a widening and philosophical strengthening of the foundations of translation studies in which a future field devoted to inter-systemic relationships could develop, especially when viewing the work of Latour. Another solution could be to use the term *inter-systemic studies* or something in this vein for the wider field of interest and retain translation and translation studies for semiotic inter-systemic relationships, due to the historical connection of translation with the semiotic and language. However, some may legitimately argue that it is time to finally sever the umbilical cord between translation and language. Personally, I am not much of a manager and planner and am thus not sure which way would practically work at the level of organizing fields of study. In my own thought, I would in the meantime use the term translation for all kinds of inter-systemic relationships and narrow it down later if need be. Also, in the meantime, one could talk about semiotic translation, physical translation, mathematical translation, biological translation, and so on, if needed.

I thus suggest that, within the field of translation studies, we retain the notion of translation for all inter-systemic phenomena and actions, while simultaneously indicating the systemic level at which you are working, that is, a relativized conceptualization. I also suggest that we use the term *semiotic translation* for the categories subsumed under Jakobson's classical definition. This hybrid or complex way of thinking, complemented by Tymoczko's inductive conceptualization of translation seems to be, at least, reflective of the complexity of the field of study. My own conceptualization has provided an explanation for the similarities between translations. Her view calls our attention to what is different between translations. These two views, taken together, help us to think about translation in a complex way, considering and respecting both similarity and difference, stability and change, one and many, necessity and contingency. Combining these approaches, we cover both the deductive and the inductive. I do not claim that they fit neatly into one another or that they do not have internal tensions. What I do claim is that they respect the complexity, meaning both the neat categories (order) and the disturbing differences (chaos), of the complex phenomenon that we know as translation.

To my mind, the conceptualization above holds a number of advantages. It complexly delimits semiotic forms of inter-ness from non-semiotic forms of inter-ness without drawing absolute distinctions between the two. Semiotic forms of inter-ness are still forms of inter-ness, and translation scholars, who in my view work with only a small part of all the inter-ing phenomena in reality, can learn much from studying other forms of inter-ness. At the same time, however, the preceding conceptualization has suggested that not all inter-ness phenomena or inter-ing processes need to be called translations. One could reserve the concept of translation for its use in translation studies, for semiotic inter-ness only. In this way, I have tried to maintain the complex relationship between sameness and difference of all inter-ing phenomena.

3.2 Translation and Emergent Semiotics

This section is a further attempt to conceptualize translation in terms of the framework set out in Chapters 1 and 2 and in the arguments presented in this chapter thus far. In this program, semiotic translation is a particular semiotic phenomenon emerging from a substratum of phenomena in cases in which one has an interaction between semiotic systems or subsystems. As indicated in Chapter 2, the semiotic emerges from the psychological, which emerges from the biological, which emerges from the chemical, which emerges from the physical. The semiotic is thus simultaneously and paradoxically emerging from all of its substrata and not reducible to these substrata. It shares aspects of the physical, chemical, biological, and psychological as Jousse (2000) argued quite long ago, but it also has features that are unique to the semiotic. For its part, semiotic inter-ness is a particular instance of inter-ness in general, that is, the inter-ing between systems and subsystems of reality.

If one then zooms in on the semiotic, it consists of various subsystems. I contend that conceptualizing of the semiotic in terms of complex adaptive systems allows one to think about the relationships between semiotic subsystems, not only about the systems themselves. I thus contend that the semiotic system, as a complex adaptive system, contains a number of subsystems, of which language is but one. Also counting as semiotic subsystems could be the kind of phenomena that are called arts, such as painting, sculpting, music, drama, and many others. Technology has made even more of these possible, such as film, television, radio, the Internet, and various forms of social media. Apart from that, semioticians have convincingly argued that all of reality has a semiotic aspect. Thus, architecture is one of the physical subsystems with the most visible semiotic aspect (M. Taylor, 2001). Other phenomena in reality, however, also have meaning, that is, a semiotic aspect. Thus, a dam can be a sign of cultural domination over nature or, if it has run dry, of human and animal suffering. Even a remote physical object such as the moon could have a semiotic aspect, that is, being related to lunacy or being in love.

To return to translation, I argue that, for a phenomenon such as translation to emerge, one has to assume subsystems. Translation is a complex phenomenon emerging from a number of subsystems (see Figure 3.5).

Thus, in the traditional translation, one has to assume language as a subsystem, which itself could be conceptualized as consisting of phonetic, morphological, syntactical, textual sub-subsystems, but one also has to assume the pragmatic, discourse, sociolinguistic, psycholinguistic, and critical linguistic, among other, subsystems. These I would call the substrata of translation proper. Put simply, for translation proper to obtain, its substrata, for example, language, have to obtain. The theory I am putting forward here thus also explains why translation can be studied from a linguistic perspective or a pragmatic perspective, for instance. It is precisely because these features form the substrata of translation. Translation thus has a language

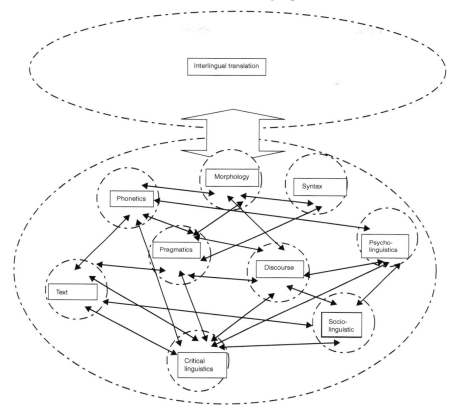

Figure 3.5 The emergence of translation

aspect, a pragmatic aspect, a textual aspect. Each time one of these is taken up as "the" field of study for translation, scholars reduce translation to one of its aspects. It is thus not impossible to study translation as language—but it is reductionist, and it mutilates the phenomenon by claiming that the part is enough to explain the whole. What we need to understand better is translation as translation, as an inter-ness phenomenon in a particular medium with particular concomitant features.

Simultaneously, I argue, semiotic translation itself, the inter-ness semiotic phenomenon, is a substratum in the emergence of social reality. It is thus both a system with subsystems and a subsystem within systems. Let me try to be clear again: One finds semiotic translation as a phenomenon in which semiotic inter-ing relationships among social systems or subsystems obtain. Thus, the economy, in part, emerges from semiotic interactions between human beings. The same holds for law, medicine, engineering, the academe, sport, politics, culture—in short, for all forms of social reality (in Figure 3.6, the arrows connect systems and subsystems, indicating the inter-connectedness

108 *Translation Theory and Development Studies*

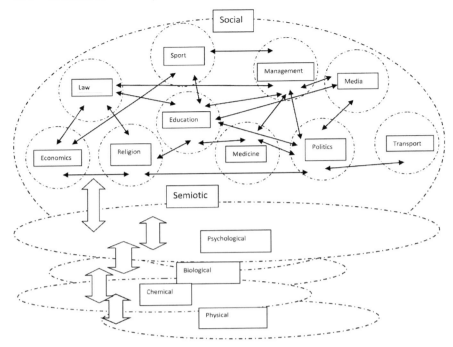

Figure 3.6 The role of translation in the emergence of social reality

of the whole of reality). This explains why semiotic translation could also be explained "as" culture, ideology, sociology. It is not because translation "is" these things, but because it partakes in the emergence of these things—seeing that reality is a whole. Partaking in the emergence of culture, semiotic translation shows features of culture; partaking in social reality, semiotic translation shows features of social reality. Thus, I am arguing that, up to now, translation has mostly been conceptualized in terms of its aspects or in terms of being an aspect of larger systems, that is, in a reductionist way. This is why one finds the numerous turns and "translation as" conceptualizations. It also explains why metaphor (St. Andre, 2010a) is currently so popular in conceptualizing translation. It focuses on a part of the whole and makes for relatively easy conceptualization where one does not have to consider the whole. It has become time to conceptualize translation as translation. This will not mean that I am trying to reduce everything to translation. Remember, I am working with the notion of emergence that is the opposite of reductionist thinking.

Similarly, social reality emerges from the semiotic interactions between humans (Figure 3.7). These semiotic interactions can take many forms, that is, talking to one another, drawing up contracts for political or economic agreements, drawing plans for architectural or engineering projects, and so

Developing Translation Studies 109

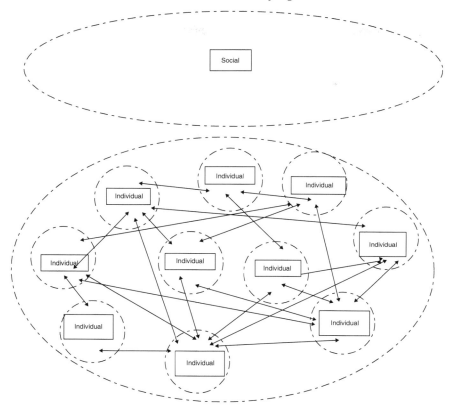

Figure 3.7 Agency, translation, and emergence

on. All of these may entail intersemiotic inter-ing processes, that is, inter-ing among semiotic systems or subsystems such as turning ideas conceptualized verbally into a building plan. In cases where humans speak different languages, the typical interlingual form of semiotic interactions, which is seen as translation proper, can be conceptualized.

To my mind, the conceptualization above provides translation scholars with a framework within which to conceptualize their field of study across culture, time, space, and ideology. In a complexity way, it maintains both difference and similarity, views the world it conceptualizes as one and many and provides a philosophical space from which to conceptualize the agency role of translation in the emergence of social reality. It points out that translation is a parasitic phenomenon. You have nothing in reality that is only a translation. You have language that has been translated, or texts that have been translated, or legal documents that have been translated. Being semiotic, that is, the substratum of social reality, translation is the inter-ing of other systems, the inter-ing among other systems. Translation is not something; it is a particular relationship among systems in which both similarity and difference obtain.

In schematic form, the conceptualization I propose concurs with that of most complexity theorists. I do suggest, however, a number of changes with the main aim of providing semiotics, and language as a semiotic subsystem in particular, with a constitutive position in the conceptualization. Sawyer and Latour have argued convincingly that symbolic interaction is a necessary level in the emergence of social phenomena. However, they did not theorize this strongly enough. Following Sawyer, I suggest the mind/brain/individual as the basic level from which social phenomena emerge, itself emerging from physical, chemical, and biological substrata. In essence, I agree with his second level, that is, interaction. However, because I believe that Jousse has theorized the scope of human interaction fuller than Sawyer has done, I substitute interaction with propositional gest, that is, the bodily ways in which the anthropos interacts with both other anthropoi and its environment (Jousse, 2000; J. Marais, 2010). I have argued elsewhere that this conceptualization opens up possibilities for an ecological perspective on human interaction, including all modes of interaction from muscular twinges to the internet. Social reality emerges out of these gests.

Theories of social emergence have been lacking in their ability to describe or explain the emergence of social phenomena from individual interactions, partly, claims Latour (2007), because they have assumed the social rather than proven it. In order to address this lacuna, Sawyer proposes two more intermediary levels of emergence, that is, ephemeral emergents and stable emergents. This move focuses on the process nature of social emergence; that is, getting to the (relatively) fixed structures of a society is a process that goes through various phases of human interaction. Out of the symbolic interactions among humans emerge first ephemeral emergent phenomena. These refer to situated, local, and temporary "structures" in the process of an emergent social structure. Sawyer (2005, p. 213) includes interactional frames, participation structures, and so on. He argues that these are the phenomena typically studied by sociolinguistics. Out of these ephemeral emergents emerge more stable emergents, which may be subcultures, conversational routines, and shared social practices, among others. They are only relatively more stable, and out of them emerges the relatively fixed social structures, such as written texts as seen in laws, and material systems and infrastructure, such as architecture and so on. It is my contention that, in cases where speakers of mutually inaccessible languages interact in this process, regardless of the level, some form of semiotic translation takes place. This could be oral translation (e.g., interpreting), multimodal translation (e.g. dubbing), digital translation (e.g., websites), or interlingual translation (e.g. forms of rewriting, faked translations, etc.).

This means that I can conceptualize semiotic translation as having emerged out of lower hierarchical levels, not being predictable from its constituent parts, having novel properties that are not found in its constituent parts, and having a downward causal effect on these properties. The main advantage of this position is that it allows one to stop depending on reductionist definitions of translation. With this conceptual space opened, one does not have to think of translation as "actual" language, literature, direct speech, or anything else. As an emergent phenomenon, translation can be studied as a phenomenon in its own right, that is, translation as translation. This could free up conceptual energy for scholars to look at translation as translation, conceptualizing it in the fashion indicated by Tymoczko. Second, this view of translation explains the downward causative effects that translation has on its constituent parts, in particular language and literature. Thirdly, because this conceptualization is grounded in "human interaction", that is, a form of anthropology, it should be able to hold for all kinds of societies as Tymoczko has required.

As important, however, is the scope this conceptualization offers for semiotic translation to take a rightful conceptual space in the emergence of social reality. In an ever-increasing global world, interaction among humans from mutually inaccessible languages is becoming more frequent (Cronin, 2006), and the relative importance of acts of translational human interaction is growing. My philosophical stance makes it possible not only to conceptualize the theories of agency seriously lacking in the theoretical underpinning. It also conceptualizes semiotics, in particular language and interlingual communication, as foundational to the emergence of social reality. In translation studies, this has implications for the debate on the visibility of the translator, agency theories, translation, and culture and for the education of translators. However, as far as the relationship of translation studies with other disciplines in the social sciences and humanities is concerned, it posits translation studies as a cluster discipline, which may not be best practiced in an academic department but rather in or as an interdisciplinary cluster. Because the various forms and fields of social reality emerge out of (translational) linguistic interaction, semiotic translation is, at least to some extent, part of the emergence of those fields. In other words, just as one needs some knowledge of physics, chemistry, and biology to understand the brain, without reducing the brain to those substrata, one may need knowledge of semiotic translation to help you understand politics, history, economics, and religious organizations, without reducing those fields to language or semiotic translation. This view is a philosophical underpinning of the notion of the "translation turn" in the humanities. Second, the emergent social structures will exert downward causation on semiotic translation. For translation scholars, this means that they cannot understand semiotic translation without considering the downward causal influence from social fields such as those named earlier. Translation scholars can thus never be purely or solely interested in semiotic translation. Interest in semiotic translation implies an interest in the social structures that, in turn, exert downward causation on semiotic translation.

Against the preceding background, I now set out to argue in more detail that semiotic translation is an emergent phenomenon. I base my argument on that of Queiros and El-Hani (2006), who have convincingly argued that semiosis is an emergent phenomenon. To my mind, it follows logically that all semiotic phenomena, including semiotic translation, are then emergent. In what follows, I explain the assumptions and features of semiotic translation as they relate to emergence. Queiros and El-Hani (2006, pp. 82–83) demonstrate that the following notions are usually prevalent in discussions on emergence: physical monism and naturalism, systemic versus nonsystemic features, hierarchy of levels, synchronic determination, and diachronic determination. As far as semiotic translation is concerned, it seems to be an advantage to conceptualize semiotic translation within a worldview of physical monism and naturalism; that is, only natural entities are considered. This would allow one not only to consider all forms of semiotic translation, including the oral and the electronic as Tymoczko (2006) has argued (also see Jousse, 2000), but it would also open up the possibility of conceptualizing semiotic translation within a fundamentally ecological philosophy. The second feature of emergence is that a property is emergent only if it is found on the level of the system, not on the level of the parts. This holds for semiotic translation as the features of semiotic translation have been shown to be unique to semiotic translations and do not occur at the level of, say, language or literature. In this regard, one can refer to the "third code", for example, Baker (1996) on simplification, explicitation, normalization, and leveling out. The third assumption is that of synchronic determination; that is, if the parts change, the whole changes. The fourth assumption of emergence relates to diachronic determination, which, as Queiros and El-Hani (2006, p. 83) rightly point out, causes problems because it seems to be deterministic. It refers to the emergence of new structures based on rules. The fifth assumption with which emergence works is a hierarchy of levels of emergence.

The following four features of emergence, I argue, apply to semiotic translation. First, the whole is irreducible to the constituent parts. In this case, one would not be able to reduce semiotic translations to language, that is, explain all features of semiotic translations in terms of linguistic theory only. Second, it has been proved that semiotic translations exert downward causation. Semiotic translations do not only influence the use of language and literature, but also exert downward causation on culture and other forms of social reality. Third, the emergent phenomena should be novel, that is, have properties not found in the constituent parts. This has been proved of semiotic translation in various studies. Last, emergence implies the unpredictability of the whole from knowledge of the parts. In this regard, I argue that one would not be able to explain features of semiotic translation from knowledge of linguistics or literature or culture, for that matter.

3.3 Complex Adaptive Systems and Agency

Recapping the argument so far, I have been arguing that semiotic translation is an emergent semiotic phenomenon. I built most of my argument on the work done by Tymoczko (2007), arguing that I would like to amend her inductive conceptualization of semiotic translation with a deductive conceptualization in an attempt to conceptualize translation complexly.

So, my conceptualization of translation starts by arguing deductively with the focus on the concepts of universality, finiteness, unity, knowability, stability, and necessity that one finds a set of phenomena in reality that is characterized by the notion of inter-ness. These phenomena are characterized by change based on stability, and a broad definition of translation studies (or inter-systemic studies) would take as its perspective this notion of systemic inter-relationships. This set of phenomena appears all over reality, that is, in the physical, the chemical, the biological, the psychological, and the social.

I then suggest that one could narrow this set of inter-ness phenomena down to the field of semiotics, which leaves one with a conceptualization of translation that considers the inter-systemic relational nature of semiotic phenomena. Semiotic inter-ness is thus deductively arrived at as the lens through which translation scholars in the traditional sense, as defined by Jakobson (2004), look at reality to determine their field of study. These acts of semiotic inter-ness are found all over reality and thus form one of the substrata for the emergence of social reality. As a field of study, the lens that translation studies uses to view reality is thus semiotic inter-ness. Nowhere in reality, I claim, does one find a phenomenon that is "a translation" only. Rather, one finds categories of phenomena that share inter-systemic semiotic relatedness as a feature. Translation scholars thus study this feature of reality in all kinds of objects.

Simultaneously, I argue inductively, with Tymoczko, with a focus on the concepts of individuality, infiniteness, diversity, unknowability, change, and contingence that the phenomena we study in semiotic translation studies cannot be defined sufficiently and necessarily. Thus, I conceptualize of semiotic translations as a cluster of phenomena that share semiotic inter-ness as a feature, but which are as divergent as reality itself. With Wittgenstein, we point at "this and things similar" to this when we think about translation.

Next, I find it useful to think about translation in terms of complex adaptive systems (CAS) theory. Of all the reasons for this choice considered in the previous two chapters, two stand out for my current argument. The first is the fact that CAS considers both system and agent in a complex way, refusing to provide primacy to either (a view supported vehemently by Latour, 2007). The moment semiotic translation turned to cultural studies, ideology studies and sociology to consider semiotic translation within these wider frames, the relationship between agent and system or structure was added to the agenda of semiotic translation studies. Up to now, studies on semiotic translation and agency have focused mostly on personal ethics (see as an example volume 5, issue 1 of *The Interpreter and Translator Trainer*) and literary translation (Gentzler, 2008; Milton & Bandia, 2009a), with the focus on the individual agent. The implications of the conceptualization set out above is that one now has theoretical space to consider semiotic translation as social phenomenon in all of its complexity, that is, cultural studies and ideology studies, but also all aspects of sociology and even further. The role of translation in every single facet of social reality can now be considered. This includes the role of translation in the development of societies (Lewis & Mosse, 2006).

The second for my selection of CAS is that it deals with systems that are open, that is, in interaction with other systems or their environment. I have not seen works in which translation scholars deal theoretically with the problem of open systems and nonlinear causality (Chesterman, 2006). Current work on the agency of translators seems to me too quick to assume a causal relationship between the intentions of an individual agent and the social effects (Tyulenev, 2011a, p. 3). In Chapters 5 through 8 of this book, I try to work out the implications of the tension between agent and system for translation studies, from a CAS perspective.

4. CONCLUSION

In summary, I would like to indicate briefly what I believe to be the advantages of thinking about translation from a complexity perspective, in particular in terms of the notion I have suggested of emergent semiotics.

- It assists in the discussion on conceptualizing translation. Reductionist theories and linear logic are not able to account for a complex, culturally determined phenomenon such as translation (Tymoczko, 2006, 2007).
- It provides a theory of agency, explaining the relationship between agents and society, or individuality and universality.
- It conceptualizes translation within an ecological framework. In this sense, it subsumes the binary oppositions in contemporary thought, that is, capitalism versus socialism, empire versus postcolonialism, globalization versus localization.
- It points to complexity studies and emergent studies as well as computer simulation as a future field of study in translation.
- It allows for a theoretical framework within which to conceptualize both micro- and macro-level translation problems and the relationship between them, as argued by Tymoczko (2002).
- It explains the "third code", that is, translation language that cannot be explained in terms of linguistics alone, the lower-level components.
- Complexity theory can enrich notions of agency by arguing that they currently assume one cause for the complex phenomenon of culture creation, for example, Gentzler (2008).
- A complexity approach questions the use of linear logic in explaining translation, for example, Chesterman (2006).
- Complexity theory challenges the divisions of critical theory and the one-sidedness of deconstruction. It should include the paradox of deconstruction/construction and good/bad.

- Complexity theory makes it possible for translation studies to conceptualize translation as a factor in the development of societies, thus allowing for studies in this regard.
- The conceptualization explains why one could basically claim everything for translation that you could claim for original writing, thus explaining the "translation as" attempts at defining translation.
- This conceptualization should explain how and why translation is to be organized not as a discipline but as a transdiscipline.

The philosophy of translation I have forwarded earlier allows for the particular contextualization of translation in particular contexts, while paradoxically considering the implications for the rest of humanity. It should thus strongly favor a contextualized curriculum, paradoxically juxtaposed with a global curriculum. It should propel research on contextual data for teaching and research, but it should also propel the theorizing in the context of the implications of the data for the global phenomenon of translation.

As the reader would have noticed, I am reticent about the practical, managerial, and organizational implications of the broadened conceptualization that I have presented. At present, I prefer to keep it open because I am aware of the fact that success can never be predicted, only acclaimed a posteriori.

Part II

4 Translation and Development

I have a cousin who worked in London as a hairdresser for a number of years. When I attended the Translation Studies Research Summer School at University College of London in 2007, we had lunch together. Inevitably, the discussion veered towards his and my experience of London/England. Being Afrikaans-speaking, and having had the horrors of the Anglo-Boer War impressed on me from an early age, one of my experiences while walking the streets of the city center of London was the following. Noticing the age of buildings and the advanced level of civilization that England must have had while South Africa was still "in the bush", I was wondering why the English, who seemingly had it all, felt the need to come to Africa to oppress and pillage other peoples who had much less. When I voiced this naive observation, my cousin told me the following story. One day, at their hairdressing salon in an up-market part of London, a fellow South African colleague of his tended to an English lady's hair. All the while, she was complaining about all the foreigners in London: Polish, Pakistanis, Chinese, Russians, Hungarians, Nigerians, Somalis, etc. The woman claimed that these foreigners were taking all the jobs, running all the shops and disadvantaging the English. At a point in the conversation, the colleague responded: Lady, for centuries your country pillaged and ravaged the world, taking gold and diamonds and labor as much as you needed. Now, it's payback time!!

1. INTRODUCTION

With this somewhat vulgar story, I wish to introduce the notion and contestations of development into translation studies. In this chapter, my main aim is to expand or develop the current cultural studies strand in translation studies to include development in its purview. My argument is, in line with the complexity philosophy of Chapter 1, that the focus in translation studies on ideas and the analysis of power should be supplemented by an equal focus on an analysis of the material basis of social reality in which translation plays a role (see Said, 1993, pp. xii-xxv, 4–7). Said's (1993, pp. 66–67) notion of contrapuntal reading in this regard, that is, an understanding that holds together more than one "tune" or line, expresses the complexity perspective outlined in Chapter 1. Over the last three decades, translation studies has attacked virtually every evil on the planet and argued in favor of the agency role that translation has played and can play in redressing wrongs. Apart from the fact that one can question the relevance of this critical fervor, a glaring exception in this list of evils under attack is capitalism and the way in which it makes "the West" possible, and, importantly, the role that translation plays in maintaining capitalist society. In fact, what is needed in translation studies, even more than judgment, is an understanding of how translation makes modern economic, political, and social life possible. Following Rist (2002) and Latour (2007), my argument is that entering the battle against ideas of power will change nothing unless the material base of power is changed. Although it is true that ideas are powerful, Rist (2002, p. 232) points out that centuries of critical scholarship has changed very little about the power of empire, and he (Rist, 2002, pp. 162–164) argues that as long as the focus is on the poor and powerless and not the rich and powerful, development will remain an imperialist endeavor. It is my contention that, both to understand translation better and to be able to have a better picture of the ethical challenges facing translation, translation scholars need to expand their view from one focused on high culture to one that includes the everyday economic, political, and social systems and their material substructure (Moss, 2007, p. 3) that make the world go round.

I attempt to make this argument in the following way. First, I provide an overview of the current development debate. The overview is provided in sections on the macro-, micro- and human-centered approaches to development as well as a section on some of the serious questions that are being asked about development. Last, I propose an agenda for the interface between translation studies and development studies.

I have to hedge my effort here. Development studies is a vast field of interest, combining sociology, political science, and economics and having numerous sub- or specialized fields of interest. I do not claim to have read comprehensively in any of these fields and subfields. As my aim with this book is setting an agenda or a framework for future work, I cannot do more than introduce what I understand to be the main debates and issues. These I use to make my particular argument, that is, that translation studies should widen its scope to add the social, political, and economic aspects of reality to its cultural focus.

My argument in the previous section of the book has been as follows: If it is true that societies emerge from the complex interactions and links between individuals (Chapters 1 and 2), and if it is true that these interactions are of a semiotic nature (Chapter 2), and if it is true that in multilingual contexts these interactions need to be facilitated by means of translation (Chapter 3), it follows that translation has a role to play in the way in which societies emerge. At this point, I am assuming to have made the previously mentioned argument, although the reader will be the judge of the validity of the argument. Based on this argument, I now conceptualize the relationship between translation and development in greater detail, or the role that translation plays in development and the role that development plays in translation.

2. CONCEPTUALIZING DEVELOPMENT

In simple terms, development studies grapples with the observation that some societies seem to be better off than are others. As a field of study, it tries to come to grips with this notion of "better off", which certain development scholars have conceptualized as developed in contrast to undeveloped or underdeveloped, while others, like Nussbaum (2011) are of the opinion that all societies are confronted with problems of development. It seems obvious that a notion such as 'better off' entails a value judgment. Proponents of development judge it better to be rich than poor, industrialized than pastoral, educated than noneducated, urban than rural, scribal than oral, and so on. In short, it is better to be developed than un- or underdeveloped. These proponents usually assume that the kind of society that has emerged in what is known as the first world or Global North is a developed society—also assuming that developed means good or better. This ideological fixation on the benefits of Western society or the Western version of modernity for the rest of the world (Global South) underlies much of development thinking. It seems clear to me that development as a notion, and development studies trying to conceptualize this notion, entails a minefield of differing values, philosophies, and judgments about what is good for society. Engaging development studies from the perspective of translation studies, I try to not to become trapped in all the internal battles of the field because it is simply impossible to be an expert in all fields. Rather, this discussion is an invitation to translation scholars to take up the baton and take the debate further. It is also an invitation to development scholars to engage in the study of translation as one of the subsystems of their field of study. At the same time, I cannot discuss theories of development without becoming involved in a discussion on the value of development. So, let us start with the overview of development theory as I have promised. I hope to be able to navigate between the two extremes of merely providing an overview without attention to value and only judging value without helping the reader to understand the rationale behind the current development discourse.

Rist (2002) provides an excellent overview of the history of the notion of development, locating its roots in ancient Greek thought about history and change (Gillespie, 2001, pp. 1–14). He also links it to the Enlightenment and its belief in science, technology, and capitalism. Furthermore, it has its roots in nineteenth-century anthropology, social Darwinism, and imperialism, which have confirmed Western civilization as the epitome of civilization (for overviews, also see Said, 1993; Dutt & Ros, 2008). Brett (2009, pp. 25–27), however, argues that development should be seen more narrowly as a discourse that arose after the Second World War and the widespread demise of colonialism and empire. Its aim, within this particular context of postcolonialism, is to develop the whole world to the level of the first world, with obvious economic and political gains for the first world (Haynes, 2008, pp. 2, 33–34). Cronin (2006) has also argued that globalization exerts a major influence on development as borders are vanishing and transnational companies are becoming increasingly powerful. In this section, in order to provide an overview of thought in development studies, I follow Brett's focus on development studies as a particular discourse without necessarily agreeing with him. In the next section, where I intend providing some of the criticism against notions of development, I again revert to Rist and others.

Traditionally, development studies is an interdiscipline comprising three fields of study, that is, sociology, economics, and political science. For its theoretical tools, it makes use of philosophies, theories, and methodologies from those three fields. This means that, despite its interdisciplinary aims (e.g., Brett, 2009), some theories of development tend to focus more on economics, some focus more on political science and some focus more on sociology. In their discussion of the history and development of the field itself, one also finds this bias; that is, development economists explain development in terms of theories of economics that followed one another whereas development sociologists explain development as a series of theories of sociology that followed one another. I do not engage in the battle for primacy among these three fields. From the complexity perspective propounded in the first section of the book, I would argue that development is as much a complex emergent phenomenon as is translation. This means that it is not reducible to any one feature of its substrata. Also, it cannot be explained by one causal factor only, and its success cannot be predicted from any one of the features of which it is comprised. After the development failures of the last half century, it does not seem very innovative to call development "complex". Although much has been written about the failure(s) of development, what I regard as reductionistic tendencies underlying the development debate have not received much attention. Some of the latest works, for example, Brett (2009) and Otsuka and Kalirajan (2011a), acknowledge the complexity of the interrelationship between state, economy and society, though they still seem to assume the necessity and attainability of their development outcomes (for notions of nonlinear systems and complexity in economics, see Leydesdorff, 2006; for considering both domestic and external factors in development, see Haynes, 2005, p. 5; also the human capabilities approach seems to think more in terms of a bouquet of solutions [Nussbaum, 2011]).

For the sake of organizing this section, I distinguish between theories that operate on a macro level and those on a micro level. The last two or three decades have seen strong arguments for conceptualizing development on a micro level—to which I return later. It suffices at this stage, once again, to argue from a complexity perspective that one needs both, and even multiple, perspectives. Philosophically speaking, development cannot be reduced to or predicted from a reductionist perspective on either the macro or the micro level.

2.1 Macro-Level Theories of Development

When one considers development theories, you can look at it either as a succession of historical developments in thought or you could group approaches together thematically under headings which do not necessarily relate to historical developments. Brett (2009), who conceptualizes the history of development theory mostly in terms of economic theory, is an example of the first approach. For him, development is a particular discourse that originated after the First World War and went through particular stages (Brett, 2009, pp. 17–32):

- between 1945 and the mid-1970s, the initial, optimistic structuralist-functionalist phase where it was assumed that, if the right structures are in place, development would follow automatically;
- from the mid-1970s to 1990, a phase of market liberalism where state control over the economy was forfeited in favor of market control and countries from the Global South were expected to rigidly follow this shift;
- since the 1990s, a neoliberal phase with massive criticism against the notion of development from, amongst others, deconstructionists (see Rabbani, 2011; Rist, 2002); and
- currently, a phase which he calls liberal pluralism, which assumes an interplay between state, market, and society for development to be successful.

Currently, authors such as Brett (2002, p. 205) and Otsuka and Kalirajan (2011b) advocate a macro approach to development that (1) conceptualizes a complex relationship between state, market and society; (2) cedes some influence to cultural relativity, that is, the influence of locality on development; and (3) emphasizes historical relativity, that is, the particular historical trajectories through which societies move, that cannot be replicated (Brett, 2009, p. 240; see also Castells, 2004). In this complex approach, the market needs to operate with some state intervention as well as the influence of civil society (Brett, 2009, p. 213). Although his complexity thinking concerning state, market, and society is commendable, I have to note here that Brett's historical relativity holds only for non-Western societies. To him, the West is clearly the pinnacle of economic civilization, and he openly suggests that the rest take note and learn from them (Brett, 2009, p. 79). He is not able to bring to the table a sophisticated discourse on historical relativity such as Castells (2004, pp. 1–13), who points out the ebb and flow in the well-being of societies. Furthermore, Rabbani (2011) compounds the problems in this debate by questioning the value of cultural relativity in development because it leaves no room for questioning the abuse of power.

In general then, Brett (2009, p. xiv) argues that development is all about structural institutional, that is, macro-level, change and the impact of capitalism on the modern world. He is of the opinion that the macro factors need to be in place for development to take place. For him (Brett, 2009, p. 2), there are two reasons why development is necessary: (1) for the survival of the global system as we know it and (2) for the eradication of poverty. He does not argue why the first is necessary or whether the second is attainable. For him, the principles of freedom, equality, scientific objectivity, and cooperative interdependence are the drivers of successful developed societies, and these principles are, basically, beyond debate (Brett, 2009, p. 3). The reason why development fails is because good ideas are implemented badly (Brett, 2009, p. 4). Furthermore, his use of the term *late developing countries* (LDCs) reveals his belief that all societies will eventually achieve the same goals as the West, which, as argued earlier, indicates the relativity of his approach to historical relativity. He operates on the assumption that "liberal and social democratic capitalistic institutions" should be the universal norm (Brett, 2009, p. 32). What the world needs is freedom, continuous growth, and incessant change (Brett, 2009, pp. 36–44).

One of his stronger arguments, to my mind, is his pointing out that humanity as a whole should learn from the accumulated knowledge of humanity (Brett, 2009, p. 49). One cannot fault such a claim because it assumes the very mutuality that Rabbani (2011) and Said (1993) have argued for, but the problem is that the accumulated knowledge of humanity á la Brett is only Western knowledge, and capitalist at that. Rabbani is thus correct in pointing out the problem: Who decides? What leads Brett into these conceptual troubles is his social evolutionism that causes him to argue simplistically, despite his notion of historical relativism, that capitalism has been proved by natural selection to be the best economic model (Brett, 2009, p. 72). In the process, he forgets that the "now" during which capitalism rules may be one fleeting moment in the history of economic systems. It is clear that, for Brett, the values have been determined. He is only looking for ways of implementing them successfully in different spatial and historical contexts (Brett, 2009, p. 81). His argument that cultural relativism does not allow a universal debate on what is good for humanity because of its particularizing tendencies is supported by Rabbani (2011). He also points out that no society can claim to be "pure" and uninfluenced by other societies. Hybridity, as far as economic development is concerned, thus seems to be the norm (Brett, 2009, p. 244; Said, 1993, p. 15). The question is then, How should the whole of humanity agree on what is good for it? This is a question Brett assumes to have been answered, whereas Rabbani (2011), Nussbaum (2011), and Rist (2002) argue that it is precisely this question that has not been answered (see also Hettne's [2005, p. 45] call for an inter-civilizational dialogue concerning development).

Where Brett (2009, p. 219) also differs from earlier approaches to development is that he wishes to replace individual liberalist approaches with approaches based on social analyses that take the different value systems, understandings and endowments of each society into account. A question that arises on reading Brett (see 2009, p. 226) is whether prejudice in development terms is not just as undesirable as prejudice based on race, sect, family, and patriarchy? Are people in Western societies who are free from familial fetters but bound to market fetters more free than people from "underdeveloped" societies who are free from market fetters but bound to familial fetters?

As the title of his book indicates, Brett (2009) makes an attempt to salvage macro-level development theory after a decade of serious criticism against it. His argument basically runs as follows: What the West has attained as a civilization should be attained by the whole world because time has shown it to be the best. This can only be done if the whole world has the means to do so, which means that development is basically an endeavor of economics, politics, and institutions. As capitalism is the only candidate left standing, history has proved capitalism as the best, and therefore, all of the world should follow capitalist principles, in particular Brett's liberal pluralist version thereof, in order to develop. Against the background of his philosophy of social evolution, he advises that societies should learn from the winners of evolution and then find ways to deal with the tensions that it causes (Brett, 2009, p.79). It is clear that he has taken note of some of the criticism against development and therefore his suggestions consider the cultural and historical specificity of societies other than Western ones. One also has to grant that, in a complexity approach, one cannot do away with macro-economic, macro-political, and macro-social thinking about development. However, as to the goals of development, it seems that the work of people such as Rist (2002), Nussbaum and Sen (1993), and Sen (1999) has passed him by.

In Coetzee et al.'s (2001) compilation, development is explained from a number of sociopolitical perspectives, including both macro and micro approaches, and they use a thematic division of material to present the reader with various philosophical, theoretical, and methodological approaches to the study of social reality. If one takes Coetzee et al. (2001) as an example, it can see the vast array of socio-political-economic topics that pertain to development, though his compilation focuses more on the sociological. Once again, I have to be selective for the sake of the argument I am making, and therefore, I cannot cover everything here.

On one hand, as far as macro approaches are concerned, one has the modernization theories of development. These could be categorized as right wing, being based on structural-functionalist theories of society and neoclassical economic theory (Graaff, 2001, p. 5). These theories assume that all societies should modernize to the same extent that the First World has done and that this can be done through economic growth and industrialization (Coetzee, 2001a, p. 21). In this theory, modernization is the final stage in the social, political, and economic development of societies, which, as indicated earlier, is problematical in itself. The modernization theories are built on a belief in change and progress that is dominant in Western thought. It also relies on the Western philosophy of control over reality; that is, by enhancing human capacity, one could solve or reduce problems that you find in your physical and social environment (Coetzee, 2001a, p. 29; see also Sen, 1999, pp. 249–281). This control is made possible by developing a society in all facets, based on economic development that provides the money for other forms of development (Freund, 2010, p. 3; Haynes, 2005, p. 314; Moss, 2007, p. 3). Coetzee (2001a, p. 29) quotes Nisbet when listing the deep-rooted assumptions behind the modernization theories of development:

- a single, linear time frame, within which it is possible to improve the quality of life;
- social reform founded in a strong conception of the past and its contribution to the present;
- the inevitability of the future, including aspects of hope and expectations regarding the future;
- the controllability of welfare, stability, equality, freedom, peace, and justice;
- a reciprocal relationship between rationalism and idealism; and
- confidence in the autonomous contribution of future generations.

A lack of control over the environment is thus seen as a sign of underdevelopment. In contrast, developed societies are born out of premodern societies by means of a transformation resulting in new forms of technology, organization, and society (Coetzee, 2001a, p. 30). This process is viewed as part of a historical continuum, always getting better. Modern societies, according to one definition, are characterized by the following (Coetzee, 2001a, p. 31):

- increasing social complexity;
- control over the environment;
- increasing specialized adaptation;
- production and absorption of knowledge;
- rational understanding and flexibility; and
- social maturation.

Modernization also implies greater differentiation, integration and adaptation (for a detailed discussion, see Coetzee, 2001a, pp. 34–37). Together, these and other yardsticks such as a growing systemness comprise the idea of modernization, in which humanity believes it can solve any problem with which it is confronted. Obviously, the yardsticks all originate in the first world that, in this debate, never seems to question the relativity of its own development. Coetzee (2001a, p. 39) makes one last important observation when claiming that modernization theory has originated from colonial history. This claim needs to bring caution to any effort to endorse any program of development.

Coetzee (2001a, pp. 40–42) ends his discussion with criticism on the modernization theories. He criticizes it for operating with a linear model of development, for assuming that external factors can stimulate the development of a society, for assuming in a deterministic fashion that development will occur if outside stimuli are correct, for assuming that differentiation is inevitable and will always be progressive, for assuming that economic betterment solves all human problems, and for ignoring that fact that modernism is in itself a tradition.

On the other hand, one has the dependency theories. These could be categorized as left-wing, being based on Marxism and theories of anti-imperialism (Graaff, 2001, p. 5). They assume that the economic and political systems of the world are set up in such a way that they force the Third World to remain dependent. Non-development, in this view, is a structural problem caused by the dominant powers in the world.

Dependency theories tend to focus on either an evolutionist assumption or a functionalist-structuralist assumption (Graaff, 2001, p. 6). Thus, it locates the causes of and obstacles to development in either the nature of human-centered development, in an evolutionist explanation, or the structures of the (globalizing) world economics, in a structuralist explanation. The problem is thus evolutionary or structural, beyond the scope of individuals, and thus by definition of a macro nature. These theories are usually of a political or economic nature, putting the blame for underdevelopment on political choices and/or macro-economic policy.

The evolutionist theories views social change as

- moving through a set number of predetermined stages;
- taking place along a single path, that is, linear and repeatable;
- gradual;
- irreversible; and
- good, that is, advanced societies are better than more primitive ones.

The determinism underlying the above views is clear. In a similar, deterministic argument, Marxist theories explain development as the (necessary) changes that modes of production undergo.

Since the 1980s, neoliberalism has been a prominent macro-economic approach to development (see Hayami & Godo, 2005, pp. 242–309; Haynes, 2008, pp. 19–40). Although a highly complex term with a complex history and used differently in varying contexts, the latest views on neoliberalism assume that the free market is the best mechanism for economic growth and thus for development. State intervention should be limited to providing the framework within which the market could operate to its potential (contrary to the later work of Brett [2009], who does argue for a degree of state intervention). The assumption is that a macro environment with the least state intervention, a market-driven economy, and democratic principles are the best soil for the growth of development.

In Chapter 6, I attend to the knowledge economy, networks, and the translation of knowledge in more detail. It will suffice to note here that the influence of globalization on development has and is being discussed widely. This includes wide-ranging overviews such as that of Castells (2004), critical views such as Davids (2007) and Gillespie (2001), and positive evaluations such as I. Taylor (2005, p. 268). In this book, my focus, time, and space do not allow me to venture into globalization, which have already been covered in translation studies (e.g., Cronin, 2006). The same holds for issues of ecology and the environment that have already been placed on the agenda of translation studies (IISD, 2012).

At this point of transfer to the next section on micro-level theories of development, let me briefly discuss Korten's generational framework of development projects as an indication that the distinction between macro- and micro-development approaches may not be as clear as my numbering suggests. Korten (1990, pp. 115–131; for a summarized table, see Swart & Venter, 2001) has identified four generations of development initiatives, which could be conceptualized as his way of looking at the movement from very local and macro approaches to more globalized and macro approaches. According to him, first-generation strategies mean the direct delivery of services to meet the needs of people. This usually entails food, health care, shelter, and so on and is often found in crisis situations. Second-generation strategies refer to efforts to build capacity in order to help people to meet their own needs. This could include training, and it is usually focused on groups. Third-generation strategies involve attempts to change local, national, and global policies and institutions. Fourth-generation strategies focus on mobilizing people's movements around the world. It can thus be seen that the dividing line, if one needs one, between micro and macro approaches lies somewhere between the second and third strategies.

2.2 Micro-Level Theories of Development

The approaches discussed above can thus be categorized as macro approaches. Since the 1990s, many scholarly voices have been heard advocating a micro approach to development. This follows on the failure of many of the macro approaches. A blend of critical theory, micro-sociology and participatory action research, the micro approaches claim that development should be about people. In their view, top-down development does not work and has to be replaced by bottom-up development (Coetzee et al., 2001; Kotzé & Kotzé, 2007; Theron, 2007a).

Micro approaches to development have their origins in the perceived failure of macro-economic and sociological approaches to achieve the desired effects. Furthermore, it is connected to the criticism against grand narratives, the rise in participatory research and action programs and the mushrooming of development agencies acting regionally or locally (Coetzee, 2001b, pp. 119–138; Theron, 2007a).

Since the 1990s, the development debate has heard a third set of voices, that is, the proponents of human-centered development, with a concomitant focus on social capital (Payne & Phillips, 2010, pp. 149–150; Prozesky & Mouton, 2001; Roodt, 2001). This approach, based on critical or humanist or critical-humanist philosophy (Nussbaum, 2011; Romm, 2001, pp. 141–152) and often part of neoliberal economic theories (Le Roux & Graaff, 2001, pp. 195–212), argues that humans should be in the center of the development debate and development interests. It also argues that development cannot take place if there is not enough social capital, that is, if the people of a country have not been developed by means of education, for instance, to be able to support the economic ideals. The United Nations has played a significant role through some of its reports, in particular the Brundtland report (IISD, 2012), to enhance the spread of ideas concerning human-centered development. Their definition of sustainable development, that is, development that meets the needs of the present without compromising the ability of future generations to meet their own needs, has become common knowledge in development circles and clearly reflects the move toward a human interest in development.

The purview of human-centered development extends in at least two directions. On one hand, it tries to change the purely macro-economic and/or macro-political focus of the development debate into a focus on the benefits or detriments of development for humanity. On the other hand, it sprouts from the realization that even hardcore economic development is based on the ability of human beings to perform economic activities with particular skills and that, without human skill—seen as capital—no development will take place; that is, without social capital, development is doomed. Its negative side is that it has turned human beings into a factor of the economy, that is, social capital, rather than turning the economy into a factor of human well-being (which Nussbaum and Sen have been trying to do as we shall see in the next section).

The human approach thus, to a large extent, entails a turn toward a micro-level look at development in which scholars advocate a bottom-up approach (Payne & Phillips, 2010, p. 176; see, however, Theron [2007c, p. 2], who argues that development will always be a top-down approach initiated by institutions). Coetzee (2001b, p. 119) provides the following definition:

> The micro-foundation is based on a people-centered approach. Development does not only imply the satisfaction of basic needs, but also the right to live a meaningful life. Development is therefore based on human well-being, and action plans should aim at providing the opportunity for people to become more than they are. An important implication of

this emphasis is that it places the meaning and the special circumstances within which action takes place at the center of the analysis.

The human-centered development approach questions the assumption that economic growth equals development. It is critical of the assumed connection between material welfare and human welfare. Coetzee (2001b, pp. 119–138) explains the following six features of the human-centered development approach:

1. People can be more than they are: Development should not only be about material benefit but also about providing a better life based on human well-being. This means that the human-centered development approach sees development as the creation of opportunities for increased humanness. It thus includes "soft" ideals such as human rights, social justice, environmental sensitivity, and freedom of expression.
2. Meaning: The human-centered development approach stresses the fact that development is about people finding or constructing meaning for their lives, creating meaningful lives. In this sense, development is a hermeneutic endeavor, as is also argued by Olivier de Sardan (2005) and Chambers (2007). I shall later on argue that this hermeneutic dimension of development is one of its points of connection with translation. Suffice it to say now that language and multilingualism have largely been ignored by development scholars and practitioners. The effect of this is, just as a matter of logic, that development has remained a foreign phenomenon.
3. The emphasis on the experience of the lifeworld: As indicated earlier, this approach sees development as much more than economic development. If development is about humans, it relates to the lifeworld of the individual, that is, family, religion, and culture. One cannot conceptualize development without considering culture, locality, and the symbolic universes that people occupy.
4. Desirable direction: The human-centered development approach is of the opinion that development should take place from below. In this perspective, development is about the well-being of people, and it should take cognizance of people's own definitions of well-being. From the complexity theory perspective that I have outlined in Chapter 1, it seems clear to me that we have another paradox here. Should development agencies decide what is good for people, or should they decide for themselves? Do development agencies know what is good for people? Do people know what is good for themselves? A philosophy of complexity will reject any of these reductionist views and look for a paradoxical solution to the problem. It is not good enough to claim that both are what are needed. The question is how. Here the dialogic concepts of Bakhtin (1982) could become useful. Development should

be a linguistic dialogue between two worlds, a boundary where two worlds meet, a *lekgotla* where two value systems are in interaction, looking for human well-being (Rabbani, 2011).
5. Consciousness: If people are involved in development, this has cognitive implications. Development cannot take place, as it were, bypassing the consciousness of the people it involves. It has to be grounded in consciousness, which once again stresses the hermeneutic nature of the development endeavor. The entire symbolic universe of participants needs to be involved in this process.
6. Participation and self-reliance: The human-centered development approach assumes that people need to participate in their own development and that they need to take responsibility for it (Maathai, 2009). The beneficiaries of development are not conceived of as recipients but as contributors.

In this approach, argues Coetzee (2001b, p. 127), the central factor is the act of interpretation (see also Kotzé & Kotzé, 2007). The participants in development should all interpret the development; they should make it accessible to themselves and be able to create meaning out of it, make sense of it. It entails a process of "complex interaction and interpenetration of meaning structures" (Coetzee, 2001b, p. 127). It is a linguistic encounter, out of which emerge new forms of social reality. It is through individual human interactions or encounters that social structures emerge. Once emerged, these structures exert downward causation on individual interactions. In this sense, development interactions give rise to the emergence of new, probably hybrid forms of society. A development theory of translation or a translation theory of development should trace these borders, hybrid forms, and new developments. This then focuses on the local, on particular times and particular spaces; that is, it is historically and geographically grounded. It takes an interest in the experiences of people. In this sense, development is a translation in more ways than one. It relates to the linguistic, whether oral or written, interactions between individuals or even groups, but it also deals with the translation of concepts, ideas, lifeworlds, and value systems into new times and spaces.

Olivier de Sardan (2005) argues that anthropology should also become part of the debate on development (see Lewis & Mosse [2006], who argue that development should be drawn into mainstream anthropology). For him, development studies are represented by two streams of thought. The first, he calls the deconstructionist theories that have criticized Western discourses on development as being imperialist (Olivier de Sardan, 2005, p. 8). The second he terms populist theories that popularize the indigenous (Olivier de Sardan, 2005, p. 9), theories through which intellectuals discover the people, pity their lot and marvel at their capacities and decide to avail themselves for the welfare of the oppressed (Olivier de Sardan, 2005, p. 35; see also Lewis & Mosse's [2006, pp. 2–5] analysis of the intellectual influence on development). Much of the postcolonial work currently done in translation studies can be regarded as populist in Olivier de Sardan's definition. Over and against both deconstructionism and populism, Olivier de Sardan (2005, p. 15) proposes a comparative approach that takes seriously the acts of adaptation in each context through which people are trying to cope with the claims of development. For him, development is thus adaptation to social change, taking place always and everywhere because society is always changing (Olivier de Sardan, 2005, p. 23). Although it is true that this change takes place under conditions of unequal power differentials, development studies needs to break away from ideological populism that studies only power differentials (dare I once again point out the relevance of his claim for translation studies). It also needs to maintain a historical attitude (also see Brett, 2009) to deal with continuous changes in communities.

For Olivier de Sardan (2005, p. 32), development situations are typical border situations where, in this case, a "cosmopolitan, international culture and sub-cultures meet the local culture and subcultures". This border situation, also aptly described regarding the South African frontier history of the eighteenth and nineteenth centuries by Legassick (2010; also see Ranis, 2011), is a complex phenomenon in which politics, economics, religion, the law, nature, and so on play a role. Olivier de Sardan (2005, p. 49) criticizes systems approaches to development because they do not provide enough conceptual space for thinking about actors and agency. I am convinced, however, that the complex view on systems that I have put forward in Chapter 1 to 3, which emphasizes both agent and system, covers his critique. The facts of development are facts that bear testimony to the relationship between heterogeneous norms and cultures (Olivier de Sadan, 2005, p. 60). These facts are syncretistic or hybrid. Olivier de Sardan (2005, p. 62) also argues that anthropology is able to conceptualize of development in a holistic fashion, relating social actions simultaneously to economic, social, cultural, political, and religious dimensions.

Olivier de Sardan (2005, p. 53) puts forward a more localized approach to development which allows him to focus on the micro and meso levels, with an emphasis on actors and agencies as well as their strategies and stakes. His approach seems to overlap with complex systems approaches as his "interactionist" approach suggests an analysis of strategies and structures, that is, individuals and collectives (Olivier de Sardan, 2005, p. 52). The interaction between 'systems of constraint and processes of adaptation' is what development scholars need to understand.

So, why do development efforts fail? Whereas Brett (2009) ascribes the failure of development plans to the bad implementation thereof, Olivier de Sardan (2005, p. 69) reckons that the expectations of development practitioners concerning development are misguided, and people usually have good reasons why they do not respond to development opportunities. Development thus represents a clash of both expectations and values. I return to this in the next section.

What then should development achieve? For Olivier de Sardan (2005, p. 70), development is grounded in two meta-ideologies: Development seeks the welfare of others, that is, it has a moral connotation, and it implies technical and economic progress, that is, it has evolutionist and technicist assumptions. The problem, which he (Oliver de Sardan, 2005, p. 72) clearly recognizes, is who decides what societies should be. Mbembe (2001) has argued that Africans need a debate on alternative ways of being modern. With this, as I interpret it, he grants that one cannot *not* be modern in these days. The question about modernity is not whether but how. I would like to rephrase: We (the whole world) need a debate on options of being modern hybridly. The present needs to be a hybrid of past and future, old and new, North and South. Without a hybrid (dis)continuity at the edge of chaos, a hybrid (dis)continuity which provides enough stability for people to remain human and enough change for them not to stagnate, development will either lead to unbridled change and its fundamentalist reactions (as is currently seen) or the evils of "underdevelopment" (as is also currently seen). What kind of society do we want? Do we all want to live to the age of 100, or do we want the 50 or 70 years we have to be meaningful? Do we all want to hasten to work in our sports utility vehicles (SUVs), visiting our shrinks over lunch to teach us to cope with stress or could we be content riding a bicycle to work, eating a less sumptuous meal and having time for our kids? I am not saying that all of the above-mentioned options are necessarily mutually exclusive. What I regard as the most important contribution by Olivier de Sardan (2005, p. 91) is his insistence that innovation or development or social change is a hermeneutic process. It cannot be impressed on people; it has to pass through their consciousness. The implication of this insight is that development is a semiotic activity. It is imbued with symbolic value. It entails a struggle between different values. Studying language and translation in development could help us to get a better understanding of the process.

Development relates to a diachronic comparativism in which neighboring phenomena operating at a regional level are studied. If one grants that development relates to a hybrid phenomenon, it means that the diffusion of developmental advantages will not be well defined. In Olivier de Sardan's (2005, p. 92) words, it will be a "nebulous notion of embeddedness of extremely variable cultural traits". Development is not a matter of technical nature; it is a matter of cultural borrowing. Within a society, agents from outside come in with their new ideas, technology, and so on, and they cause a conflict of interests because they do not enter into a vacuum but into a social space that already has its own interests. Thus, from this interaction, new social realities have to be constructed.

In development projects, one has to reckon with the meeting of two "cultures", that is, with translation. Olivier de Sardan discusses various points of contention that arise from development work. The history/context of the particular site at which you want to work is relevant. So is the difference, especially in rural areas, between technical rationality and other registers of coherence, which may be fragmented and focused on individual behavior in the case of peasants (Olivier de Sardan, 2005, p. 144). As any kind of intervention in a society requires a reconsideration of the whole social ecosystem, selective appropriation, sidetracking, seeking safety, seeking aid, and the monopolization of aid are ways through which a local community could appropriate aid (Calvert, 2005, p. 48; Handelman, 2005; Olivier de Sardan, 2005, pp. 146–149). The clash between a local popular knowledge system and the scientific knowledge system brought in by development agents causes a major tension. This once again calls for time, for mediation between the different systems of knowledge and values, and for translation. If you take the argument for development as a hybrid phenomenon, the coexistence of two or more systems of knowledge should not be a problem. This leads Olivier de Sardan (2005, pp. 166–167) to conclude that the development process is at its base a mediated process. In fact, Haynes (2005, p. 314) calls it a site of struggle because it always has resource implications. It is about passing on the message; it is missionary, which means that it constitutes a clash of values (Davis, 2006, p. 18). It is about agents speaking on behalf of their authorities, and they speak in different languages in many ways. When one further considers the process of development brokering, language matters become even more complex because now you not only have the different natural language of participants and the difference between popular and local language but also have the language of brokerage, of project management, and of development itself (Olivier de Sardan, 2005, pp. 170–184).

The micro approaches to development could then be conceptualized as participatory approaches with the focus on actors and actor networks (Lewis & Mosse, 2006, p. 10; Olivier de Sardan, 2005, pp. 137–152, 166–184; Shaw, 2005). Development agencies make use of development brokers and development agents to do their work. These agents interpret the situation on the ground, creating cognitive and performative spaces in which they can operate (Lewis & Mosse, 2006, p. 13). It is here that Latour's notion of translation as the process through which various stakeholders come on board and how interests are negotiated becomes of interest. In this respect, Lewis and Mosse (2006, p. 14) view translation as the negotiation of meanings and definitions and mutuality, whereas Salemink (2006, p. 102) calls it the attempt to find a common language in a development context. The encounters at the site of development, encounters between people who speak different languages, literally and figuratively, need to be translated into one common goal. This is a point of contestation par excellence. Nauta (2007, p. 163) uses the notion of translation in development encounters to indicate the research, workshops and reports used to manage tensions. In this sense, translation is once again seen as the point of contact to (through technical managerial expertise) unify the diverse points of view and interests that meet in a development project. In this regard, Theron (2007c, p. 2) argues that development is usually done on behalf of somebody else. As in translation, this poses the problem of representing someone else's views. The point I wish to make is that micro-level approaches to development offer translation scholars the opportunity, if they have a broad enough conception of translation, to study the interface of cultural systems linguistically and conceptually. Following Theron (2007, p. 7), one could then conceptualize of development as the complex meeting of numerous open-ended systems that are themselves complex. The implication of this is that predicting the outcome of a development intervention is basically impossible. Furthermore, Theron (2007a, p. 44; see also Kotzé & Kotzé, 2007, pp. 78–79) argues that the disciplinary nature of Western knowledge is not suited for a complex phenomenon such as development (which is basically what I argued in Chapter 3). Kotzé and Kotzé (2007, p. 79) particularly question linear assumptions about the context in development. Disciplinary knowledge thus needs translation to make it understandable, accessible, and adaptable to particular contexts. Kotzé and Kotzé (2007) also focus on the hermeneutics of development, arguing that the work of development agents is focused on understanding development, understanding the particular context and then engaging these two. The theoretical framework that I have set out for translation, that is, complex adaptive systems, in which both individual agent and social structure are conceptualized as nonlinear factors in the emergence of social (developmental) reality, also seems relevant for development situations, although much work is needed in this regard.

If one then follows Theron (2007b, pp. 222–223) by arguing that development is a conceptual issue, it follows logically that it is also a semiotic issue (see also Chambers, 2007, p. 185).

2.3 Human-Centered Approaches to Development

Although it may be true that micro approaches to development are also human-centered approaches, I think that human-centered approaches deserve a discussion of their own because they have become extremely powerful and relevant and because they are trying to also include macro approaches to development. Within the space I have, it is impossible to provide an overview of all literature on this approach. I shall limit my discussion to the work of Nussbaum and Sen, who are the two main proponents of the capabilities approach, one of the most popular human-centered approaches to development.

Despite some differences between them, Nussbaum and Sen have in common the argument that a purely statistical or economic approach to development does not fulfill the aims of development. Nussbaum (2011, pp. 46–50; Sen 1999, p. 19) argues that the gross domestic product (GDP) cannot be an indication of the decency of human living in a particular country, as was claimed by macro-economic development theorists. What is needed is an approach to development that is able to measure quality of life, decency of life, in short, human-centered development. In his approach, Sen (1999) sees development as freedom in the sense that development should enhance the freedom that individuals need in order to make choices. Unfreedoms, or a lack of choice, thus mean a lack of development. In other words, the aim of development should not be limited to economic development, and one should not assume that when you have developed an economy that you have automatically provided people with a more decent, meaningful, and dignified life. Although it is true that the material substratum to human-centered development is provided by economic development, humans and their development cannot be reduced to economic well-being. Also, freedom is never absolute. As Latour (2007, p. 230) says, "freedom is getting out of *bad* bondage, not the *absence* of bondage" (italics in original). The aim of development should thus be to limit the existence or influence of bad unfreedoms on people, but to think that one will be totally free is unrealistic because reality, which we cannot escape, exerts various restrictions on us, be they "natural" or "social". On one hand, Nussbaum thus questions the assumption that a high GDP or high per-capita income, which divides the total income of a country by its number of people, indicates that everybody has enough. In cases in which the gap between rich and poor is excessively large, such as South Africa, Brazil, and Equatorial Guinea, for example, GDP says very little about the dignity of a large portion of the population. On the other hand, she questions the notion that wealth will inevitably trickle down to even the poorest (Nussbaum, 2011, p. 13). Sen (1999, pp. 35–53) adds to this debate by requiring of development to sort out its ends and its means. Economic growth cannot be the end of development; it is only a means to another end, that is, human freedom. This seems to be the central tenet of human approaches to development. They have restored human dignity as the end of development, not the means to it.

Therefore, Nussbaum (2011, p. 4) suggests that one should rather measure development in terms of the opportunities that are open for every person in a country. In this sense, all nations are developing nations because they need to develop the dignity of their populace further. Instead of applying one yardstick to measure development, Nussbaum (2011, p. 18) proposes a number of yardsticks, which she calls capabilities. She thus proposes comparing the development progress in countries by comparing their performance as far as these capabilities are concerned. For her, human-centered development means that people should be free to make choices, and it is the responsibility of societies to make it possible—create the opportunities or capabilities—for people to make choices according to their own values (2011, p. 18). In simple terms, human-centered development is interested in what people can be or do or become. She suggests that there be a number of these capabilities, that is, combined capabilities (2011, p. 21).

Nussbaum (2011, p. 21) also distinguishes between internal capabilities and innate equipment. In other words, innate equipment or basic capabilities refers to the physical and mental abilities with which someone is born, whereas internal capabilities are socially acquired traits and abilities. Although not everybody has the same innate equipment, the aim of development is to support the development of every person's internal capabilities. Having developed these internal capabilities, the combined capabilities make it possible for someone to choose according to her value system, to be able to make choices.

A strong point in Nussbaum's argument is that she refuses to reduce the capabilities to one or two central ones (Nussbaum 2011, p. 35). For her, human dignity is a complex phenomenon that requires a complexity of conditions to do well. Thus, she lists ten capabilities which could be expanded depending on the particular society (Nussbaum, 2011, pp. 33–34). Also, these capabilities, though generally assumed to be universally valid, could be applied differently in different cultural contexts (Nussbaum, 2011, pp. 101–112). To be fair to her thinking, I quote her in full on these capabilities (italics from the original):

1. *Life.* Being able to live to the end of a human life of normal length; not dying prematurely, or before one's life is so reduced as to be not worth living.
2. *Bodily health.* Being able to have good health, including reproductive health; to be adequately nourished; to have adequate shelter.
3. *Bodily integrity.* Being able to move freely from place to place; to be secure against violent assault, including sexual assault and domestic violence; having opportunities for sexual satisfaction and for choice in matters of reproduction.
4. *Senses, imagination and thought.* Being able to use the senses, think, and reason—and to do these things in a "truly human" way, a way informed and cultivated by an adequate education, including, but by no means limited to, literacy and basic mathematical and scientific training. Being able to use imagination and thought in connection with experiencing and producing works and events of one's own choice, religious, literary, musical, and so forth. Being able to use one's mind in ways protected by guarantees of freedom of expression with respect to both political and artistic speech, and freedom of religious exercise. Being able to have pleasurable experiences and avoid non-beneficial pain.
5. *Emotions.* Being able to have attachments to things and people outside ourselves; to loves those who love and care for us, to grieve at their absence; in general, to love, to grieve, to experience longing, gratitude, and justified anger. Not having one's emotional development blighted by fear and anxiety . . .
6. *Practical reason.* Being able to form a conception of the good and to engage in critical reflection about planning one's life . . .
7. *Affiliation.* (A) Being able to live with and toward others; to recognize and show concern for other human beings, to engage in various forms

of social interaction; to be able to imagine the situation of another . . .
(B) Having the social bases of self-respect and nonhumiliation; being able to be treated as a dignified being whose worth is equal to that of others. This entails provisions of nondiscrimination on the basis of race, sex, sexual orientation, ethnicity, caste, religion, national origin.
8. *Other species.* Being able to live with concern for an in relation to animals, plants, and the world of nature.
9. *Play.* Being able to laugh, to play, to enjoy recreational activities.
10. *Control over one's environment. (A) Political.* Being able to participate effectively in political choices that govern one's life; having the right of political participation, protections of free speech and association. *(B) Material.* Being able to hold property . . . , and having property rights on an equal basis with others; having the right to seek employment on an equal basis with others; having the freedom from unwarranted search and seizure . . .

It should be clear from this very brief and limited discussion that (1) development is relevant to translation studies and (2) translation scholars will have to do much more work to understand development and its relationship to translation. In the last section of this chapter, I try to provide some direction in this regard.

3. CRITICAL PERSPECTIVES ON DEVELOPMENT

As in any field of study, development studies makes use of a number of assumptions on which to build its house. Over the last two decades or so, a critical debate has arisen, not only about how to go about development but also particularly about the very assumptions underlying a discourse on development. As it is nowadays taken as a given that translators are ethically involved in their work through the choices they make, a presentation of development theory for translation studies would not suffice without listening to the critical voices.

I shall start by presenting the scathing attack that Rist (2002) has leveled against "the faith" of and in development. Based on an insightful overview of the history of the notion of development, arguing convincingly that it is a distinctly Western notion, he questions humanity's faith in its ability to continue to develop (read grow economically) ad infinitum (Rist, 2002, p. x), which Goudzwaard and De Lange (1995, pp. 1–3) have also done. Development, he argues, rests on a particular view of history, humanity's control over it, and a religious belief in continuous change. The belief is also that change is good, and its results are necessarily better than what came before. What is challenged is not the pervasive nature of change in reality but the assumptions that it is always for the better and that it can be engineered or controlled. Rist's historical analysis also poses the question whether there is a difference between social change and adaptation (Olivier de Sardan, 2005), in general, and the particular mode of social change that is called development. Development, as a Western form of thinking and doing, is thus also inevitably tied to colonialism and empire (Rist, 2002, p. 52). In his work on culture and empire, Said (1993, p. 282) argued in similar fashion that development is actually a guise for imperialism.

One of the most destructive lines of thinking in development is the biological or social evolutionist thinking, which presented development as natural and thus inevitable (Rist, 2002, p. 54; see also Brett's [2009] use of social Darwinism to justify development). Rist argues that the current development debate started with President Truman's inaugural speech in which development became a new way for the United States to think about international relationships and where development changed its status from intransitive to transitive, that is, something that does not merely happen but what can be done (Rist, 2002, pp. 72–73). Development thus became a way of colonizing the mind by being a legal and peaceful way of telling people how they should act if they want to be cast in the image of the successful (Brett, 2009) West (Rist, 2002, p. 74). Based on Rist's analysis, I would suggest that the distinction developed/un(der)developed has become a politically correct way of continuing the racist bias of which Said (1993, 1994) has so convincingly written.

Rist's argument is that development theorists have and are asking all kinds of questions about development except those that really matter. To him, the real question is not why some are poor, but why some are rich. The real question, put differently, is about an economic system other than capitalism (Rist, 2002, p. 246) for which development scholars need to look much wider than the here and now. What we need to find out is not how to make everybody as prosperous as an American but how we can ensure that all people have enough, materially, to live a meaningful life (Rist, 2002, p. 148). What we need to discuss further is what we lose when we modernize and/or Westernize, how far we want to go with that process, and whether we are prepared to live with the consequences either way. On one hand, what is lost could be merely vested power, that is, paternalism, but on the other hand, if modernization is done in only one way, it amounts to Westernization. Thus, Rist (2002, p. 102) also suggests a debate on alternative ways of being modern and on the hybridization of development.

To my mind Rist (2002, p. 146ff) correctly identifies the development discourse as a faith. Its continual claims of new insights, of "if-only" arguments and of restating the same values and ideas in different ways point in this direction (see Puuka et al. [2012] for a development text that is, once again, little more than a wish list [read utopia] of what an ideal society should look like or how a nonideal society should go about becoming an ideal one).

In his discussion on the report of the Hammarskjold foundation, Rist (2002, pp. 155–157) grants that focusing on people, that is, people-centered development, rather than economic structures and proposing limits to consumption are positive developments. However, he argues that the plight of the poor is just a morally justified pretext for outside intervention in countries and that the needs debate is reducing humanity to its biological substructure (Rist, 2002, pp. 167–168). Furthermore, he questions who decides what human needs are because they are not necessarily universal but could be co-determined by social contexts.

After his somber review of development discourse, Rist (2002, pp. 242–246) suggests three possible future sets of action. The first is to maintain the search for growth but with reforms to the global economic system, although he cannot foresee any control over the global system. The second entails that the Global South should stop expecting anything from development and make do with what they have, in this way at least breaking with the dominant world system. Thirdly, economists could go looking for new economic theories (contrary to Brett, 2009) in an interdisciplinary effort with historians and anthropologists. Are there ways of exchange other than the market, Rist (2002, p. 247) asks, and are there noneconomic factors in the economy, for example, prestige, that could counter the materialist bias of capitalism to truly develop human existence in all of its complexity?

Rabbani (2011) engages in the debate between pro- and anti-developmentalists, arguing that both make use of the same problematic arguments. Her argument entails that both pro- and anti-developmentalists operate at the level of values and not at the level of truth, the former because they believe they are right and the latter because they believe nobody can be right. She points out how the antidevelopment debate tries to protect (local, Global South) communities against the empire of development by claiming cultural relativism. In so doing, they give up the notion of truth, which implies that they are merely interested in maintaining the status quo in their own ranks, as do pro-developmentalists. Rather than operating at the level of values, which can never be contested, she proposes a dialogic and mutual relationship between humans in which everybody is able to contest everybody else's truth claims (Rabbani, 2011, pp. 3–5). It is her opinion that giving up the notion of truth to safeguard yourself against mutuality and the other is too high a price to pay.

In her analysis, both pro- and anti-developmentalists operate based on freedom. The pro-developmentalists assume individual freedom to be their highest value, whereas anti-developmentalists operate on the level of social or community freedom, that is, the right of a community to be free of development or whatever is imposed on it (Rabbani, 2011, p. 10). She rightly points out, however, that both these approaches insulate the human being from the other, resulting in the legitimization of the established order, be that order developed or non-developed (Rabbani, 2011, p. 11). This insulatory move means that communities forever remain as they are, never having the option of discussing or reconsidering their future. It leads to a position that is as futile as that of pro-developmentalists who argue that everything and everybody must change (in their image).

Rabbani (2011, p. 19) tries to move development discourse out of the pro- and anti-impasse by arguing that mutual recognition is a basic feature of humanity, be that individual or social mutual recognition (also see Said, 1993, p. 41; Castells, 2004, p. 7). Of particular interest for translation studies is her argument that the recognition of the other as superior, equal, or inferior is mediated by the interpretation of symbols, which need continuous reassessment and recognition (Rabbani, 2011, p. 34). She also tries to move the debate from the mere legitimization or questioning of power to understanding by claiming that mutual recognition and self-understanding go together (Rabbani, 2011, p. 37). In this, one clearly sees her dependence on Habermas and the effort to escape from the quagmire of power by arguing for understanding, truth, and rationality to at least play a role in the development dialogue. Her argument is especially powerful when she claims that when truth goes, the fight against oppression goes. To put it in a more sophisticated way, she argues that "the problem with postmodernist arguments against universality, is that, if there is no universal right or wrong, anything goes anyway, so how can one then be against oppression?" (Rabbani, 2011, p. 54). Power cannot be contested at the level of value, is her claim (Rabbani, 2011, p. 70). One must have some recourse to truth, which, in her definition, is not a grand narrative but the product of mutual recognition and interdependence. To my mind, she is pointing in the right direction. Arguing only for the contingency of truth, as has also become fashionable in translation studies, leaves one with no response to power. From the perspective of a philosophy of complexity, truth and value will obviously hang together "at the edge of chaos", as will universality and locality, as will necessity and contingency. At this stage, I still need to work out exactly how, but these paradoxes need to be maintained. Thus, I suggest that Rabbani is actually recommending a debate about the truth of values in development, because development is ultimately a faith, as Rist (2002) has argued.

When development is conceptualized of as a dialogue focused on mutual recognition and self-understanding, it enters the domain of hermeneutics, which is related to translation. Rabbani (2011, p. 100) claims that humanity will remain undeveloped as long as it does not universally validate its self-understanding and as long as "my" and "your" forms of development are mutually exclusive. She thus argues that "we" need to develop, whatever that means. The dialogue she foresees is "a process of giving and demanding reasons for the sole purpose of reaching understanding" (Rabbani, 2011, p. 107). With this hermeneutic move, she tries to connect people, to put understanding and insight before judgment and use. In her view, freedom does not exist. It is a social construct, a gift of the other's friendship, as she calls it (Rabbani, 2011, p. 145). What we need to do in development studies, and in translation studies and all kinds of "inter"-studies, is to balance at the edge of chaos our current obsession with the right to be right, with the right to know and to understand (Rabbani, 2011, p. 156).

Although Said did not write about development per se, his work is relevant to thinking about the world as it is today. In his analysis, it is the human flaw in all projects, that is, selfishness, which is "turning complexity into simplicity, turning the other into my other, turning contingency into inevitability" (Said, 1994, p. 115). This is a deep-cutting criticism of development as development discourse often operates at the level of macro theories, programs, and values. It seldom asks questions about the human condition, and it seldom asks about the psychological price that humanity is paying when selling its soul to capitalism, development, growth, freedom, change, and o on in order to buy some reprieve for its body. Just like Rist (2002, pp. 230–232), Said (1994, p. 202) questions the evolutionist assumptions behind development, namely that everything gets better with time. His observation on orientalism, that is, that it reduces the Orient to a kind of human flatness in which every community is the same and has the same future, also holds true for development, because development flattens the world by posing one goal for all societies. His advocacy for historical relativism, that is, that the difference of every epoch be appreciated, goes far deeper than that of Brett (2009, pp. 18, 79, 240–252), who allows for historical relativism only as far as the pragmatics of the implementation of the universal, ahistorical values of Western society are concerned. In Said's (1994, p. 204) view, imperialism, racism, and ethnocentricity were the only mechanisms that "advanced" cultures had for dealing with the other. In this sense, it seems fair to argue that development is just a sophisticated form of colonization (see also Gillespie, 2001). What needs to be addressed in any debate on the state of human society is synchronic essentialism (Said, 1994, p. 240). As Castells (2000a, pp. 1–13) has vividly pointed out, through history, societies change with some being "better off now" and "worse off then". Turning the "better off now: into some sort of essential, never-changing value, such as Brett does with capitalism, lies behind empire.

One of Said's insightful comments, which relates directly to translation studies, concerns the modern social sciences. He argues (Said, 1994, p. 290) that, with modern quantitative research, social scientists believe that they can get to understand humanity—and thus propose theories of development about what is best for humanity—without factoring language into the equation. This is one of my main arguments concerning the development debate. The development debate is purportedly about human betterment, about the poor, about a better life, but, according to Said, it does not pay enough attention to language, the way in which you "get to" the people you are studying, the way in which you are to know the people who are involved in development. In this sense, he argues that development is a "people-less" field of study and activism. It does not matter what your conceptualization of development is and whether you are for or against it. A meaningful discourse on development should entail the role of language, differences in language and hermeneutics/understanding as a crucial part of its endeavor. To my mind, it is precisely because social scientists do not sufficiently factor language and interpretation into their equation that they tend to essentialize societies (Said, 1993, p. 32).

The implications of Said's (1993) ideas on the pervasiveness of empire have been taken up in various strands of postcolonial translation studies that have studied the role of translation in making empire possible and in maintaining it. What is lacking in this regard is to turn the gaze from culture alone to include the economy, politics, and social institutions in the purview of translation studies. How did and does translation continue to make capitalism possible and to maintain it? How did and does translation continue to make political domination and the creation of the social institutions that maintain development discourses possible (see Said, 1993, p. 223)? Said (1993, pp. 327–334) thus suggests that the vicious circle of conflict between empire and the colonized, in which both make use of the same strategies to oppose one another (and which is fuelled by the cultural relativism of scholars such as Baker [2006]), needs to be overcome. Opposing empire in a way that will continue empire even if empire has been destroyed, is not what we are looking for. We need ways to deal with power and injustice that will not institutionalize the use of power and injustice. For Said (1993, p. 328), these ways are the ways of "a critical, intellectual style, not professional competence". We are looking for man, at the edge of chaos, in cultures that emerge and that are noncoercive.

4. TRANSLATION AND DEVELOPMENT

So, how is one to think about the relationship between translation and development? I think the first, somewhat obvious, point is that this relationship has been neglected by both translation studies and development studies, to the detriment of both. Except for the work of Lewis and Mosse (2006), who have based their work on that of Latour (2007) and Callon et al. (2011), I could not find any title in which translation and development have been combined. Although it is true that scholars in translation studies have worked on issues that can be regarded as developmental, that is, various aspects of technical translation, community translation, and the entire branch of postcolonial translation studies, they have not theorized development itself in their thinking. In other words, they have not thought about development as a conceptual category and its relationship to translation. To foster this interdisciplinary relationship between translation studies and development studies is thus the second main aim of this book.

With the large bias for critical studies in translation studies, I need to point out that, in my work, my aim is not first and foremost liberation or activism, but understanding. Or, as Latour (2007) suggests, it is accounting for the relationship between translation and development. In translation studies terms, my aim is descriptive. I am of the opinion that even those translation scholars who argue most vociferously against prescriptive approaches to translation are themselves prescriptive when it comes to ethical and ideological matters. For now, I suggest that translation scholars rather work empirically to trace and account for the interfaces of translational and developmental actions. I do not suggest a total ban on judgment and criticism, but instead a temporary moratorium, until we know and understand enough. I would not want my work to be suggesting yet another crusade to save the world.

Studying development from a translation studies perspective will require more thinking on agency. The type of activist agency currently advocated in translation studies will have to be revisited. As (a part of) translation studies frees itself from its bondage to critical theory and academic activism, it will be able to see that perhaps there are many other ways of being agents than being activists. Consider the millions of pages of translated text that go into the construction of the European Union. Also consider the billions of translated spoken words that make the running of the informal economy in developing countries possible. Further consider the translation of ideas on economic reform from Washington to Kampala or on plant breeding from the University of the Free State to a rural farm in Ethiopia and its role in developing the latter. The kind of agency involved in these actions needs to be thought about, and to refer to Latour (2007), agency is the one thing we know virtually nothing about. Thus, for now, I am not judging a particular theory of development to be better than others. I am not suggesting a particular way of developing through translation. My aim is to understand and account for what people do when they need to communicate, in whichever mode, with other people who do not speak the same language as they do. Furthermore, my aim is to understand and account for the ways in which these communications contribute to the creation and maintenance of social ties or "the social".

I thus contend that the focus on agency in translation studies is part of a Western analysis of reality. You can only contribute if you are actively for or against something. It also rests on a very strong belief that your actions matter and that you are in control of history and nature, that is, humanism. Nonlinear systems theory relativizes the importance of human agency. The outcome of your input cannot necessarily be predicted.

I am not arguing that one should forego the notion of agency. What I suggest is that we look for other modes of agency, that is, translation that serves or translation that builds. These forms of motivation for action are also agentive in nature. What I am trying to say is that agency in the critical theory definition of the word is not necessarily the only kind of agency contributing to the construction of social reality. The typical anonymous, voiceless, invisible translator slaving away in a stuffy little office, translating boring municipal regulation after regulation, is contributing as much if not more to the construction of social reality than the verbose literary translator who performs an aggressive feminine translation of a literary classic. Western notions of high visibility, branding, and status should not be the only ones defining the agency of translators.

My advocacy for a development focus in translation studies has another implication. It should redirect the perspective of translation studies to the informal sector of economic activity. The linguistic and especially the comparative literature bias in translation studies has had the result that translation scholars mostly focus their attention to high culture, that is, literary translation, scientific translation, and conference interpreting. Although this is not exclusively the case, as examples of work on community interpreting has shown, the informal economy, which entails a large part of the world economy, has not been in the purview of translation studies scholars. This means that the picture we have of translation is skewed and is not representative of all translation activities across the globe. In particular, it is skewed toward developed countries, which have a larger formal economy than developing countries (see Chapter 8 for statistics in this regard).

So my interests are simple. Do we know what the role of translation is in development? Do we know which texts are being translated? Do we know how people communicate in development projects where various cultures, values, and languages meet? Do we know what happens in oral translation in development? Do we know what constraints developing contexts place on translators and their translations? And, can we know these things and how can we know them?

In the next three chapters, I try to answer some of these questions. In Chapter 5, I trace the (non-)translation of policy documents for local economic development. In Chapter 6, I account for the role of translation in the knowledge economy, once again tracing the translation of knowledge in its spread from a university to its end users in other countries. In Chapter 7, I provide an account of a very short study I did on translation in the informal economy.

5 Translation, Local Economic Development, and Border

1. INTRODUCTION

The first set of empirical data that I wish to present pertains to the translation of policy documents concerning local economic development (LED). I should point out here that the South African government itself has made the choice to use the term *development* in its economic policies. Thinking about this situation in complexity terms, it means that a particular development process is one set of constraints or enablers influencing translation. It also means that translation could be studied as a factor inhibiting or enhancing development, particularly local economic development. I thus conceptualize of translation as part of the substructure for the emergence of social reality, in this case local economic development. Simultaneously, I conceptualize of social reality, in particular local economic development, as a constraining and/or enabling factor in translation. In this chapter, I thus attempt to answer two questions: What is the role of translation in local economic development in a rural South African context (Donaldson & Marais, 2012, pp. ix–xi; Hoogendoorn & Nel, 2012)? and What constraints do the development context place on translation in South Africa?

This focus, however, is still too wide to be manageable in the scope of one chapter. In line with the views on development put forward in Chapter 4, I further limit my scope to "local" economic development (for an overview, see Lund, 2008). This is a purely pragmatic choice with no ideological or theoretical intentions whatsoever. However, as with all choices, it will definitely exclude some data, and this unintended consequence cannot be countered, only acknowledged. Future studies in this field, if other scholars deem it worth their while, could take up the translation of development on a larger scale.

The research that I propose in this chapter entails the following. Policy documents on local economic development follow a very interesting route that allows one to study boundaries and the travel of ideas across boundaries (Susam-Sarajeva, 2006) in what I hope to illustrate is a unique context. Broadly speaking, one finds international policy documents such as Agenda 21 or The Millennium Development Goals in which a number of participants agree on consensual guidelines or policies for economic development or climate change. These policy documents are then usually taken to a national level by signatory countries, and they become part of the national policy framework of each country. In the case of South Africa, the national policy framework then becomes the guideline for each of the nine provinces in South Africa to compile their own development plan, thus localizing it even further. In the South African context, these plans are known as Integrated Development Plans or IDPs (see Figure 5.1 for a map of the South African provinces).

On their part, the South African provinces are divided into district municipalities, that is, combinations of a number of local municipalities (see Figure 5.2, which indicates the district municipalities in the Free State province).

The local municipalities, for their part, consist of a number of (usually) small towns, and in each town, one finds a unit manager that acts as the head municipal official for that town. The !Xhariep District Municipality, where I did the research for this chapter, indicated in the map in Figure 5.2, consists of three local municipalities: Letsemeng, Kopanong, and Mokohare (indicated in Figure 5.3). Figure 5.3 also indicates the location of the Gariep Dam, at the very bottom of the map, and the location of the towns Phillipolis, Trompsburg, and Gariep Dam (in the Kopanong Local Municipality in the Free State), Colesberg (Pixley Ka Seme District Municipality) in Northern Cape, and Venterstad (Ukhuhlamba District Municipality) in Eastern Cape. The fact that the Gariep Dam and its development area are located on the border of three provinces (Free State, Northern Cape and Eastern Cape) and three district and local municipalities makes it an interesting point to study from a translation perspective.

What interests me in this is (1) the localization of ideas on local economic development, (2) the different voices vying for power in this localization process, and (3) the language in which this takes place and the role of translation proper in this process. Put simply, is development translated? Does it essentially remain a foreign concept, or is it indigenized?

In what follows, I first provide a comparison of a number of policy documents by means of discourse analysis. Then I present the data of some open-ended interviews I conducted with a number of development officials, as well as my observations during my visit to the particular towns. Last, I try to conceptualize the implications of the data for translation theory.

I follow an inductive logic in this chapter, first discussing the data and then detecting the emerging patterns. I conclude by trying to theorize the implications of the patterns found. I am not naive enough to believe that I did not have ideas or theories before I set out on the fieldwork. These have been set out previously. I literally went into the fieldwork with my existing knowledge and some reading work on LED. My main aim was, in the style of ethnography, to observe and listen to people on the ground, while simultaneously, in the style of critical discourse analysis, comparing the various existing policy documents.

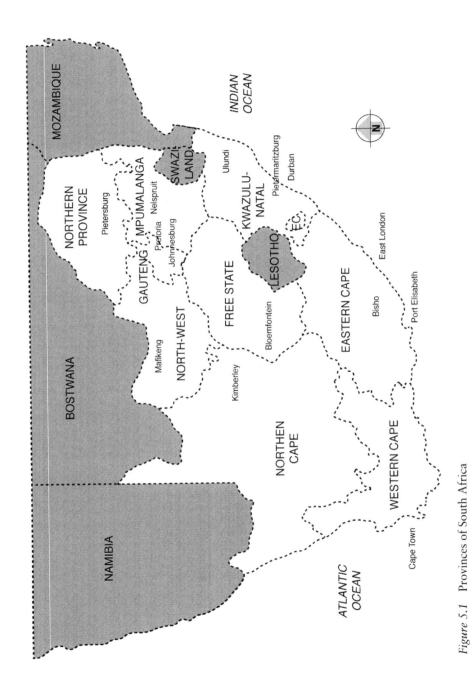

Figure 5.1 Provinces of South Africa
(*Source*: Du Plessis, 2000, p. 99)

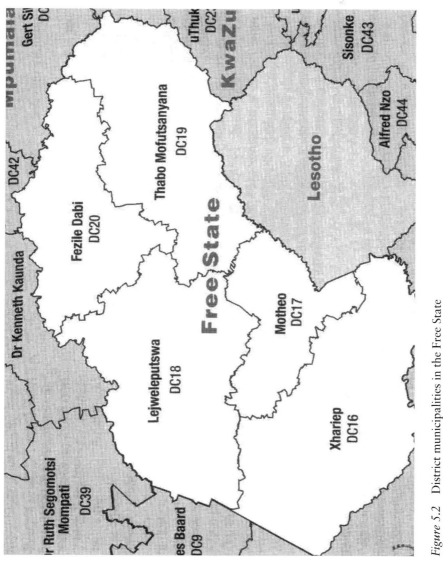

Figure 5.2 District municipalities in the Free State

(Source: *Gaffney's Local Government in South Africa, 2009–2011* (Gaffney's Local Government, 2009, p. 596)

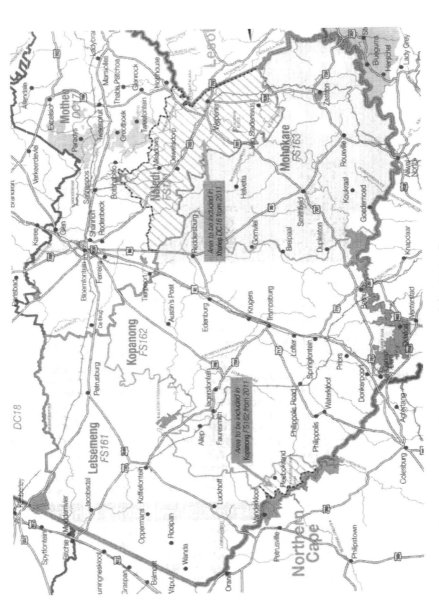

Figure 5.3 Provinces, municipalities and towns around the Gariep Dam
(*Source:* Gaffney's *Local Government in South Africa, 2009–2011* (Gaffney's Local Government, 2009, p. 227)

On a point of definition, I need to make clear that when I refer to translation here, I also include what is sometimes referred to as interpreting, that is, oral translation.

2. TRANSLATING POLICY DOCUMENTS FOR LOCAL ECONOMIC DEVELOPMENT

Before I go into a discussion of the data, I need to provide some context. First, the geopolitical context of the data I am discussing is as follows: The Free State province is the central province of South Africa (see Figure 5.1). It has one metropolitan area, the capital, which falls under the Mangaung Metropolitan Municipality. Further, it is mostly a rural province with small towns centered around agriculture, tourism, some mining in the northwest of the province, and industries in Sasolburg in the north (Puuka et al., 2012; see also the Free State's Regional Steering Committee's [2010] report for a detailed socioeconomic profile of the province).

The Free State province is located in central South Africa, bordering Lesotho in the east, Gauteng and North West in the north, the Northern Cape in the west, and the Eastern Cape in the south (see Figure 5.1). It is governed by an African National Congress (ANC) government with its administrative headquarters in the Mangaung Metropolitan Municipality. The Free State province is divided, first, into district municipalities, of which there are five. These are !Xhariep in the south, Mangaung in the center, Lejweleputsa in the northwest, Fezile Dabi in the north, and Thabo Mofutsanyana in the northeast (see Figure 5.2). Each district municipality consists of a number of local municipalities. These local municipalities are usually representative of a number of small towns. For instance, the !Xhariep District Municipality, on which I focus in this chapter, consists of three local municipalities: Kopanong, Letsemeng, and Mokahare (see Figure 5.3). Each local municipality again consists of a number of small towns. Kopanong, where I conducted part of the research, includes Phillipolis, Trompsburg, and Gariep (see Figure 5.3).

At this stage, it is necessary to motivate my choice of district and local municipality. In the southern Free State, we have the Gariep Dam, the largest reservoir in South Africa. Around this dam, a tourist industry of some sorts has developed, but it remains, to a large extent, unfulfilled potential. The interesting factor is that this dam is located at the junction of three provinces. To its north, it is part of the Free State province and to the south, to Eastern Cape province. To the west, it borders Northern Cape province (see Figure 5.1). Thus, the development of this area is the joint responsibility of three provinces, three district municipalities, and three local municipalities. All of the provinces, district municipalities, and local municipalities are controlled by the ANC, but as indicated earlier, the provincial boundaries and histories do not provide for a mono-ideology ANC with the same set of interests. To my mind, the interesting question posed by this dam is that of borders and the travel of ideas. There is one entity, the dam with its tourist and development potential, cut in three by borders. What happens here is that the development policies of central government travel from its headquarters via provincial headquarters, via district municipalities to local municipalities to each little town. How then do the borders influence the development? How does space influence the travel and localization of ideas? What happens when development policies travel from one central point, via power centers far apart to local centers close together? What, in other words, is the influence of space on the travel of ideas?

The second point of background refers to the compilation of the documents I discuss. Space does not allow me to attend to this issue in detail and studying the voices in these documents should render interesting results, but the main point here is that, apart from the ideas that have travelled to find a home in these documents, one also has to consider the other voices in them. These include, at least, the voices of development agencies, academic advisors to government, factions within the governing party, consultants' perspectives, and the views of the community. I point out one or two voices that are of interest to my argument, but on the whole, the situation reflects a paradox between the monolingual text creating the illusion of one voice and the cacophony of voices vying for supremacy in the document itself.

2.1 Provincial GDPs

During the next step in the localization process, the National Growth and Development Plan (NGDP) is supposed to be used as a basis for each provincial government in South Africa to draw up their own development plan, in my case the Free State Growth and Development Plan (FSGDP). Two interesting factors come into play here. The one is that, although the ANC is the majority party in the country, the provincial system and historical factors contribute to a situation in which one actually finds ANCs, not an ANC. The provincial borders thus sometimes lead to competition for scarce resources between provincial governments. Second, in one province, Western Cape, the ANC does not have the majority vote. Comparative work could provide an understanding of a number of factors in this regard. Firstly, in the translation of development policies from national to provincial level, do local needs override national needs? Second, what is the driving force behind localization, that is, economic or political, or as it is stated in South African parlance, "grassroots interests" or ideological interests? Third, how would the thinking in the non-ANC province compare to that in the ANC provinces? Here I am not necessarily referring to obvious ideological differences but particularly to the way in which the localization process is seen. What happens when the ideological soil of the place to which a policy travels differs from the soil at its place of origin?

As one of my students is comparing the policies on local economic development in the Free State and Western Cape, including the two metropolitan areas, I do not perform an analysis to compare provinces.

As far as the FSGDP is concerned, I was not able to locate any translations of this document. It is available in English only.

2.2 IDPs at the District Municipal Level

Once again, the first observation should be that none of the development policies in the area I studied is in any other language but English. Now, if one considers the fact that, according to the Integrated Development Plan (IDP) for the !Xhariep District Municipality (IDP-!Xhariep, 2012), both Afrikaans and Sesotho are spoken by 35% of the population, respectively; isiXhosa by 19%, Setswana by 4% and English by only 6%, it is clear that the practice of non-translation has huge implications. In the ethnographic work I did, no official indicated that non-translation was a policy. Their usual reply to my questions pertaining to translation was that they were not aware of any translations and that it was merely a practical matter because they did not have the budget to have everything translated. In response to a question concerning the inhibitory nature of language in development, one official even said, "No one has ever thought of this." And, they added, significant numbers of people were illiterate and semiliterate anyway, which meant that translation of written texts would not assist them. Also, with the exception of some businesspeople and one or two politically minded citizens, very few people ever perused the development policies, and thus, it did not seem wise to have these translated, especially given the situation of limited financial resources. This matter relates to Meylaerts's (2011) distinction between language policy and translation policy. It is clear that the South African language policy as embodied in the Constitution has to be amended by a translation policy that carefully considers the use of translation in the context of local economic development. Respondents showed a strong indication, however, that if anybody from the public wanted to know the contents of an IDP, someone at the municipality would sit with the person and tell them about the contents. This would also happen with other development issues, such as questions concerning housing, the development of roads, and other infrastructure and even social security matters.

Whenever the mode of communication switches from written to oral, so it seems, the language of communication seems to turn from monolingual English into multilingualism, as needed. This multilingual communication takes place on an informal level. None of the district or local municipalities I studied had an officially adopted language plan, a language policy, or language practitioners in their service. Everybody I interviewed in official positions, however, confirmed the practice that both with individual inquiries and at community meetings, multilingualism was the practice. This claim obviously has to be studied in more detail. Some nonofficials whom

I interviewed, for example, people from the tourist industry, indicated that this was true. However, they also indicated that multilingualism was used selectively for power reasons. In municipal council meetings, members of the ruling party would suddenly change from English to an African language if they did not want opposition members to understand what they are talking about. Furthermore, in public meetings, the interpreting/translation is not always up to standard, and on other occasions, it is used selectively to the point of excluding opposition views. At this stage, my study did not go into the detail of this issue, but another of my students is busy with an ethnographic study in which he will live in one of these communities for long periods to observe this informal working of multilingualism and translation.

I now compare the IDPs of the three relevant district municipalities to look at the way in which the ideas on local economic development have travelled. I studied the IDPs of the Ukhahlamba (IDP-Ukhahlamba, 2004), Pixley Ka Seme (IDP-Pixley Ka Seme, 2010) and !Xhariep District Municipalities (IDP-!Xhariep, 2012). The little town of Venterstad in Eastern Cape falls under the Ukhahlamba District Municipality whereas Colesberg in Northern Capes falls under the Pixley Ka Seme District Municipality, and the Free State towns fall under the !Xhariep District Municipality. Obviously, much more can be done than what I have done and what is presented here. For instance, one could look at the way in which an IDP translates its own views from written into table or figure form. Alternatively, one could look at the way in which broad visions are translated into work plans, ideas into money, and so on.

For the sake of space, I have limited myself to comparing the structure of the three IDPs. What I want to establish is how the one set of ideas has travelled from the ANC's headquarters in Johannesburg to these localities and how space and borders have influenced this travel process.

If one uses the index of each of the IDPs as a point of departure, you find significant differences. The Ukhahlamba IDP (2004) goes straight into practical matters, that is, what they regard as important is needs (2.1 in Table 5.1). The document gives the impression of being practical. Evidence of this is found in its 38 pages compared to the 141 of the Pixley Ka Seme document (IDP-Pixley Ka Seme, 2010), which uses the first five points of the document to provide an institutional and legal framework. The framework in the Ukhahlamba IDP is a general planning framework, which does not in any way seem related to the NGDS or the FSGDP. It seems that planning per se dominates development. The question on the table seems to be planning, not development. If one then looks further at the large focus on needs, it seems that fulfilling needs has supplanted the search for development, or at least, has been equated to development.

In contrast, the Pixley Ka Seme IDP is focused on authority, the law, and due processes (see Table 5.2). It has a seemingly endless introduction in which lines of authority are stipulated, in which a long list of relevant laws is related to its work, and in which the process of writing an IPD is set out. It creates the impression of a much more complicated and official document,

Table 5.1 Table of contents of the Ukhahlamba IDP

1 STRATEGIC RESPONSE TO NEEDS

2 UNDERSTANDING THE UKHAHLAMBA DISTRICT

  2.1 WHAT ARE THE DISTRICT- WIDE NEEDS OF UKHAHLAMBA?

    2.1.1 Water and Sanitation Provision Across the District

    2.1.2 Road Access

    2.1.3 Stimulation of the Economy

    2.1.4 Address Social Issues

    2.1.6 Building of Partnerships and Relations

    2.1.7 Institutional Capacity Development

    2.1.8 Democratic Governance

    2.1.9 Natural Environment Awareness

  2.2 WHAT ARE THE CAPACITY AND SUPPORT NEEDS OF THE LOCAL MUNICIPALITIES?

  2.3 WHAT ARE THE ROLES AND RESPONSIBILITIES OF THE DISTRICT MUNICIPALITY?

    2.3.1 District Municipality's Role

    2.3.2 Powers and Functions

    2.3.3 Additional Responsibilities

3 UKHAHLAMBA DISTRICT: THE FUTURE

  3.1 HOW DO WE DREAM THE FUTURE?

  3.2 HOW ARE WE GOING TO GET TO THE DREAM?

    3.2.1 Mission Reasoning

  3.3 TARGETS FOR ACHIEVING THE VISION

  3.4 WHAT DO WE WISH TO ACHIEVE? (GOALS)

  3.5 WHAT IS OUR APPROACH TO GETTING WHAT WE WANT? (STRATEGIES)

    3.5.1 Stimulating the District Economy so as to Retain and Increase Income in the Area

    3.5.2 Improving Service Delivery Quality (through efficiency, economy, effectiveness and ethics)

    3.5.3 Capacitating Local Government to Undertake their Roles, Powers and Functions

    3.5.4 Meet Basic Needs

Table 5.2 Table of contents of the Pixley Ka Seme IDP

1. Introduction
2. Reparation Process Plan: District Framework
3. Vision, Mission and Values
4. Existing Development Analysis Legal Framework Analysis
   Leadership Guide
   Technical Analysis (Basic Facts, Figures and Key Development Priorities)
   Summary of Community and Stakeholder Analysis (Key Development Priorities)
   Institutional Analysis (Strengths and Weaknesses)
   Economic Analysis (Patterns, Trends, Opportunities and Threats)
   Socio-Economic Analysis (Poverty Situations)
   Spatial Analysis (Patterns, Trends, Opportunities and Threats)
   Environmental Analysis 9Trends, Potential Disaster, Opportunities and Threats)
   In depth Analysis and Identify Key Development priorities
5. Development Strategies Key Performance Areas
   Strategies and Development Objectives Summarized list of specific identified Development Projects, Programmes and Sectoral Plan.
6. Projects
   Project, Programme and Sectoral Plan Proposals (one page each) linked to Performance Management details
7. Institutional Organogram Committees System, Community Participation, Decision-making Process (All on Diagram)
   List of By-laws
8. Performance Management System including a List of Performance Based Contracts
9. Sectoral (departments) Five Year Operational Business Plans
10. Specific Plans Communication Plan
    Financial Plan (Including Capital)
    Spatial Development Framework
    Disaster Management Plan
    Human Resource Management Plan
11. Implementation Plan Monitoring and Evaluation
    Reporting

most probably also much more illegible and inaccessible to the public. Finding the issues in the document requires quite an effort.

The !Xhariep IDP (see Table 5.3) disguises its real planning between the introductory parts that focus on legal and procedural matters and the second half of the document that is taken up by procedures and methods. The actual plan is set out in section 2.5 of the plan, setting out a relatively

Table 5.3 Table of contents of the !Xhariep IDP

---

1 INTRODUCTION
  1.1 LEGAL BACKGROUND
  1.2 PURPOSE OF THE IDP
  1.3 ROLE AND PURPOSE OF THIS VOLUME OF THE IDP

2 FRAMEWORK PLAN
  2.1 INTRODUCTION
  2.2 FRAMEWORK PROGRAMME WITH TIME FRAME
  2.3 ISSUES, MECHANISMS AND PROCEDURE FOR ALIGNMENT AND CONSULTATION
    2.3.1 List of role players
    2.3.2 Communication mechanism
    2.3.3 Establishment of Structures
    2.3.4 Logistic Arrangements
  2.4 BINDING PLANS AND PLANNING REQUIREMENTS AT PROVINCIAL AND NATIONAL LEVEL
    2.4.1 National legislation applicable to the functions of Local Government
  2.5 LOCALISED STRATEGIC GUIDELINES
    2.5.1 SPATIAL DIMENSION
    2.5.2 PEOPLE DIMENSION
    2.5.3 ENVIRONMENTAL DIMENSION
    2.5.4 ECONOMIC DIMENSION
    2.5.5 INSTITUTIONAL DIMENSION
  2.6 AMENDMENT OF THE FRAMEWORK
  2.7 CONCLUSION

3 PROCESS PLAN
  3.1 INTRODUCTION
  3.2 INSTITUTIONAL ARRANGEMENTS
    3.2.1 Roles and responsibilities
    3.2.2 Organisational structure
  3.3 MECHANISM AND PROCEDURE FOR PARTICIPATION
  3.4 ACTION PROGRAMME AND RESOURCE PLAN
  3.5 ISSUES, MECHANISMS AND PROCEDURE FOR ALIGNMENT AND CONSULTATION
    3.5.1 List of role players
    3.5.2 Communication mechanism
    3.5.3 Alignment events
    3.5.4 Establishment of Structure
    3.5.5 Logistic Arrangements

(Continued)

Table 5.3 Continued

3.6 BINDING PLANS AND PLANNING REQUIREMENTS AT PROVINCIAL AND NATIONAL LEVEL
3.7 BUDGET FOR THE IDP REVIEW
3.8 CONCLUSION
4 METHODOLOGY
  4.1 COMPILATION OF THE IDP
    4.1.1 Phase 0: Preparation
    4.1.2 Phase 1: Analysis
    4.1.3 Phase 2: Strategies
    4.1.4 Phase 3: Projects
    4.1.5 Phase 4: Integration
    4.1.6 Phase 5: Approval
  4.2 REVIEW OF THE IDP
    4.2.1 Phase 0: Preparation
    4.2.2 Phase 1: Review of comments received and compliance with legislative requirements
    4.2.3 Phase 2: Self-assessment of the IDP
    4.2.4 Phase 3: Re-Analysis of the current situation
    4.2.5 Phase 4: Review of Strategies
    4.2.6 Phase 5: Review of Projects
    4.2.7 Phase 6: Integration
    4.2.8 Phase 7: Approval
  4.3 COMPLIANCE WITH PROCESS PLAN
5 CONCLUSION

simple conceptualization concerning people, the economy, space, institutions and the environment.

If one then goes into more detail by comparing what each IDP identifies as needs (Ukhahlamba) or core issues (Pixley Ka Seme) or localized strategic guidelines (!Xhariep), the following picture emerges (see Table 5.4).

What seems to be common in all three documents is water, roads, social issues, health care, the natural environment, and the stimulation of the economy. At the same time, it is clear that each document conceptualizes of these problems in different ways, indicating some kind of localization. For instance, the Ukhahlamba IDP considers water and sanitation under one heading, whereas for the Pixley Ka Seme IDP, these are two different matters. Ukhahlamba is interested in promoting "awareness" of the natural environment, whereas Pixley Ka Seme is interested in managing the environment. The document for !Xhariep has reduced all the needs to five "dimensions" of interest. To read Table 5.4, you need to compare the

Table 5.4 Comparison of points of interest in IDPs

Ukhahlamba	Pixley Ka Seme	!Xhariep
1 Water and sanitation provision across the district	1 Sanitation provision	2 Spatial dimension
2 Road access	1 Bulk water supply	4 People dimension
3 Stimulation of the economy	3 LED, tourism and poverty alleviation	7 Environmental dimension
4 Address social issues	4 Housing	3 Economic dimension
5 Primary health care	2 Roads, streets and storm water management	6 Institutional dimension
6 Building of partnerships and relationships	5 Health and HIV/AIDS	
Institutional capacity development	3 Electricity	
Democratic governance	4 Education, youth and development	
7 Natural environment awareness	2 Land and land reform	
	4 Crime, security and disaster management	
	4 Sport and recreation	
	7 Environmental and waste management	
	7 Cemeteries	

numbers in the column to the left of all entries. Thus, all water issues are numbered 1, all spatial issues are 2, all economic matters are 3, social issues are 4, healthcare is 5, institutions are 6, and the environment is 7.

Where Ukhahlamba and Pixley Ka Seme differ is on item 6 in the Ukhahlamba IDP, which focuses on matters of governance. It has a large focus on partnerships, capacity building and democracy, which are all matters related to organization, management and governance—and which Pixley Ka Seme does not attend to at all. On its part, Pixley Ka Seme highlights land and land reform, a matter to which Ukhahlamba does not even refer, except for reference to roads. Why, one could ask, would land reform be an issue in one of the district municipalities and not in the other—seeing that they are geographically so close? And why would institutional capacity be an overwhelming issue in Ukhahlamba and not in Pixley Ka Seme? If one compares these IDPs with the NGDP, Ukhahlamba's seems to be much closer to the national plan than does Pixley Ka Seme's.

Local interests thus seem to have overruled national interests. Evaluating this is difficult, and I shall attempt such an evaluation only after I have presented the data of the interviews. One would also be able to perform this exercise for the IDPs of local municipalities, but my aim here was not a comprehensive overview of documentation. Rather, I established two points: the lack of translation at the level of written documents and a clear local bias in understanding development.

3. FINDINGS OF OPEN-ENDED INTERVIEWS

I then triangulated the preceding discourse analysis with open-ended interviews with a number of local-authority officials and representatives from the tourism industry. None of the officials I contacted refused to see me, but a small minority was nervous about talking to me. Also, one or two of the officials were out of town during the week I visited, and I was met by their deputies or by the head of another relevant department. In the Kopanong Local Municipality (IDP-Kopanong, 2003), which falls under the !Xhariep District Municipality, I spoke to officials from three of the constituent towns, Phillipolis, Trompsburg (an official from the Kopanong Local Municipality), and Gariep, and for the sake of anonymity, I shall refer to them as officials 1, 2 and 3. I also spoke to one representative of the tourism industry, to whom I shall refer as representative 1. In the Umsobomvu Local Municipality (IDP-Umsobomvu, 2010), which resorts under Pixley Ka Seme District Municipality, I spoke to one official (official 4) and two representatives of the tourism industry (representatives 2 and 3). In Gariep Local Municipality (IDP-Gariep, 2002), which resorts under the Ukhahlamba District Municipality, I spoke to one official (official 5) and one representative of the tourism industry (representative 4). In total, I thus spoke to five officials and four tourism representatives for a total of nine interviews. The open-ended discussion document I used is included as Addendum 1 at the end of the chapter. Except for one interview, I recorded all the interviews and had a colleague who made some notes.

I had two main aims with the interviews. First, I wanted to listen to different stakeholders' views on the relationship between language/translation and development. This interest refers to translation proper. Second, I wanted to gauge the localization of ideas on development in the small towns I visited. So, questions 1, 4, 5, 6, and 9 relate to the interviewees' ideas on development. Questions 2, 3, 7, 8, 10, and 11 relate to their perceptions on language and translation.

It was first clear that all interviewees were led by local interests in their conceptualization of development. This was found in response to question 1. I found no global idealism at local level. Development needs at this level include land (in particular serviced land—representative 1), employment, education, water, roads and housing. I think it would be fair to say that, conceptually, global development ideas, for example, the network society with its networks of information technology (Castells, 2000a), have been translated into local concepts, although representative 1 pointed out that many ideas were never implemented or badly implemented because of a lack of capacity. Thus, there is not always a clear distinction between a lack of implementation of global ideas and the power of localization. It is also clear, if one compares the IDPs with a global document such as Agenda 21 (Agenda 21,n.d.), that the former is driven by needs, much more than by ideas. I had considerable problems in getting officials to respond to question 9, their personal ideas of development. For instance, after I was asked to rephrase the question, official 2 said that, for him, development is "to change the life of people", after which he immediately went back to talking about housing and education. On one hand, one can deplore this seeming lack of abstract thinking on development. On the other hand, it at least points to the localization of ideas. What was noticeable, however, is that officials often talked in "development speak", overusing stock phrases such as "public participation" and "development needs". Officials could immediately identify between one and three pressing development needs in their area.

What became clear from the interviews is that, without exception, officials viewed development as service provision. In no case could I trace a distinction between the development of the area and the task of a municipality to deliver services. The very narrow tasks of delivering services in the municipal area are wholly equated with development. To my mind, this reflects a narrowing of scope as development policies travel. On one hand, this may be inevitable and actually the preferred way. On the other hand, it seems that the global ideas about development have very little if any influence on local ideas about the same. This became particularly clear when I asked officials about their personal views on development. This question was added with particular reference to Olivier de Sardan's (2005) idea that development is a hermeneutic process in which foreign ideas need to be localized through interpretive processes. Representative 2 focused his discussion on the most important development issues in his area, on very local matters such as tourism, for which Colesberg (in the Pixley Ka Seme District Municipality) is famous, and the possibility of providing a halfway station for truck drivers operating between Cape Town and Johannesburg. Representative 3 indicated that all official meetings took place in English, but if one knew that a particular official was Afrikaans-speaking; for instance, one would speak Afrikaans in one-on-one meetings. Community meetings were also held according to the language needs of the particular constituency. Official 5 gave an interesting example of how locality played a role in conceptualizations of development. In the town where he is the unit manager, an access road between different parts of the town as well as upgrading a school were the most important development issues, whereas in the larger district municipality, housing and water provision took the prime spot. This seems to confirm my impressions that locality does play a role.

As far as translation proper is concerned (question 2), a clear picture emerged in terms of written documentation. All policy documents on local economic development were available in English only, and no translations were available. As far as spoken language is concerned, the pattern differentiates. My questions in this regard tested the use of language on various levels of the municipality, from senior level through to front-office level and community meetings. Here the picture was varied. Mostly, senior management spoke English, but in Colesberg, which is dominated by Afrikaans speakers, Afrikaans would occasionally be used. Representative 2 indicated that the municipality made use of the services of one of their own employees who had previously been an interpreter in the Department of Justice. Here one thus finds another informal arrangement, but seemingly, it is one with some good luck attached to it. Representative 2 also indicated that, in his municipal area, officials would look for an interpreter if a client had a language problem. Official 4 even mentioned the priest as someone who sometimes interprets. When I asked him about the possibility of appointing a professional language practitioner, he responded in the affirmative, arguing that the municipality does not have a communications desk and that one could combine the two services. This observation points to the need for communication officers in South Africa to be equipped or educated for the multilingual situation in which they are going to work. In order for this to happen, we need to problematize language and multilingualism in many of these careers such as marketing, journalism, and communications. A lack of training in the problem of language in a multilingual society will continue to inhibit the development of that society. Middle management also mostly communicates in English.

At front-office level, officials are all at least bilingual. Official 2 indicated that their front-desk staff usually speak Sesotho but would be able to assist in English, isiXhosa, Setswana, and Afrikaans. Also in the tourism industry, the front-desk staff members are multilingual. In most cases, I was assisted in both Afrikaans and English (as I sometimes switched to test the situation). Council meetings were all held in English, but ward meetings were held according to the language preference of the group. Official 2 indicated that, because his Afrikaans was not good, he would take another more fluent Afrikaans-speaking official with him when he went to meet with an Afrikaans constituency. Public rallies were mostly held in English with either professional or lay interpreting provided. Representatives from the tourism industry were not as positive about the latter as the officials, who claimed that "everything" got translated. In Colesberg, representative 2 indicated that ward councilors would give feedback on the IDP, interpreting where necessary. When asked, he indicated that only about 40% of citizens are literate. According to him, people would ask their children to help them understand documentation that they cannot read. Official 5 indicated that, in the municipality's council meetings, English was used about 80% of the time and Afrikaans about 20% of the time. According to him, anyone could request clarification in his or her own language at any stage. Representative 4 indicated that, in his municipality, members of the ruling party would use isiXhosa to exclude opposition parties from a particular discussion. They would provide a translated version after this discussion within a discussion, but the opposition parties usually have the feeling that not everything is told and that they have been excluded. It was interesting that official 5 indicated that English made up a very small part of her constituency (she referred to these English-speaking people as "intruders"). At the senior-management level, she spoke English; at middle-management level, Afrikaans was spoken; and at the front desk, her staff spoke Afrikaans, English, and isiXhosa. When she held ward meetings, these were held in Afrikaans, but her reports on these meetings are in English. This scenario, in which the same official has to operate in different languages at different levels and in different modes of communication, has, to my mind, not been theorized within translation studies. Even more crucial is the need for data in this regard.

Concerning question 3, no official indicated that they ever had complaints about communication with the public or that they were aware of any problems. Informal arrangements are usually made to accommodate different language requirements. Representative 1 was of the opinion that English is the language of business and that he was not aware of it causing any problems. At a local level, anyway, informal processes of translation and interpreting meant that people find a way around language barriers. Sometimes they manage because they are able to communicate in more than one language, thus translating "in their heads" as it were. Sometimes they would take friends along to help them understand what is going on. Official 5 responded in an interesting way to my question about how non-English speakers were able to fill in forms that are in English only. He pointed out that "we never give anybody a form before asking first whether they need assistance in filling it in". This assistance would include assisting with language difference. Representative 4 noted that his municipality had problems with people inquiring about accounts in Afrikaans, only to be answered in English. She also pointed out that the high levels of illiteracy in the municipal area render translation somewhat irrelevant.

I used question 4 to see whether the needs identified in question 1 were translated into plans and whether the plans were influenced by a top-down decision-making process. In most cases, the projects were indeed related to the needs. Representative 1, however, indicated that top-down ways of acting do occur, for instance, when representatives from the district municipality offered to build toilets at the cemetery, while housing was the biggest local need. Representative 4 was the only one who pointed out the social problems of development. It was only when she directed my attention to these social problems that I realized that none of the other respondents had referred to the social problems caused by un(der)development. (Nussbaum, 2011; Rist,

2002; Said, 1993; Sen, 1999). Except for the fact that their conceptualization of development was limited to service delivery, they also assumed that economic development would solve all development problems, or they never thought of development outside of the political-economic field. Representative 4 pointed to HIV/AIDS, alcohol and drug abuse, fetal alcohol syndrome, teenage pregnancies, and a culture of poverty that inhibits development. For instance, although there is a good school available, children do not learn because many of them have been born with fetal alcohol syndrome.

After battling to get responses to question 5, I eventually deleted it from the interviews. I think this item was simply too abstract.

Concerning question 6, all the respondents indicated that they had received assistance from their respective provincial governments in compiling the IDP, but that these governments were not forcing them in any direction. They had a huge say in the compilation of the IDP, which was usually compiled by consultants in cooperation with the officials. Representative 3, who was seemingly not a supporter of the ruling party, was of the opinion that Colesberg was an example where local interests override national and/or provincial interests. What became interesting in his observations was that, because documents were only in English and many citizens were illiterate anyway, this put more power into the hands of the local politicians who were responsible for telling people about the content of the IDP. This made me think about the situation in the church during the Middle Ages when average members could not read the Bible and had to rely on priests to do so. This lack of multilingualism and multimodality in communication thus clearly holds implications for democracy and carries notions of an adult electorate. The lack of professional interpreting/translation could further exacerbate this problem. Further study into the ways in which IDPs are represented to the public may shed light on this matter.

Concerning public participation and feedback (question 7), the pattern that emerged was that of informal interpreting. Official 2 indicated that his municipality had decided that, apart from the consultants compiling the IDP, one official from the municipality had to be involved in this process. This enhanced communication as he sat in on all meetings and could interpret when necessary. He did indicate, however, that language problems resulted in the fact that the community did not really take ownership of the document once it had been compiled. First, the document is only in English, and second, it is in written form and quite technical at that, which means most members of the public, who are semiliterate or illiterate, cannot access it in any case. Although none of the officials thought that people had problems communicating with the municipality, because they were very confident about the fact that lay interpreting was always available for any language, some of them did agree that speaking a language other than English may sometimes disadvantage speakers in obtaining services (question 11). In response to question 7, concerning public participation in a document that is always in English, officials indicated that professional or lay interpreting services were provided at consultative meetings and that so few people ever read the final document that language was not a factor in the feedback. None of the respondents was aware of any translation of any of the documents, and only one official thought that it may be a good idea to have it translated. Here, official 5 indicated that officials from her local municipality would visit for planning meetings and would not be able to speak Afrikaans. She would then sometimes have to interpret herself, and "sometimes my attention gets drawn away and then I have to make up something to say, but luckily I know the IDP environment".

The responses to question 8 were in unanimous agreement. No IDP document has been translated. Official 2 indicated that his municipality does have their accounts in both English and Sesotho but in no other language. He did, however, indicate the need for translation. Despite the fact that many members of the society he serves are semiliterate, he argued that they would at least be able to get some information had the documents been in their first language. He told me about cases where training was offered by SEDA (a government-sponsored training provider). However, because the advertisements were in English, many people did not attend because they knew that they would not be able to cope in English. When prompted, he also indicated that the municipality was considering appointing a language practitioner and was willing to appoint such a person on the same level as its chief accountant, for a salary of about R260 000 a year (about $35 000). It must be mentioned that much work has been done in his area over the past decade or so by the Multilingualism in Development Project (MIDP V, 2012). This research-and-development project seems to have had an influence because he was the only official who showed sensitivity to language matters. Official 4 indicated that some of the documents in his municipality have an invitation at the bottom for people to return to the municipal offices for help if they were not comfortable with the language on the document. He did not indicate the language(s) in which this invitation was written. Official 5 said that all notices from her office went out in Afrikaans. However, if she was aware that a notice on an important topic had to go out, she would translate it into English (with the assistance of one of the front staff members, who is English), and because they are a small community, she would then have the English notices delivered to the particular houses.

As indicated, I had serious problems in obtaining responses to question 9. Official 5 was the only respondent who referred to the negative implications of development. When asked about her philosophy about development, she indicated that it was to make the town better and to make service delivery easier, which seemed very practical and nonphilosophical ideas. She then turned to enhancing tourism, but indicated that the larger the town became, the more it was losing its rural, uncomplicated character (see also Donaldson & Marais, 2012, p. xi). Especially during holidays and weekends, "those elements" would visit the town, "shout and make noise", and disturb the peace and quiet that brought many people to settle there in the first place.

Concerning question 10, respondents all felt that language was not a problem in cross-border communication. Many other problems complicated the problem, but these are not related to translation or the travel of ideas. They were rather on the level of boundaries, political will, and so on.

Responses to question 11 varied. Official 2 was quite vocal about the fact that language does pose barriers for development. According to him, someone who does not speak English will not have the same development opportunities as someone who does. He said that non-English speakers are marginalized and told me about the already quoted incident about training opportunities that were advertised in English only. Representative 2 agreed that language creates barriers for development and at first suggested English courses to solve the problem. When I suggested the possibility of a language practitioner, he agreed that it may help and again pointed out that monolingualism is a disadvantage to development in South Africa. Representative 3 also pointed to the fact that they needed a public-relations officer and that a person able to multitask in this regard, for example, handling media releases and inquiries from the public but being able to do so in the context of multilinguality and multiculturality would add value to the services rendered by the municipality. Although official 4 was uncertain about the barrier posed by language, he later on acknowledged that it did pose certain problems. He admitted that he was not as capable of expressing himself in English and that, although he had been "afraid of English and never spoke it", he was now somewhat more comfortable with it. He also felt that the municipality could afford the appointment of a language practitioner for about R120 000 ($15 000) a year and with an embarrassed chuckle admitted that nobody had thought about it yet.

Official 5 provided an interesting perspective. On one hand, he was adamant that language acted as a barrier to development. He told me about an incident when he had just taken over as unit manager. He wanted everybody in town who had small businesses to be on the formal list of suppliers of services and goods to the municipality. However, to achieve this, people had to fill in lengthy English documents, which totally demoralized them, and the plan failed. On the other hand, he said that he could not see that the municipality would appoint a language practitioner within the next 10 years because there were many needs more pressing than language. Anyone who has visited this little village and has seen abject poverty could understand his point of view. This dilemma highlights one of the developmental problems in South Africa. You cannot develop if there is no basic infrastructure. You cannot get an infrastructure development if there is no money to do it. You cannot get money if there is no development, constituting a catch-22 situation.

Representative 4 argued that language is not really a problem in development. She was also somewhat ambiguous in her responses. On one hand, she kept on emphasizing the fact that they were living in a small community and that people had a feeling of community. This would lead to people interpreting for one another at a meeting or even protecting others by telling the interpreter when something had not been interpreted correctly. This audience participation in interpreting is something that has not yet been considered in interpreting theory. At the same time, she acknowledged that people may "deep down resent English" and the foreignness that it brings to development ideas. Yet, she claimed, people do understand that "we are living in a larger world now and that it is better to have one language of communication". Official 5 indicated that language acts as a distinct barrier to development. In her case, a Chinese company had received a contract for a certain development project. Because the inhabitants of her town are mostly Afrikaans speaking, the Chinese company decided to make use of labor from a neighboring town, which incidentally falls in another province, from where they could obtain English-speaking laborers. She is in favor of her municipality appointing a language practitioner.

4. THEORETICAL IMPLICATIONS

The first conclusion that is overwhelmingly clear from the data is that no written policy document on local economic development has been translated. All documents are available in English only. This means that, as far as development documentation is concerned, South Africa has a de facto non-translation situation. It is not a policy, as both the Constitution and laws provide for multiple languages. This multiplicity of language is, however, not supported by a policy on translation, which has led to non-translation becoming the de facto translation policy. The implications of non-translation are the following: First, it enforces a perception of foreignness. Development, its terminology, and its ideas remain foreign to the majority of the South African public for the mere reason that it has not been translated (Olivier de Sardan, 2005). As one of the respondents said, South Africans now need to realize that they are part of a larger world, which means that they are not the only voices in this world and that there are powerful people speaking in languages other than their home language. I suggest that the phenomenon of non-translation and the perceptions of people from all walks of life warrant thorough future study, not from a sociolinguistic or language policy point of view but from a translation studies, hermeneutic point of view.

Second, the lack of translated development documentation creates the illusion that "his master" speaks with one voice. Development ideas reach communities in one language, foreign to most of them. It comes as a dominating, hegemonic perspective in which they have little say. It never becomes "theirs" (Olivier de Sardan, 2005), but it is always about what government will be doing, playing into the culture of dependency on donor aid to which Castells (2000b, pp. 105–121) refers. Thus, language and the multilinguistic nature of the constituency does not feature as a problem in any theoretical discussion on local economic development that I have read (refer, for instance, to the work by Rogerson, 1997, 2004, 2008, 2010). It is seen neither as a factor that could enhance development nor as a problem that can constrain it. Although no official translation policy (Meylaerts, 2011) seems to be in place, the practice in the context of policy documents on local economic development in the areas I have studied seems to be one of non-translation. As is the case in other countries where non-translation seems standard practice (Gentzler, 2008), the monolingual nature of communication has the function of creating homogeny, which is not always easily distinguishable from hegemony.

However, third, this seeming homogeneous voice of whoever's voice in which the master speaks, splits into 11 the moment it hits the ground. The moment these documents come into connection with the public, various formal and mostly informal strategies are used to facilitate multilingual requirements, for example, informal translation and interpreting and even transpreting.[1] It has become clear from my fieldwork that local, rural communities in South Africa operate based on high social capital and low technological capital (Florida, 2005, pp. 1–45). The social capital is used to substitute for the lack of technological capital in society. In all cases, respondents emphasized the fact that people help one another to understand. This form of translation/interpreting, which I call "communal translation" to distinguish it from community translation, supports Tymoczko's (2006) views that not only professional acts of translation should fall within the purview of translation studies. Thus, one has a clear example of a community taking responsibility for understanding matters that apply to them, a view that deconstructs the typical Western notion of a translator as an individual professional behind a computer in an office. The extent to which this communal translation is localizing and to which it deals with the foreignness of development speak has not formed part of my research and needs further investigation.

The fourth implication of the data from the fieldwork concerns the conceptual translation of travelling ideas. On the face of it, it seems that locality overrides globality and that the translation actions that I have described achieve the mediation function of connecting the global and the local. For instance, Lund (2008, p. 4) points out that local economic development should be focused on creating jobs, which in many of the cases I have been studying seems not to be happening due to, among others, the over-indigenization of development policies. Because the local and immediate needs override the hermeneutic process or the process of the translation of the social (Latour, 2007), the links to more foreign concepts such as how to provide economic growth and jobs do not develop. However, one could also look at it from another perspective. The translation action could also serve the maintenance of the *status quo*, or, at least, the dominance of local, vested interests over social change. The ways in which nuanced development policies from the international community are "translated" into local needs testifies to this (see Section 1.2 in this chapter). In Western translation theory, translation is usually seen as an agent of change—for the better, that is. The data I have presented could just as well be construed to argue the opposite (see Rabbani's [2011] criticism that both development and antidevelopment proponents actually support the status quo).

Theoretically, I then suggest that the data challenges ideas about translation as the action of an individual, and it questions any unequivocal equation of translation with development. In fact, I interpret the data as indicating that the line between localization and the self-serving maintenance of the status quo is indeed very thin. Translation is not necessarily an agent of progressive thought, but could, for better or for worse, also be an agent of conservation (see Cronin, 2006, p. 48). The cultural and literary bias in translation studies may have predisposed it to finding translation acting on behalf of progressive forces in society. Having another look at the opposite could be worth our while.

Addendum
Open-Ended Interview for Discussions on Translation and Local Economic Development

1. In your opinion, what are the most pressing development needs in your municipal area?
2. What languages are spoken in your municipal jurisdiction? What languages do your officials speak:
   - at senior level, e.g. Municipal Manager and Department Heads;
   - at middle level, e.g. unit managers in the different towns;
   - at front-office level, e.g. payment offices;
   - in council meetings;
   - in ward meetings; or
   - at public rallies?
3. Do you think that some people in your municipal area may have difficulties in communicating with the municipality? Examples?
4. What do you think are the two most important projects of your development plan?
5. Which idea in the plan is most important for your area of jurisdiction?
6. Who compiled the IDP? What was the role of COGTA in the IDP?
7. Given that IDPs and other strategies are always written in English, how does the public participate in its drawing up and feedback on it?
8. Have the IDP or any LED documents in your area been translated from English to other languages? Do you think there is a need to do so?
9. For you personally, what is development? If you think of your constituency, how would they define development?
10. How do you cooperate with neighboring local municipalities in your provinces, across provinces? Is language a factor here?
11. In your view, do the different languages that people speak create barriers for development for:
    - Sesotho speakers;
    - Afrikaans speakers;
    - English speakers; and
    - Xhosa speakers.

6 Translation, the Knowledge Economy, and Development

1. INTRODUCTION

The idea that translation assists in the diffusion and/or creation of knowledge is not new. In translation studies, this idea has been propounded in various forms. Examples are Susam-Sarajeva's (2006) study on how translation has aided the travel of ideas on semiotics into Turkey, Milton and Bandia's (2009) compilation on the use of translation as an agent for modernization, Gentzler's (2008) book on the creation of new forms of culture through translation, Tyulenev's (2012) views on the role of translation in the Westernization of Russia in the eighteenth century, and Sturge's (2007) study on the role of translation in the travel of anthropological knowledge.

In this chapter, I want to conceptualize what is usually understood as travel theory in terms of the knowledge economy, learning regions, and the network economy. This is in line with the aims of the second part of the book, that is, to consider the role of translation in the development of societies. My argument in Chapter 4 was that the cultural/ideological side of development has been studied in the comparative-literature approaches to translation studies. My aim is to expand this debate to include the economy, politics, and sociology, that is, development studies.

First, I provide an overview of the concept of the knowledge economy and follow this with a section on learning regions, which focuses on regional development. Third, I look at the network economy and close the chapter with a discussion on some empirical data that I gathered.

2. THE KNOWLEDGE ECONOMY

Scholars in economics have differences of opinion as to whether there is such a thing as the knowledge economy (Brinkley, 2006, p. 5), how to define it, and how to measure it. My aim in this section is not to take part in their debate, because I am not qualified to do that, but to trace the debate and its implications for translation studies, particularly concerning the first two points of the debate.

In general, the argument about whether there is a knowledge economy entails claims that we have entered a new type of economy that is based on the operation of knowledge on knowledge (Castells, 2000a), whereas the counterargument claims that knowledge has always been a part of the development of any economic activity, even agrarian ones. Thus, Houghton and Sheehan (2000, p. 1) claim that the definition of the knowledge economy is a matter of degree, that is, knowledge has always been at the basis of economic development, but now it has become the "central resource and factor in the creation of wealth". The call is then to devise ways of measuring the size and the impact of the knowledge economy. Once measured, so the argument goes, one can argue that it exists. A number of scholars have proposed such measurements with the result that I suggest one is now able to talk about the knowledge economy (Leydesdorff, 2006). For the purposes of my argument here, I shall not enter into further debate on the existence and measurement of the knowledge economy. I feel that it suffices to argue that similar "measurements" concerning the effects of translation will bring credibility to claims concerning the role of translation in society. What I have in mind is that we should try to understand the extent of economic, political, and social activities depending on translation. For instance, how much business would Toyota or BMW or McDonald's lose if none had access to translators? Castells (2000a, p. 100) views the core characteristic of the change towards a knowledge economy to be the human ability to process symbols. Thus, for him, the technological ability to use semiotics as a productive force is driving the development of the knowledge economy.

So, what is the knowledge economy? I think it is best described by Castells as an economy in which knowledge is applied not to nature or natural resources, but to knowledge itself. David and Foray (2001, p. 6) define the knowledge economy as follows: "A knowledge-intensive community is one wherein a large proportion of members is involved in the production and reproduction of knowledge". Smith (2002, p. 6) thinks that the knowledge economy refers to an economy that is directly based on the production, distribution and use of knowledge and information. According to Powell and Snellman (2004, p. 200), studies on the knowledge economy focus on three main fields: (1) science-based industries, (2) whether particular industries are especially knowledge intensive, and (3) the role of learning and continuous innovation inside firms. They (Powell & Snellman, 2004, p. 201) thus define the knowledge economy as "production and services based on knowledge-intensive activities that contribute to an accelerated pace of technological and scientific advance as well as equally rapid obsolescence" (see also Florida, 2005). All of the definitions seems to share the aspect that, in the knowledge economy, one finds a much larger focus on knowledge than on physical labor or natural resources (see Cooke, 2003, p. 5; Houghton & Sheehan, 2000, p. 2) or, as R. Florida (1995, p. 528) puts it, the means of production has changed from physical labor to the human mind and innovation in particular. Brinkley (2006, p. 4) cites a number of definitions with which different institutions work:

- "Although the pace may differ all Organisation for Economic Co-operation and Development (OECD) economies are moving towards a knowledge-based economy" (OECD).
- "[O]ne in which the generation and exploitation of knowledge has come to play the predominant part in the creation of wealth. It is not simply about pushing back the frontiers of knowledge; it is also about the most effective use and exploitation of all types of knowledge in all manner of economic activity" (DTI Competitiveness White Paper).
- "[T]he idea of the knowledge driven economy is not just a description of high tech industries. It describes a set of new sources of competitive advantage which can apply to all sectors, all companies and all regions, from agriculture and retailing to software and biotechnology" (New measures for the New Economy).
- "[E]conomic success is increasingly based on the effective utilisation of intangible assets such as knowledge, skills and innovative potential as the key resource for competitive advantage. The term 'knowledge economy' is used to describe this emerging economic structure" (ESRC).
- "[T]he knowledge society is a larger concept than just an increased commitment to R&D [research and development]. It covers every aspect of the contemporary economy where knowledge is at the heart of value added—from high tech manufacturing and ICTs [information and communication technologies] through knowledge intensive services to the overtly creative industries such as media and architecture" ('Kok Report').

Houghton and Sheehan (2002, p. 9) provide a helpful overview of the features of the knowledge economy:

- There is an enormous increase in the codification of knowledge, which, together with networks and the digitalization of information, is leading to its increasing commodification.
- Increasing codification of knowledge is leading to a shift in the balance of the stock of knowledge—leading to a relative shortage of tacit knowledge.
- Codification is promoting a shift in the organization and structure of production.
- Information and communication technologies increasingly favor the diffusion of information over re-invention, reducing the investment required for a given quantum of knowledge.
- The increasing rate of accumulation of knowledge stocks is positive for economic growth (raising the speed limit to growth). Knowledge is not necessarily exhausted in consumption.

- Codification is producing a convergence, bridging different areas of competence, reducing knowledge dispersion, and increasing the speed of turnover of the stock of knowledge.
- The innovation system and its "knowledge distribution power" are critically important.
- The increased rate of codification and collection of information are leading to a shift in focus towards tacit ("handling") skills.
- Learning is increasingly central for both people and organizations.
- Learning involves both education and learning-by-doing, learning-by-using, and learning-by-interacting.
- Learning organizations are increasingly networked organizations.
- Initiative, creativity, problem solving, and openness to change are increasingly important skills.
- The transition to a knowledge-based system may make market failure systemic.
- A knowledge-based economy is so fundamentally different from the resource-based system of the last century that conventional economic understanding must be reexamined.

A point on which all scholars seems to agree is that the development of information and communication technology (ICT) since the 1970s has provided the material substructure for this development to take place (Brinkley, 2006, p. 5; Brinkley & Lee, 2007, p. 6; David & Foray, 2001), although the knowledge economy itself is not to be limited to the ICT industry (Cooke, 2003, p. 2). However, it also seems clear that knowledge is not produced and distributed to the same extent in all sectors because, among others, the applicability of technology is limited (Adam & Foray, 2001, p. 12). Furthermore, knowledge is becoming fragmented because it is easy to divide it and store it as information.

As I shall point out again in the section on learning regions, the technical ability to store masses of information has brought about two sets of distinctions. The one is between knowledge/understanding and information and the other is between tacit and codified knowledge (Adam & Foray, 2001, p. 4; Brinkley, 2006, p. 5; Smith, 2002, p. 7). Scholars point out that ICT has made it possible to turn knowledge into information in order to store and/or disseminate it. Furthermore, ICT has made it possible to turn tacit knowledge into codified knowledge, once again in order to store and, particularly, to disseminate it. The relevance for translation studies is that, with ICT, knowledge is translated into other forms of symbolic representation in order to store it (Adam & Foray, 2001, p. 5).

Much of the debate is dominated by the question of whether the ICT revolution means the end of geography (Adam & Foray, 2001, p. 6), a question discussed in detail in the next section.

Brinkley (2006, p. 6) points out that knowledge is seldom private. Instead, it is a public good because it tends to leak, which means that it cannot be contained in one person or one space but tends to "leak" out into other persons and spaces. He thus argues that knowledge is necessary for development, but it is not sufficient; that is, knowledge alone will not cause development.

According to Adam and Foray (2001, pp. 1–2), the features of the knowledge economy are the acceleration of knowledge production (Davenport, n.d., p. 44; Florida, 2005; Rhoades & Slaughter, 2004), the rise of intangible capital at the macroeconomic level and innovation as the dominant activity in the economy. Smith (2002, p. 13) is of the opinion that research and development are not the only indicators of a reliance on knowledge production. He introduces the difference between knowledge creation and learning, that is, the supply and demand sides of knowledge (Smith 2002, p. 15).

3. LEARNING REGIONS

Hauser et al. (2007, p. 76; see also Smith, 2002, p. 15) argue that, in the knowledge economy, knowledge is the most important resource and learning is the most important process. These two factors, the production of knowledge, and the learning process, form the core point of interest in studies on the knowledge economy. Although the general assumption is that the advances in information and communication technology have made the travel of knowledge easier, and some have even pronounced the death of geography (K. Morgan, 2004, p. 5), it was soon discovered that knowledge does not travel so easily.

The main reason for knowledge being "sticky" is its tacit nature (Hauser et al., 2007, p. 76; K. Morgan 2004, p. 7). If knowledge could be reduced to information, it would have been easy to store and transfer it. However, knowledge is always embodied, which makes space a relevant factor in the production and distribution of knowledge. K. Morgan (2004, p. 3) draws a further distinction between knowledge and understanding, claiming that the former travels easily and the latter does not. This is largely in line with Olivier de Sardan's (2005) hermeneutic approach to development. According to Morgan (2004, p. 5), human interaction cannot be replaced by technology, and he further claims that arguments concerning the death of geography are confusing spatial reach with social depth. The latter is obviously the more sought after as a scarce resource. Thus, standardized transactions could be done in virtual space, but complex, ambiguous, and tacit transactions need social space (Morgan, 2004, pp. 5, 7). Apart from being embodied, tacit knowledge is also collective in nature and thus cannot be translated easily (Morgan, 1997, p. 495).

Furthermore, codified knowledge does not represent an economic advantage because it is available everywhere, while tacit knowledge is valuable because it is a scarce resource (Hauser et al., 2007, p. 76). Houghton and

Sheehan (2000, p. 13) also made the important observation that, unlike materials in the manufacturing economy, knowledge is not destroyed in consumption and can be reused. Although the up-front costs of knowledge production may thus be high, the costs of reproduction, storage, and distribution, especially if the knowledge can be turned into information, are low. Economic geography has thus come up with the notion of learning regions, arguing that people still prefer to group together. Also, the knowledge that is relevant to a particular industry does not necessarily reside in the industry; it might be distributed across various technologies, actors, and industries (Smith, 2002, p. 19). Thus, R. Florida (1995, p. 528) argues that learning regions are places where knowledge and ideas are deposited and collected. Furthermore, with knowledge being a resource, regions with clusters of knowledgeable institutions, such as Silicon Valley in California, become the infrastructure for the further development of knowledge. In this kind of regional development, foreign direct investment serves as a way of diffusing knowledge (Florida, 1995, p. 529), something that is in need of research from a translation studies perspective. With foreign direct investment comes the movement of personnel, who move with their tacit knowledge and transfer it into new regions.

K. Morgan (2004, pp. 8–9) points to another very relevant point for translation studies. In the production process, one needs teams of engineers, production staff and sales staff, each coming to the table with an own "language", which often causes them to talk past one another. This is a further argument in favor of the need to study the semiotic substructure of the economy, politics, and development in much more depth and from a complex systems, that is, inter-ness, point of view. K. Morgan (2004, p. 13) could be taken for a translation scholar in his claim that "[t]hese two tendencies—standardization and localization—constitute a permanent dialectic in the spatial economy, making geographical outcomes a two-way street between localization and diffusion, not a one-way highway to dispersion."

Hassink (2005, p. 6) provides the following principles for the development of learning regions:

- carefully coordinating supply of and demand for skilled individuals;
- developing a framework for improving organizational learning, which is not only focused on high-tech sectors, but on all sectors that have the potential to develop high levels of innovative capacity;
- carefully identifying resources in the region that could impede economic development (lock-ins);
- positively responding to changes from outside, particularly where this involves unlearning;
- developing mechanisms for coordinating both across departmental and governance (regional, national, supranational) responsibilities;
- developing strategies to foster appropriate forms of social capital and tacit knowledge that are positive to learning and innovation;

- continuously evaluating relationships between participation in individual learning, innovation and labor market changes;
- developing an educational and research infrastructure for the knowledge society;
- encouraging openness to impulses from outside;
- fostering redundancy and variety; and
- ensuring the participation of large groups of society in devising and implementing strategies.

The reason why regions have become important relates to the demise of the power and influence of the nation state in the process of globalization and the rise of regions and cities as the organizers of economics (Florida, 1995, p. 531; Hauser et al., 2007, p. 76; MacKinnon et al., 2002, p. 294). See also Puuka et al. (2012) and the Free State's Regional Steering Committee (2010) for detailed studies on the knowledge economy at a regional level. Because capitalism is based on competition, and the knowledge economy on the competition of ideas, regions that are able to mobilize human infrastructure, that is, knowledge and ideas, are the regions who will win (Florida, 1995, p. 532). If it is true that social capital triggers the output of innovation processes, translation comes to play an important role in innovation in the context of transnational companies that have to bring together people with tacit knowledge from various linguistic backgrounds. If, furthermore, globalised networks of people moving and communicating as needed are required, i.e. if social capital is paramount, it means that we are living in a world that is increasingly symbolic and in need of the mediation of symbolic universes. If, as Hudson (1999, p. 65) claims, regionality focuses on space, this means that culture, language and the social (semiotic) underpinning of economic success is becoming increasingly important. MacKinnon et al. (2002, p. 301) puts it simply: "Places where tacit knowledge can be accumulated have an advantage."

Because of the importance of knowledge as a means of production, regions have to become learning regions, that is, regions that accumulate the means of production (Florida, 1995, p. 170). The relationships within these learning regions need to be stable and there needs to be trust between institutions and people for learning to take place (MacKinnon et al., 2002, p. 302). Furthermore, there must be networks to link the various producers of knowledge with one another but also to link producers and users of knowledge. The role of knowledge in development is one of those things that cannot be precisely determined. It is intangible, pervasive and morphs its form continuously, which is why the network and the breaking down of the silo approach to research is important (see Free State's Regional Steering Committee, 2010, p. 78). It also seems clear that, with the focus on the knowledge economy, education has become increasingly important (Houghton & Sheehan, 2000, p. 21) because the kind of labor that the knowledge economy requires is asking for investment in people with broad-based problem-solving skills and with social and interpersonal communication skills. This state of affairs makes it possible to argue for including translation courses in business and economics courses to enhance the ability of the educated to communicate cross-culturally. For instance, Cooke (2003, p. 12) claims that the systemic nature of interaction between production and exploitation is massively assisted by "boundary crossing" competence", which is the field of expertise of translation studies. He (Cooke, 2003, pp. 12–14), just like Morgan, sounds like a translation scholar when he argues that

> at key points where epistemic communities like "academic engineers", "civil servants" and "business managers" must communicate on policy-related matters there are "boundary crossing" buffers like Fraunhofer Institutes, Business Associations and Science Park Incubator Centres that interpret among distinct communities of practice thus enabling (international) regional knowledge flow from exploration through examination to exploitation knowledge categories.

4. THE NETWORK ECONOMY

In his magisterial trilogy, Castells (2000a, 2000b, 2004) provides a comprehensive overview of the implications of the shift to a network society. I provide a brief overview of his ideas to sketch the broad background to the implications of the network society.

Castells's (2000a, pp. 408–409) central view of the nature of the network society is that the space of place has been replaced by the space of flows. Although geography has not become irrelevant, the intentions of the network society are to minimize the implications of space and time to the extent that all that remains are the virtual flows (Castells, 2000a, p. 463). Within the network society, places function only as nodes in a network, losing their importance as a place and deriving their importance from their position in the "hierarchy of wealth generation, information processing, and power making that ultimately conditions the fate of each locale" (Castells, 2000a, p. 445). Thus, the network economy is organized around global networks of capital, management, and information, which are not operated by human agents but by electronically operated, random processing of information (Castells, 2000a, p. 505).

For Castells (2000a, p. 4), this move toward a network society has been made possible by the developments in information and communication technology that has changed the material base of the social reality that we inhabit. The major implication of this network society is its ability to cut off nodes that do not add value (Castells, 2000b, p. 1), which is one of the reasons why an un(der)developed area such as sub-Saharan Africa finds it difficult to reconnect to the world economy. This results in what Castells

(2000b, p. 165) calls black holes of isolation because, once you have been cut from the network and landed in such a hole, there is no way to escape from it. Furthermore, not only individuals but regions and countries can also be cut off from the network. Rist (2002, p. 165) claims that there is an escape, but only if the rules of the game are changed. Thus, isolation seems to be the largest threat to technological development because if you are not connected to the network, you miss out on the flow of knowledge, which leads to innovation and ultimately wealth (Castells 2000a, p. 13).

The importance of the flow of information or knowledge, which has to be in some sort of semiotic form, and upon which the network society is based, thus argues in favor of the importance of translation. By translation, I mean all kinds of inter-systemic semiotic movement. Castells (2000a, p. 171) argues that the network economy requires "bridges of transfer to connect tacit to explicit, explicit to tacit, tacit to tacit and explicit to explicit". Because the network economy has not obliterated space but is instead connecting spaces in its network, and because culture is an effect of the way in which symbolic human interaction has crystallized in a particular geographic space (Castells 2000a, p. 15), the interaction between local and global will ask for much deeper thinking on inter-systemicness, the crossing of boundaries and the translation of knowledge.

5. TRANSLATION, THE KNOWLEDGE ECONOMY, AND AGRICULTURE DEVELOPMENT

In this section, I report on empirical research that I conducted on the role of translation in the knowledge economy and the way in which it could influence particular aspects of development. In particular, I wish to trace a few of the links of a research project on *The Influence of Heat, Drought and Cold Stress on Gluten Proteins and Baking Quality in Hard Red Spring Wheat*, in which the Department of Plant Sciences at the University of the Free State (UFS) was involved. The UFS leader of the research team is Professor Maryke Labuschagne (project leader). She and some of her students graciously provided me with information on their work. As with all of my empirical work, my aim is not to provide a comprehensive covering of the topic but to illustrate a case study to provide some initial insight into the particular topic at hand with the aim of stimulating further research on this topic.

In this case, I looked at the translation of the researchers' ideas in various contexts. On one hand, I analyze the way in which the research team translated their ideas when talking to different links in the knowledge economy. On the other hand, I looked at how they translated their knowledge to the consumers of knowledge in various contexts. For the first aim, I relied on texts the project leader provided me. For the second aim, I referred to additional texts that I received from two interviewees, as well as the interviews that I conducted with two senior students in the project (a PhD and a postdoc student). See addendum for open-ended questionnaire.

From the project leader I received, among others, a document in which the relevant research project was conceptualized for internal use. I also received a funding application in which the project was submitted to an overseas funder. Last, I studied PowerPoint presentation where the project leader communicated her ideas to farmers and agricultural business people in South Africa. In terms of the knowledge economy, the first text represents the views of the knowledge producer, the second is aimed at the funder of knowledge production, and the third is aimed at the knowledge consumer.

On studying the three texts in detail, it became clear that the one aimed at the producer, a Microsoft Word document written in the form of an academic article (text 1), starts with a conceptual problem, stating "Gluten is produced by the interaction between wheat flour proteins in the presence of water, which confers the unique viscoelastic properties essential for making bread", followed by a reference. Environmental matters are only mentioned in the third sentence of the second paragraph. The text aimed at the funder, an Microsoft Word document that is a template provided by the donor and completed by the applicant (text 2), starts and ends with environmental problems that are said to cause social problems: "Heat and drought stress are increasingly proving to be major production constraints in sub-Saharan Africa" and "The data will be very relevant to the wheat and baking industry". The text that addresses the knowledge consumers, a PowerPoint presentation (text 3), starts with matters of definition in the first slide, asking, "What is a gluten", which is assumed knowledge in the previous two texts. According to the authors' perception of the role of their readers in the knowledge economy, the problem to be addressed is thus respectively translated into either a conceptual/academic one, a social/industrial/development one, or a "how knowledge benefits industry" one.

Text 1 has a significant bibliography and uses references frequently, thus claiming its authority by means of its links to sources. Text 2 has no bibliography and no references but most of the document is devoted to the curriculum vitae of participants, proving their competence and authority. Text 3 assumes authority by starting with the question, "What is a gluten?" It assumes to know and to tell what it knows.

Text 1 solves its problems by means of technical scientific equations. Under the heading "Materials and methods", it has a subsection "Size Exclusion High Performance Liquid Chromatography (SE-HPLC)", under which it claims to measure its results by an equation such as

100[(SDS-insoluble LPP and SDS-insoluble SPP)/SDS-soluble and SDS-insoluble LPP and SPP)]; the percentage of large unextractable polymeric protein (%LUPP), 100[(SDS-insoluble LPP)/SDS-soluble and SDS-insoluble LPP)]; the percentage of small unextractable polymeric protein (%SUPP), 100[(SDS-insoluble SPP)/SDS-soluble and SDS-insoluble SPP)].

Unless you are a plant breeding specialist, you would have no clue as to what this is all about. The problem of data analysis, which in the funding application was translated as "The trial will be done under controlled conditions for two consecutive seasons to confirm the data" and "A representative main tiller sample of each replication will be analyzed in France using a two dimensional gel", has in text 1 been translated into chemical or microbiological equations. It has become technical, a matter of proving particular chemical and microbiological equations, whereas in text 2, it is a matter of solving environmental influences on production processes that may have social ramifications. Text 3 solves its problems by providing visual aids, such as showing a picture of three slices of bread of different sizes and the explanation that the difference in size is related to the differences in gluten content. In each case, the proof has thus been translated into a different semiotic system, that is, chemical formulae in text 1, environmental rhetoric in text 2, and pictures of products in text 3.

Text 1 plays a particular role in the knowledge economy, answering the question, What do we need to know? Text 2 plays its particular role in the same knowledge economy, translating the technical questions concerning the content of knowledge concerning gluten to industrial, social, and developmental issues that would motivate a funder to contribute to the production of knowledge. Text 3 plays its particular role in the knowledge economy by taking the scientific knowledge, envisioned in text 1 and that have been funded by the convincing argument concerning capacity in text 2, to the consumers of knowledge, that is, the farmers and agricultural businesses, explaining from the potential benefits of this knowledge to them. By means of the translation of the project leader's ideas into three different texts, knowledge is being produced and disseminated. Without the translation, the funder would not have been able to judge the project leader's competence to do the research, and the consumers would most probably not have understood her. These texts, as translations of the same set of ideas, become the links that keep the social institution we call research together and which forms part of the knowledge economy.

I now turn to a discussion of the two interviews I had with the project leader's cooperators. One was a postdoctoral student from Zambia (respondent 1) and the other an Ethiopian doctoral student (respondent 2) nearing the end of his studies.

In response to the question concerning the networks through which their knowledge travelled, respondent 1 indicated that his institution has connections with the agricultural extension department, nongovernmental organizations (NGOs) and community-based organizations (CBOs). Concerning the first, they would hold annual planning meetings to which all extension officers are invited. At these meetings, the researchers share their new knowledge stemming from research during the past year and, with input from the extension officers who are knowledgeable about the farmers' problems, plan the fields of research for the next year. This network thus has a dialogic structure with knowledge moving both ways. With the NGOs, they would hold demonstrations in which farmers are also involved. These demonstrations are held regionally and are adapted to the needs of each region. They would also hold field days during which they go to farms and demonstrate (another translation of knowledge into technical expertise, products, and tacit know-how) new technology to farmers. On these days, they would distribute written documentation that would be translated into the vernacular of the region.

The institution of respondent 1 makes much use of regional radio stations to reach various communities. Respondent 1 would write a text in English to be broadcast at regional level. The regional radio stations would then translate the text into their particular languages, send it back to respondent 1 for checking, and then broadcast it. With the regional radio stations, knowledge is already localized because it is translated into the language of the region, but it is also knowledge that is relevant to that particular region, because the regions differ in their needs. Respondent 1 indicated that translations were of the "indigenized" type, steering away from English technical terminology and rather making use of examples of paraphrases to translate technical terminology. Respondent 1 received feedback on the travel and relevance of his knowledge because the radio station often interviewed farmers, hearing from them about the success of new technology.

Brochures would often go out in vernacular languages. Respondent 1 indicated that a significant number of farmers in his country would not be able to read these brochures, but their peers would read it and translate it for them. This relates to my notion of "communal translation" as expounded in Chapter 5. Translation strategies are usually simplification. They do not make use of professional translators but use colleagues in their research network to perform the translations.

Respondent 1 was of the opinion that knowledge that was tested and working, that is, shown to farmers to be advantageous, would travel. In his words, "The more you are with end-users, the better". Thus, one already needs some kind of translation of the knowledge from theoretical knowledge into a form of embodied knowledge or practice before you can communicate with the farmers.

Respondent 2 has a very specific network with which knowledge is disseminated. First, he would speak to extension staff who would then further disseminate information. They would work primarily with development agents who will work with farmers. These development workers are seen as a bridge to the farmers as they usually speak the regional vernacular, know the culture, and have enough technical knowledge (they usually have a four-year, BSc qualification). Thus, they are translators in more than one sense of the word. Respondent 1 was strong in his opinions that one "does not talk jargon in front of the farmers" but that you translate your knowledge into local knowledge systems. For instance, using metric measurements would not be understandable in his context as many farmers have traditional units of measurement for land size and volumes.

Respondent 2 has been doing translations for about five to six years, translating promotional and informational material, supporting Tymoczko's (2006) claims that translation is not always done by professionals. His company also makes use of public-relations officers who are trained in communications and culture but not in language and translation. They often have to create new terminology or make use of paraphrase, for example, translating "quality protein maize" by "nutritionally enhanced maize". They do not make use of professional translators.

A very important node in their network is field days, to which farmers are invited. In these cases, communication would be oral and in Amharic. They would also use interpreters to translate into smaller languages. Respondent 1 also confirms the practice of neighbors telling one another about the new technology, that is, communal translation, those who can read interpreting it for those who cannot. With field days, they make use of a government structure called "One to five networks". With these networks, innovative farmers are identified, and they are then targeted with new technology, with the expectation that they would diffuse the knowledge to five other farmers in their vicinity. Although efficient to some extent, these networks sometimes hinder the uptake of knowledge as it is seen as ideologically compromised by being sponsored and used by government for political purposes.

Respondent 2 also makes use of radio, which is more efficient than TV in his country. National and regional radio stations are also responsible for translating information. He referred to the use of an SMS (Short Message Service) system in Kenya where information about new technology is distributed via SMS.

Farmer training occasions take place on farms and are of an oral nature. Demonstration plays a large role, thus translating pure knowledge into a product. This is also done by means of what they call a demonstration plot, where they demonstrate their knowledge on an experimental plot of land, and farmers will then decide about the uptake of the product. Once again, knowledge is translated into enhanced products, which communicate better than do lectures.

Obviously, in a country with many languages, as is the case in most African countries, everything cannot be translated into all languages as time and finances are scarce resources. Thus, the respondents indicated that they at least tried to have their knowledge translated into the most important languages.

An interesting translation phenomenon was pointed out to me by respondent 2. In an effort to accommodate illiterate and semiliterate farmers, they use symbols on their seed packets to indicate the days between seeding and maturity and the area in which these seeds would be of optimal use. In one such example, a poster for maize seed, a monkey symbol is used for seeds that mature faster and a zebra symbol for seeds that take up to 10 days longer to mature. This is a case of inter-semiotic translation. Although I do not have enough data to make strong claims in this regard, I am suggesting, based on the linguistic anthropology of Jousse (2000) and on some initial observations, that the common practice of simplifying texts for semiliterate readers is not the most effective. In the context of developing countries, we need to look at multimodality and inter-semiotic translation as one of the solutions to this problem.

6. CONCLUSION

It seems to me that the knowledge economy offers a particularly rich point of connection between translation studies and development studies—and even economics. Further empirical work in this interdisciplinary point of connection is needed to confirm or disprove this claim.

It seems clear to me that, when knowledge travels, it has to be translated. Different spaces and different nodes in the network require different forms of knowledge. In particular, with illiteracy and semiliteracy at high levels in developing contexts, the multimodal translation of knowledge could provide the crucial links that people in developing contexts need in order to prohibit them from falling into the black holes of which Castells (2000b) speaks.

Last, so much translation is taking place outside of the professional sphere that I do not think we have the slightest idea of what our field of study really entails. In this regard, ethnographic studies, on one hand, and sociological studies that are concerned with flows and economic activity, on the other, are necessary to help us understand this fascinating set of informal activities.

Addendum
Translation, the Knowledge Economy and Development

Dear Participant

Thank you for taking the time to assist me by providing me with information concerning the travel of your knowledge in your community. Hopefully, your participation will lead to a better understanding of the way in which knowledge travels, which is a crucial prerequisite for development.

As far as confidentiality is concerned, I undertake not to mention any names in my work. I also undertake to give you due recognition for your contribution. If you do not wish to be named, please let me know.

Firstly, may I thus request some documentation from you regarding the following:

1. PowerPoint presentations you may have used to present your knowledge to audiences other than academic audiences.
2. Popular articles you may have written for, for instance, agriculture magazines.
3. Handout sheets or pamphlets you may have compiled.
4. Blogs, Facebook pages or websites where you have or are disseminating your knowledge.
5. Translations that you or someone may have made of any of the above. Here, I am also interested in things like sketches, models, etc. in which you have transferred your knowledge into other forms.

Secondly, may I request your response on the following questions?

1. Could you briefly describe the networks of people or organizations through which your knowledge travels further, e.g. government working groups, policy councils, businesses, farmers' groups, agricultural organizations?
2. In particular, could you describe the networks of people or organizations through which your knowledge travels to grass-roots level?
3. Could you briefly describe how you would adapt (if at all) your knowledge to localize it in your country/area/community?

4. Could you also briefly comment on how much of your knowledge gets translated (orally and in writing) into any local language in your country?
5. Would you care to comment on the importance (or not) of translation for disseminating your knowledge?
6. Lastly, would you care to comment on the role of the travel of knowledge and translation on development?

7 Translation in the Informal Economy

1. INTRODUCTION

Quite often, when one reads about translation practices such as those in South America, where literary translators have used translation as an anticolonial instrument (Gentzler, 2008), and you compare this to similar practices in India or Canada (Brisset, 2005; Simon, 2012), where translation was used to promote cultural identity, you come on striking similarities: People translate novels to achieve particular ideological aims, mostly to free their country or culture from colonial hegemony. Another example would be to compare translation practices in Turkey, where translation was used in the modernization of Turkey on a scientific level (Susam-Sarajeva, 2006), to some of the practices presented by Milton and Bandia (2009a), where translation is presented as an agent in cultural, educational and political modernization (see Uchiyama, 2009). Again, these practices show similarities: People translated large volumes of text to expose the people in their country to (better) views from elsewhere. These similarities, to me, are due to either the comparative literature or postcolonial frameworks that have been imposed on the interpretations of the data. In other words, because the theoretical expectations of researchers are framed by a near-dogmatic critical and postcolonial interest in translation studies, the findings largely reflect those expectations.

The similarities could also be due to most, if not all, research in translation studies focuses on the written, formal, high-culture part of social reality in the various countries. Furthermore, they usually focus on the work done in cities (for an approach to rurality, see Donaldson & Marais, 2012, pp. ix–xi), to the exclusion of rural areas. Although I do not think one can fault scholars for this focus, I deem it necessary to add another perspective to translation studies, that is, translation in the informal economy. In other words, the focus on high culture is not wrong but limited. Translation studies has focused, similar to literary studies, postcolonial studies, and even history, on power struggles and, in particular, on where the powerful struggle (on developing conditions in developed countries and vice versa, see Haynes, 2008, p. 5). What happens when the poor, who constitute by far the largest proportion of the global human population, eke out their living has up to now not fallen within the purview of translation studies scholars, with the exception of studies in community interpreting.

How the poor, and concomitantly less educated, survive in multilingual contexts survive a lack of language skills, both oral and written, cut them off from the networks of society is the focus of this chapter. In development studies, and in economics in particular, the notion of the informal economy has been conceptualized to indicate exactly this. Turning its gaze toward this informal economy will afford translation studies scholars a whole new perspective on social reality and translation practices.

I start with an overview of the literature concerning the theory of the informal economy. Then I shall present some research done by two of my students on aspects of translation in the informal economy. Lastly, I present some of my own data in this regard. My aim, as with Chapters 5 and 6, is to suggest an agenda for future research, not to provide a full-scale research report myself.

2. DEFINING THE INFORMAL ECONOMY

A variety of definitions has been suggested for the informal economy. In this section, I provide some of them to introduce the reader to the notion of the informal economy, with the eventual aim of arguing why the informal economy is relevant to translation studies (and development).

The notion of an informal economy has been in the making for quite some time, but the term was coined by Hart (1972), at basically the same time that it was used in a report on Kenya by the International Labour Organization (ILO; 1972). Initially, it was known as the informal sector, but since 2003, the term *informal economy* has become the standard designation.

Chen (2007, p. 1) defines the informal economy as economic units and workers that remain outside of the world of regulated economic activities and protected employment relationships. The latest definitions of the informal economy thus focus on employment relationships that are not legally regulated and protected, and it includes all kinds of unregulated employment and unincorporated enterprises (Chen, 2007, p. 7). The latter would include employers, own-account operators, and unpaid family workers. The definition would also include wage employers in informal jobs, that is, workers without formal contracts, worker benefits, or social protection, that work for formal, or informal, firms; for households; or for people without a fixed employer.

In the case of South Africa, Statistics South Africa defines the informal sector as follows: The informal sector consists of those businesses that are not registered in any way. They are generally small in nature and are seldom run from business premises. Instead, they are run from homes, street pavements, and other informal arrangements (Devey et al., 2006, p. 4).

The ILO (2009, p. III; Samson, 2004, p. 6) defines the informal economy as "all economic activities by workers and economic units that are—in law or in practice—not covered or insufficiently covered by formal arrangements". These activities are not included in the law, which means that they operate outside the formal reach of the law; or they are not covered in practice, which means that—although they operate within the formal reach of the law, the law is not applied or enforced; or the law discourages compliance because it is inappropriate, burdensome, or imposes excessive costs.

Theron (2011, p. 9) points out that the Quality Labor Force Survey defines the informal sector somewhat differently: It comprises businesses that are unregistered, that do not have a value-added tax (VAT) number, that are generally small in nature, and that are seldom run from business premises but often run from homes, street pavements or other informal arrangements.

For the sake of this chapter, I make use of the ILO's definition as my working definition of the informal economy, although, as the next section shows, I am aware of academic differences of opinion on the matter.

3. CONCEPTUALIZING THE INFORMAL ECONOMY

Chen (2005, p. 5) lists what she calls interested observers of the informal economy in the *research* community, who are the people who create new knowledge:

- *neoclassical development economists:* who see small-scale enterprises as using the "right" combination of labor and capital for developing countries;
- *agricultural development economists:* who see agricultural growth as the engine of development in developing countries, in part because it creates demand for rural small-scale enterprises;
- *informal sector scholars:* who study the divisions and linkages between large/formal and small/informal firms in developing countries; and
- *industrial relations scholars:* who study the changing patterns of production and labor relations in formal manufacturing in developed countries (e.g., flexible specialization literature).

Interested observers in the *practitioner* community, who are the people who make use of the knowledge, include, according to Chen (2005, p. 5),

- *microfinance and microenterprise practitioners:* who recognize the economic growth and/or poverty reduction potential of microenterprises;
- *sustainable livelihoods specialists:* who are concerned about the erosion of the natural resource base for livelihoods of the poor;
- *labor advocates:* who are concerned about the erosion of employment relations and working conditions of the global workforce; and

- *fair trade proponents:* who are concerned about the competitiveness of small producers and the protection of workers under specific trade agreements and trade liberalization more broadly.

At first, under the assumptions of modernization theory, it was assumed that the informal economy would disappear as countries developed to the level of Western economies (Chen, 2007, p. 1; Dutt & Ros, 2008, p. 483). The fact that this did not happen and that the informal sector in developed countries has, in fact, grown over the last three decades is an indication that the informal economy is here to stay. In fact, Chen (2005, p. 8) claims that the informal sector will become a feature of modern capitalist development. So, what causes the informal economy? The first obvious cause would be a lack of opportunity in the formal economy. In this regard, reasons abound. The formal economy sometimes simply does not have enough job opportunities for everybody in a country. Also, job opportunities require certain entry-level skills and education, which many people may not have. People entering the informal economy or remaining in it usually, but not always, seem to be forced by a lack of human capital (Ibourk, 2012, p. 42). A second reason for the growth in the informal economy is the rise of neoliberalism in the 1980s (Chen, 2007, p. 6; Devey et al., 2006, p. 9), which, because of its informalization approach and structural adjustments (Delvaux, n.d., pp. 15–17), caused major job losses across the world. This forced people into the informal economy to secure a living. The 2008 financial crisis and subsequent recessions also played a role in this regard (Theron, 2011, pp. 10–11). Xaba et al. (2002, p. 20) argues that, in Africa, the economic disruption caused by colonialism also contributed to the formation of the informal sector.

Another second school of thought on the informal economy is the dualist school, claiming that the two economies basically run on parallel, never-to-meet lines. Over the years, it has, however, become clear that one cannot conceptualize of the formal and informal economies in a dualist fashion. Rather, the two facets of the economy depend upon one another and play into one another (Chen, 2005, pp. 3, 17; Samson, 2004, p. 19; Theron, 2011, p. 8). In South Africa, the dualist approach was made popular by the ANC's concepts of the first and second economy, which, according to them, ran parallel with basically no interface (H. Marais, 2011, pp. 194–195). According to the ANC (Presidency, 2006; Rogerson, 2007), the first economy is basically the formal economy that is structured and regulated whereas the second economy is unstructured and unregulated. In this view, the informal or second economy is seen as undesirable, and everything in the economy needs to be similar to what it is in the first economy. The rejection of the informal economy by the ANC hampered the opportunities for the emergence of a small-business sector in South Africa.

Third, the structuralist school of thought on the informal economy claims that the informal economy is caused by the nature of the economic structure, that is, capitalism, which structurally excludes certain people from its purview (Chen, 2005, p. 3). Davis (2006, p. 7) claims that the tendency over the last decades has been to create middle classes by channeling wealth away from the poor rather than by creating new wealth. This has led more poor people to informal survivalism. Thus, Dutt and Ros (2008, pp. 486–487) explain that the structuralist school of thought would attribute the informal economy to rapid population growth, migration to cities, and insufficient employment.

Fourth, the legalist school of thought claims that the informal economy finds its origin in the overregulation of the economy (Chen, 2005, p. 3). People choose to operate outside of this regulation because it has become too cumbersome, too costly and providing too little value for the effort and money put in. A point that is relevant for translation studies' interest in the informal economy is that the regulating environment is usually a written one, whereas many people participating in the informal economy are not able or are only partially able to operate in a written environment (ILO, 2009, p. 30). It is not only a matter of people being semiliterate, but in a country such as South Africa, you need to be bilingual to take part in the regulating environment as most written documents are available only in English or perhaps also in Afrikaans. The ILO report on development in Africa (ILO, 2007, p. 15) argues that the informal economy is a rich source of knowledge that can be tapped into. This could be related to the previous chapter on the transfer of knowledge.

The main debate at this moment rages around the lack of protection of employees in the informal economy (Chen, 2005, p. 6). In this regard, the ILO has been playing a significant role. In this labor perspective, the labor relationship becomes the category for describing the informal economy, and the implication is that the informal economy is not only a phenomenon found in developing countries but in all countries across the globe (Dutt & Ros, 2008, p. 488).

It is also clear from the literature that the informal economy plays a significant role in development and the reduction of poverty or, at least, in keeping people alive (e.g., Chen, 2005, p. 1). Castells (2004) has argued that the demise of the state in many countries causes people to look after themselves because there are no institutions to do it for them. Lund (2008, p. 3) argues that a focus on the informal economy, keeping in mind the link between the formal and the informal economy, could lead to growth and development. Such a focus would, among others, extend credit to people working in the informal sector because they have already proved that they are trying to provide for themselves and should therefore be supported (Lund, 2008, p. 20). Samuels (2005, p. 1) argues that the informal economy has become important because of the shift of interest from the macro economy to the micro economy and the concomitant growth in interest and the importance of NGOs. In such a micro approach, the focus is on sustainable, community-based, people-participatory policies, and programs (Samuels, 2005, p. 2), which relates to the movement in approaches to development that I have discussed in Chapter 4. These types of human approaches to development take the agency role of people seriously and they become the interventionists of their own development (Maathai, 2009). What is important in this regard, argues Samuels (2005, p. 7), is that the UN Habitat agenda should be localized to each context where people need to take responsibility for its implementation. In a human-centered approach such as this, the state is required to create an enabling environment, not to perform the development.

The literature also points out that the informal economy is not a monolithic phenomenon. It is highly segmented and differentiated as far as economic sector, place of work, employment status, social group, and gender are concerned (Chen, 2007, p. 2; Rogerson & Preson-Whyte, 1991, p. 1). Devey et al. (2006, pp. 4, 8) concur that the informal economy is heterogeneous, including different types of economic activity, different employment relations, and activities with different economic potential. Rogerson (1996, p. 171) points out that one finds a variety of enterprises in the informal economy, from survivalist to micro to growth enterprises. Thus, some enterprises are for mere survival, for example, some waste pickers (Schenk et al., 2012), whereas others are of such a nature that they may even grow into larger enterprises.

One of the great debates in studies on the informal economy is whether people join it voluntarily or out of necessity. On one hand, it has been proved that jobs in the formal sector generally pay better than those in the informal sector. On the other hand, the entrepreneurial spirit in humans causes some of them to prefer to work for themselves. Reasons why people would enter the informal economy include the following (Devey et al., 2006, p. 3):

- ease of entry;
- reliance on indigenous resources;
- family ownership of enterprises;
- small scale of operation;
- labor-intensive and adapted technology;
- skill acquired outside of the formal school system; and
- unregulated and competitive markets.

In contrast to the claims that ease of entry makes the informal economy attractive, Ghandi Kingdon (2003, p. 403) argues, however, that entry into the informal economy is not that easy. It still requires skill, and then there is the problem of competition as many people compete for scarce opportunities. She asks why, when there is such great unemployment in South Africa, more people do not enter the informal economy. Apart from the two reasons mentioned earlier, she also suggests that the apartheid legacy of repression may have inhibited self-confidence that again hampers the entrepreneurial spirit (Ghandi Kingdon, 2003, p. 403).

Furthermore, the informal economy is prone to a large gender divide. Men often earn much more, whereas many more women are operative in the informal economy. Thus, in the informal economy, self-employed workers earn most and home workers least whereas men earn much more than do women (see Chen's [2005, pp. 9–10] triangle of power and income in the informal economy). Chen (2005, p. 11) suggests that men have better tools, operate from better sites, have greater access to productive assets and capital, and sell higher volumes and a different range of goods. Furthermore, Lund (2008, p. 5) argues that most of the voluntary caring work in a society is done informally by women. Therefore, one also has to be sensitive to the continuation of gender divisions in promoting community caring and the responsibility of social groups to look after the old and weak in a community. It assumes that women will always have time and energy to spend on these groups (Lund, 2008, p. 5) because community work is actually women's work. In the process, women are prohibited from earning an income.

One of the major debates concerning the informal debate relates to the legality thereof (Chen, 2005, p. 11; Webb et al., 2009) presents a thorough overview of the problems of what he calls legality and legitimacy. According to him, enterprises in the informal economy are technically illegal as they do not comply with legal regulations formally required. However, they are legitimate in terms of the value systems of certain communities. Most of the products provided by the informal economy, however, are not illegal, though they have been produced illegally. He (Webb et al., 2009, pp. 495–496) thus distinguishes between informal institutions that refer to the norms, values, and beliefs that constitute socially acceptable behavior and formal institutions that refer to the legality or illegality of institutions.

The literature on the informal economy also reflects a debate on the advisability of formalizing the informal sector. On one hand, institutions such as the ILO argue that the informal economy is not providing "decent" jobs (Ibourk, 2012, p. 1) and that formalization would be the preferred option. On the other hand, efforts at formalization may just create more of the informal economy.

4. THE RELEVANCE OF THE INFORMAL ECONOMY FOR TRANSLATION STUDIES

I argue in this section that the informal economy is relevant to translation studies scholars for three reasons.

The first reason has to do with the research agenda of translation studies in general. Although much as been made of the "de-Westernization" of the field of translation studies (especially by scholars in the IATIS camp such as Tymoczko, 2006; see the special issue of *Translation and Interpreting Studies*, volume 6, issue 2, on Eurocentrism in Translation Studies for some alternative views on this debate), the debate seems to have become stuck on an analysis of the etymology of words used for translation in different cultures and the so-called different conceptualizations of translations performed in different contexts. Despite Tymoczko's early call for rethinking the formal and written bias in translation studies, little seems to have been done in this regard. I thus argue that a focus on the informal economy, though not limited to non-Western countries, will provide at least some impetus to the search for practices of translation that are not defined by Western contexts, which are more part of the formal economy in terms of the definition provided earlier. As long as translation studies keeps its focus on the elite component of societies worldwide, that is, literary translation, translation for large businesses, military translation, media translation, and scientific translation, it fixes its purview on the most Westernized part of social reality and thus confirms the Western bias Tymoczko suggests should be deconstructed.

I contend that the informal economy provides translation studies scholars with a heuristic entry point to much more local practices, many of which are survivalist and not found in more affluent and/or developed countries. To set some sort of research agenda in this regard, the questions include the following:

- If the literature is correct in arguing for a link between the informal and formal economy, how do illiterate, semiliterate, and partially educated people engage with the regulatory environment which is mostly literate, written, and formal? In other words, how do they translate themselves and their concerns?
- How do people in especially the survivalist part of the informal economy perform their tasks or business in multilingual contexts, given the assumption that they are not linguistically skilled to obtain jobs in the formal economy (Schenk et al., 2012)?
- Does the informal economy hold job opportunities for language practitioners?
- What would the size of the language practice industry in the informal economy be?
- Is translation even a factor in the informal economy?
- How do translation practices in different contexts in the informal economy compare?

The second reason why the informal economy deserves the attention of translation studies is because of its size. Because of its being informal, the reliability of figures in this regard is always being questioned. However, I contend that the data we have are sufficient to require us to refocus our attention towards the informal economy.

Globally, Castells (2000b, p. 124) suggests that 24% of the world population is involved in the informal economy. Chen (2005, p. 13) argues that

> informal employment comprises one-half to three-quarters of non-agricultural employment in developing countries: specifically, 48 per cent

in North Africa; 51 per cent in Latin America; 65 per cent in Asia; and 72 per cent in sub-Saharan Africa. If South Africa is excluded, the share of informal employment in non-agricultural employment rises to 78 per cent in sub-Saharan Africa.

Ibourk (2012, p. 14) suggests that as many as 82% of jobs in Morocco are of an informal nature. In a recent study, the ILO (2009) is of the opinion that, in sub-Saharan Africa, 72% of jobs are in the informal economy, excluding agricultural workers. According to Dutt and Ros (2008, p. 484), 60% of jobs, excluding agriculture, in developing countries are in the informal economy. The growth in the informal economy has the implication that 7 out of every 10 new jobs created are in this sector, whereas 6 out of every 10 poor and 7 out of every 10 indigent people work in this sector (Dutt & Ros 2008, p. 484).

In South Africa in particular, Lund (2008, p. 3) suggests that 35% of all jobs are in the informal sector, while Theron (2011, p. 12) puts the figures at between 17% and 30%, depending on the category on which the calculation is based.

Whichever way one looks at these figures, the figures do vary among studies, and there are multiple ways of looking at them. The figures seem to suggest a significant point of interest for translation studies. I am not necessarily suggesting that much professional translation goes on in the informal economy. I think that translation scholars should study the informal economy in order to better understand the role of (informal or nonprofessional) translation in the emergence of society and how translation could be developed (if necessary) in the informal economy. I also wish to suggest that, because we do not know the nature of translation in the informal economy, we cannot rule out its relevance. Thus, we first need to gain a deeper understanding before we start judging or making suggestions in this regard (see also an earlier article I wrote in this regard; Marais, 2010).

The third reason why the informal economy may be relevant to translation studies relates to translator education. For instance, in South Africa, most research in translation studies is seemingly done on translation phenomena in the formal economy and, particularly, in literary translation (see, for example, Inggs & Meintjies, 2009; Kruger, 2012; Steiner, 2009). Searches on Google Scholar Advanced for the work of other well-known South African translation studies scholars such as Anna-Marie Beukes, Iliana Dimitriu, Ilse Feinauer, Alet Kruger, Jan-Louis Kruger, Jackie Naudé, and Marné Pienaar confirm this tendency. What needs to be added to this is a focus on factors of the informal economy. Although one can argue that students find jobs in the formal sector (to a far smaller extent in literary translation), we simply do not know what the situation is concerning the informal economy. This means that, in South Africa, we are educating translators for a particular market while excluding a significant possible part of the market, as I have argued previously. I am not claiming that there is a market for translators in the informal economy. I am merely stating the possibility that there may be one, but this could turn out to be untrue. I wish to criticize the apparent overemphasis on literary translation. It would seem that, given this situation, the reality of living in Africa has not occurred to the largely white research community of translation scholars in South Africa. What is more, by educating our growing numbers of black students in this Westernized tradition of translation, we (the translation scholars) are translating Africa into a Western colony for our students.

5. TRANSLATION IN THE INFORMAL ECONOMY IN SOUTH AFRICA

In this section, I present some empirical data on translation in the informal economy in South Africa. First, I briefly present the findings of three studies done by students of mine. To this I add data from my own fieldwork.

I would firstly like to refer to a study done by Makhado (2010) on the circumstances under which Tshivenda freelance translators work. Venda was one of the former homelands in apartheid South Africa, located in the northern part of the current Limpopo province and largely rural. In Makhado's study, he provided questionnaires to 31 translators who attended a local translation convention and then interviewed four translators on their practices. Of the 31 translators who received questionnaires, 11 returned completed questionnaires. The findings indicated a typical informal industry. Seven of the 11 respondents indicated that they do not have computers and that they do their translations by hand. They would then request friends or family members with the required technology to type the translations for them (Makhado, 2010, p. 57). Some translators also reported having to travel great distances to centers where they could fax or e-mail translations as they did not have the necessary technology (Makhado, 2010, p. 58). Travelling obviously has an adverse influence on their profit because public transport is quite expensive in South Africa. This practice shows the expected lack of financial and technological capital and the concomitant high levels of social capital which help translators to fulfill their tasks. The lack of technological skill was confirmed by the fact that only three respondents were aware of computer-assisted translation. Not all of the respondents had offices, and they indicated that this lack was detrimental to their work performance. In general, translators also indicated that they did not have electronic editing technology such as spell checkers. They banked on their social capital, once again, to solve this problem by asking fellow translators to edit their work and by making use of available language experts such as teachers to assist them (Makhado, 2010, p. 59).

As far as networking is concerned, some of the translators indicated that they had never previously attended a translators' conference (Makhado, 2010, p. 61) and that they compensated for this lack by their own personal networks with language experts. Some of the respondents had networks with other translators and some did not, indicating, once again, that they formed networks more locally (Makhado, 2010, p. 63). One of the interviewees indicated another problem, that is, that he or she cannot connect easily to other translators because of the cost of telephone calls. It seems clear that the lack of technology has an impact on the kind of networks to which these translators have access. What the impact on the quality of their work is remains to be studied (Makhado, 2010, p. 63).

In addition, Makhado then interviewed four translators on their working conditions, asking open-ended questions. He started with a question concerning the challenges they experienced. The lack of technical terms and/or the standardization of terms in Tshivenda was a common challenge to all translators (Makhado, 2010, p. 64), indicating that terminology training should be prioritized in contexts in which translators from "less-developed" languages are educated. Respondents also indicated that the dictionaries they had were not up to date with the most recent terms. Also, it seems from one response that the dictionaries in current use do not capture all the semantic fields of words (Makhado, 2010, p. 67).

A second study with some relevant data on translation in the informal economy is that of Motsie (2010) who interviewed the authors of informal advertisements on aspects of translation. These kinds of advertisements are created by self-employed handymen such as painters, builders, and thatchers. The advertisements, typically made from castaway cartons and painted with the finger, are put up on electricity poles at busy intersections in the city, advertising the skill of the handyman. Motsie interviewed 10 of these handymen on various socioeconomic matters relating to translation. She also interviewed a hairdresser, a car-wash owner, a businessperson, and the owner of a day-care center, all of whom had advertised in this informal way. What should be made clear is that all of these respondents are Sesotho or Setswana speaking (as first language) and that their advertisements are in English and/or Afrikaans, which would be their second, third, or fourth languages. It is also clear from their advertisements that they use especially Afrikaans, as most of their potential employers would be Afrikaans. Furthermore, the language they use is of a poor quality, reflecting the Sesotho syntax and being a mixture of English and Afrikaans.

Because it is not always possible to obtain reliable information on income, Motsie (2010, pp. 29–39) decided to categorize her respondents according to the Living Standards Measurement (LSM; n.d.), a scale adapted to South African conditions measuring a wide variety of material features of a household to determine living standards. Whereas 6 of her 10 respondents were categorized as LSM 1, which is the lowest category, 4 were categorized as LSM 5, which is relatively high (LSM 12 is the highest). All her respondents had some education, with Grade 6 being the lowest. Some of them had college qualifications, which in South Africa is between high school and university level. They earned anything from a R1000 to R5000 per month ($120-$600) (Motsie, 2010, pp. 80–88), and all were interested in more professional and professionally translated advertisements. They indicated their willingness to pay between R50 and R100 ($6 and $12) for such advertisements.

Motsie's findings lead to various conclusions. It indicates that language and particularly translation matter in the informal economy. Although the forms that translation action and the expectations concerning translation may take will differ, these are still cases of translation action that need to be studied to come to a fuller understanding of translation as a global phenomenon. Surprisingly, it also indicates that quality is not the only factor that causes a translation to be successful. In fact, word on the street is that the worse the advertisement looks, the better their chances of getting work, because the potential employers will see them as "lowly educated", believing they can obtain cheap labor. This matter of quality of language and of how it relates to economic activities warrants further study.

Motsie's study also confirms that the informal economy is not limited to the extremely poor as some of her respondents fell in LSM 5.

Furthermore, Motsie's (2010, pp. 80–88) study indicates that there may be a market for informal language practitioners who have skills levels that are not very high and who will be willing to work at relatively low rates. I am well aware, and I have been attacked for this position, that it seems I am suggesting a lowering of standards and the de-professionalization of translation. On the contrary, what I am suggesting is that developing contexts keep their high-level, professional translation practitioners for the formal, professional side of their economy. My suggestion entails that informal language practitioners with lower skills should be provided to work in the informal economy. In the South African context, they can be equipped with a one- or two-year diploma after school, which can be attained at Further Education and Training (FET) colleges. In this regard, another student of mine has done some basic work on the nature of a curriculum for such training (Erasmus, 2011). This could mean that jobs will be created and that translation will become affordable at the level where it is also needed. Providing professional services at professional rates in an informal situation where informal rates are required will not aid the development of a language-practice industry in developing contexts.

Kraay's (2011) study reports on an informal development project (Swart & Venter, 2001, pp. 487–489) in which she was involved and in which she studied the use or nonuse of translation. Her study relates to two informal groups who came together for development goals. In her first case study, the group of youths indicated that they did not need translation and did not use translation. However, her findings indicated that they were translating all the time or, that as they pointed out, they would use some kind of township vernacular (Kraay, 2011, p. 105). Because they were all able to speak multiple languages, they would interpret informally if a particular member could not understand a particular language. This once again points to the prevalence of social capital, of strong bonds among people, and of the taking of responsibility for one another that plays a role in solving the problem. I know that these kinds of findings also lie in the terrain of sociolinguistics. My point is not to claim that translation theory can explain all of it. My point is that, if one defines translation as intersystemic semiotic interaction of any kind and in any mode, the kind of phenomena described by Kraay should be included in the purview of translation studies.

In her second case study, the members of an ABET (Adult Basic Education and Training) class provided examples of both interlinguistic and inter-semiotic translation. Members would help one another verbally to understand what was said in class as the classes were partly in English, but they would also read their textbooks and then explain to one another because some were more literate than were others. These data can be used to question, together with Tymoczko (2006), the assumption that translation is always a written exercise performed by a single professional in an office situation. Within the informal economy, it seems that there are many more practices of a translational nature than have been studied up to now.

To these studies, I have added a small empirical study of my own which should be read as a case study. From the literature, I took the claim that people in the informal economy are linked to the formal economy and that the two economies are to be viewed as connected by a network. My interest lay in finding out what role translation plays in the creation of these kinds of networks. For this data, I conducted 40 open-ended interviews with self-employed people in the informal economy within the Mangaung Metropolitan Municipality of South Africa's Free State province. Of the interviews conducted, 20 were with street peddlers in the city center, that is, people trading or offering services in temporary stands or on the sidewalks. The other 20 interviews were conducted in the traditionally black and brown/colored[1] part of the city among the owners of "spaza shops" (informal shops in residential areas) and various other informal enterprises (selling motor parts, washing cars, selling tires, doing welding). As I conducted the research with the aim of understanding peoples' networks and the role that translation plays in maintaining these networks, and not with the aim of drawing statistically significant conclusions, my discussion of the findings focus on the nonstatistical data. In other words, I have focused on the unique practices against the background of the more general trends, trying to render the complexity of practices that I have experienced visible.

The first relevant point is that only 2 of the 20 respondents from the street-peddling group indicated that they spoke only one language (Sesotho). The interpreter who accompanied me confirmed afterward that their accent indicated that these two respondents were from Lesotho, and they themselves indicated that they had only six years of primary school education each. One sold maize cobs that she bought raw and cooked herself before selling them. When asked how she would deal with customers who did not speak Sesotho, she indicated that they would solve the problem by gesturing. I suggest that this kind of translation, through bodily "gestes" (Jousse, 2000), should be further investigated, especially in cases of what is called "survivalist" activities in the informal economy. It may be that much more human interaction takes place at the level of gestes than what translation studies scholars are willing to admit. And, one could ask, are gestes translated, or are they supra-linguistic or even supra-semiotic?

Of the other 18 respondents, 5 spoke at least two languages, four spoke three languages, 4 spoke four languages, 2 spoke five languages, 2 spoke six languages, and 1 spoke seven languages. What became clear from the interviews is that the indication that someone speaks or does not speak a particular language is very relative, in two ways. In one instance, a respondent indicated that he was not able to speak Sesotho (the majority language in the area), but when a client approached him and asked in Sesotho to use one of the phones he had to rent, he understood perfectly well. Similarly, some respondents indicated that were able to speak a language, but it was clear either from their own indications or the context, that this was a barely functional ability. One Zimbabwean respondent indicated that he had even learned Afrikaans because many Afrikaans people insisted on speaking their home language. The examples he cited to prove his proficiency were "Goeie more" (Good morning) and "Hoe gaan dit?" (How are you?), which are fine for creating a connection with a possible client but cannot be construed as "speaking the language". It seems to me that these informal traders or service providers work within a limited context, in which limited translation skills help them get by. If our Zimbabwean respondent, who by the way had a university degree, would have to write a paper on small business in Afrikaans, he would not be able to do it. In other words, the particular set of circumstances under which one works plays a role in the translation strategies you need to employ in order to cope. Those strategies in an informal economic situation would differ from strategies in a formal economic setting. I return to the nature of a fixed locality later.

What became clear is that the type of language that someone speaks determines the nature of their network with suppliers and clients. Respondents from West Africa who could speak French had a supply network in Mauritius, and they maintained links via cell phone. Other respondents from foreign countries sourced most of their stock from Johannesburg, serviced in English, and a Ghanaian respondent had his own Ghanaian supply network that is serviced in a Ghanaian local language (Chi). Local respondents who could speak English sourced most of their stock locally, as large sections of the rest of the world would be out of their reach, linguistically. Those who could only speak Sesotho were even more limited as they could only provide merchandise that was available from Sesotho-speaking suppliers.

As far as written languages are concerned, 2 respondents could write only one language, 13 could write two, 1 could write three, and 1 respondent could write four languages. Once again, the question did not test the quality of written abilities because I was interested in the respondents' views on how their oral and written language abilities influenced their business. In one sense, the quality of writing abilities is irrelevant as it became clear from the questions on communication that written communication features very low on the agenda, if at all, which is one of the features of the informal economy. Very few respondents indicated that they ever used written communication with their clients, and if they did, it would always be in English. Large numbers of people thus get by without written translations and even do effective business without it, but they do have strategies to cope with linguistic differences.

The data seem to indicate that respondents use their full linguistic ability when speaking to their clients. Being in the Free State province where Sesotho is the most-used language, most respondents spoke Sesotho to their clients, with many indicating that they also spoke English, isiXhosa, IsiZulu, Setswana, and Afrikaans with their clients. They very seldom use SMSs, which would represent a hybrid case of oral and written communication, to contact clients, and if they did, it would be in English.

In contrast to their communication with clients, communication with suppliers, that is, the formal sector, would be mostly in English. The exceptions would be respondents who bought locally; for example, a lady who supplied lunches indicated that she bought from the butchery on the corner of the street. Also, respondents who sold fresh produce such as fruit indicated that they bought from the fresh-produce market. In these very local cases, they may get by with Sesotho only. It is clear that the informal sector is significantly oral in nature. The few respondents who indicated that they completed written documents with their suppliers did so in English. Furthermore, most of them did not use SMSs because their dealings were so local or specific (e.g., buying fruit) that they preferred personal contact with suppliers. Only three respondents indicated that they sometimes did use SMSs, with two of them using English only.

The communication that takes place with the government sector is overwhelmingly in English. Here respondents indicated that, if they had problems with writing or with writing in English, they would request help, for example, from family members or an official. Mostly, however, the respondents indicated that they did not communicate with government, some of them quite ruefully.

The same tendency that I reported in Chapter 5 is evident here. Downstream, respondents communicated multilingually. Upstream, the communication becomes more monolingual the higher one goes. Thus, suppliers are contacted mostly in English whereas government is always contacted in English, especially in cases of written texts. The economy thus seems to show a particular linguistic pattern. The more formal, the more monolinguistic; the more informal, the more multilinguistic. In South Africa, this means that one has to translate, unless you were born in English. If you are not English speaking, you have to translate when you speak to government officials. You also have to translate between oral and written media. Similarly, whichever language you speak, if you want to do business in the informal sector, you have to be able to translate, mostly orally, but sometimes also between oral and written communication. The findings will also mean, and this has to be tested, that the ability to translate is a factor in upward mobility in business. A purely monolingual African language speaker in South Africa will experience difficulty succeeding in the informal economy and in getting out of the informal economy into the formal economy. Actually, in South Africa, it seems that English speakers are the only language group able to function successfully in both the formal and informal economy in their home language only.

Findings from the 20 interviews conducted in the townships confirm the basic trend, that is, that one of the requirements for doing business in the informal sector in South Africa is the ability to use more than one language. Furthermore, speaking to clients generally includes translation as not all of the clients speak the same language as the owner. Furthermore, speaking to government officials does not take place either, which is typical of the informal economy, or it takes place overwhelmingly in English (i.e., citizens have to translate in order to talk to government, not the other way round).

A number of significant exceptions to this trend were found. The first relates to a Bangladeshi businessman with a small shop from his home, where he sells groceries. He indicated that he spoke only Bangla, and his English was so bad that we could not continue the interview with him. He has a Malawian assistant who is able to speak Chichewa and English and who has learned a smattering of Sesotho with which to communicate with local customers. Thus, this pair, both foreigners to South Africa, has combined forces around language so that the one conducts the management and the other handles the relationship with customers. When asked how the Bangladeshi conducted the buying of stock from suppliers, he explained via his assistant that he bought from other Bangladeshis. Thus, the availability of a network in his language made the setting up of his little business possible. This seems to be an example of a strategic alliance at the level of social capital, in the link to both suppliers and assistant, to enhance the working of financial capital.

At another little shop in a shipping container, selling sweets, cold drinks, and milk, the owner indicated that she only spoke Sesotho to her suppliers. When we were already back in our car, I told the interpreter that I was wondering where she had found a Sesotho-speaking supplier of milk. The interpreter offered to go and find out and came back with some very interesting news. She obtained her milk from someone who was connected to an Afrikaans-speaking farmer as a middleman. As a middleman, he was responsible for distributing milk to many such small businesses in the township, because he knew his way around and—importantly—he could speak Sesotho. Thus, the interpreter/translator made it possible for the farmer to do business in Afrikaans and for the survivalist partaker in the informal economy to do business in Sesotho by rendering a translation service—free of charge. This example makes it clear that translation actions take many forms, that is, some take an oral form and some a written form; some are done by the person him- or herself and for some, the person needs a mediator; some mediators are professional and some are lay mediators. Also, the translation action and the business action are not separated. The one feeds into the other, and one does not find the professional model of specialization.

The last relevant observation is that some of the foreigners in the informal economy in the area I studied, from Bangladesh, Ethiopia, Ghana, Lesotho, Malawi, Pakistan, Senegal, Swaziland, and Zimbabwe, are so limited in their language abilities that the minimum or sometimes even no speaking is involved in their transactions. Because they sell simple merchandise such as fruit or food, customers often only say the brand name of what they want, put down some money and then receive change and the product. In other cases, customers will literally just point to what they want, hand over the money, and receive change and the product. This led me to thinking about a physical/material and semiotic substratum to trade that makes language not unnecessary but also not an absolute requirement (Latour, 2007). What I would like to suggest is that business has a nonlinguistic semiotic or symbolic or material substructure that means that, to a degree, it can take place without language. This is similar to international sporting events where two teams speaking mutually unintelligible languages play soccer, or any other sport, against one another or run a 100-meter sprint against one another, without having to communicate linguistically to make it possible. Similarly, when someone pitches up at your stall or spaza shop, the symbolic code and the material conditions underlying the interaction are that of buying and selling. In other words, the material world of things has already been translated into a semiotically meaningful world of trade, which is a known space and thus does not require translation at each and every instance. When entering one of these spaza shops, you enter an already translated text of agreed upon human interaction. Thus, for someone to function in an informal economic setup, internal or self-translation or the availability of people with the social capital of internal translation are an advantage, but seemingly not an absolute requirement. The symbolic or semiotic interaction more basic than language and the translated material conditions on which these rest, which determine the rules of buying and selling, seem to be able to help some people to make a living. In fact, it could perhaps be argued, and should definitely be investigated, that at least some part of the worldwide tourism industry operates in this way.

6. CONCLUSION

In my opinion, the data I have presented can be interpreted as being indicative of the need for further interdisciplinary research between translation studies and development studies scholars. There seems to be sufficient grounds for consider the role of translation as a significant factor in the creation and maintenance of links between the informal and the formal sectors of the economy, at least in South Africa.

I am not able to draw forceful conclusions at the end of this chapter, nor would that have been my aim in the first place. Instead, my aim has been to open up the notion of the informal economy and its development to translation studies scholars. Concomitantly, I have proposed the notion of translation to scholars in development studies and development economics as yet another factor pertaining to the informal economy and its development. I hope, at least, to have convinced both sets of readers of the relevance of the informal economy and translation for the both of them. Other than that, we need much more data to try to account for the role of translation in the creation of networks in the informal economy and its relationship to the formal economy.

The data that I have presented seem to confirm Latour's (1987, 2000, 2007) idea of a sociology of translation. By means of translation, that is, the turning into semiotic phenomena of non-semiotic phenomena, a social world is created, and human beings are able to function in this world because they know the semiotics, though not its particular language.

The informal economy may be quite invisible to most translation studies scholars, but invisibility, as Venuti (1995) has argued, does not imply nonexistence.

Conclusion
Developing Translation, Translating Development

1. PRESENT

I have arrived at the end. The end, not of thinking, or of the problems confronting developing contexts or translation studies, but the end that writing brings to the writer. Furthermore, it is not an end to the complexities of reality, but an end, for now, to my efforts at thinking and talking about these complexities in a scholarly way. What remains to be done is summarizing and looking ahead.

I started by arguing that a philosophy of complexity or a complexity theory approach may enrich the conceptualization of translation and translation studies. The focus of the complexity approach on non-reductionism, nonlinearity, and open systems is, to my mind, its biggest contribution. I do not claim that I have thought through all of its implications for translation studies. In fact, I think I have just scratched the surface. Much more work is needed on the implications of a complexity conceptualization in the humanities in general and in semiotics in particular.

I then considered the notion of emergence as a way of thinking about reality without succumbing to reductionism. I argued that, if Searle (1995; 1998; 2010) is correct in claiming a linguistic substructure for the emergence of social reality, one could expand his ideas concerning language to include it in semiotics (to my mind, the larger category). Semiotics, being a more general category of making meaning of material and social reality, conceptualized as an inter-system between other systems provides the conceptual framework for thinking about the translational activities out of which social reality emerges.

In the third chapter, I engaged with current views on the definition or conceptualization of translation, arguing that it is biased toward a postmodern epistemology that causes these conceptualizations to be biased toward change, particularity, unknowability, the finite, the plural, and the contingent. I tried to counterbalance this with a complexity epistemology, which holds both change and stability, particularity and universality, unknowability and knowability, the finite and the infinite, the plural and the singular, and the contingent and the necessary in conceptual paradox. By combining the seminal insights of Searle with complex adaptive systems theory and semiotics, I suggested that the term translation could be used to refer to all inter-systemic interaction, irrespective of the particular system or subsystem. Semiotic inter-systemic interaction is then one instance of the larger category and can itself be a superordinate category with smaller subcategories such as interlingual translation. I tried to overcome stable definitions of systems by criticizing Jakobson's inter- and intra-linguistic and inter-semiotic distinctions, claiming that one can only distinguish between intra- and inter-systemic interaction depending on whether you regard two systems as equal or whether you regard one of the systems as a subsystem of the other.

In Chapter 4, I provided an overview of development theory, claiming that the movement towards human-centered development entails an understanding that development is, among other things, a hermeneutic endeavor, which cannot be understood without recourse to inter-systemic semiotic interaction among people.

Chapter 5 provided some data on the translation, or, non-translation, of local development policy documents in the Free State province of South Africa. I found that, as long as the documents are in written form, non-translation is the norm. However, once these documents are communicated or needed in oral form, translation is required. In particular, I found that members of communities take responsibility for each other's understanding of these texts, giving rise to a form I coined communal translation.

In Chapter 6, I argued that when one consider the economy as a knowledge economy, linked by various hubs of knowledge, translation (conceptualized as inter-systemic semiotic interaction) plays a major role in knowledge production, knowledge transfer, and knowledge consumption. I provided empirical data to argue that various translational activities link the various facets of the knowledge economy to one another.

In Chapter 7, I provided an overview of the informal economy, arguing that it makes up such a significant part of the world economy that translation studies scholars can no longer ignore it. I provided empirical data that I used to argue that, without some form of translation, very few people could partake even in the informal economy of South Africa. The main thrust of this chapter was to argue for a much larger interest in the informal economy by translation studies scholars. I also argued that social spaces are already translated spaces in the sense that they have been imbued with meaning based on the social interaction which is invoked. These interactions can take place without the intermediate action of language.

Thus, I have tried to develop the notion of translation, to expand the borders of the field of study, to contribute to its philosophical foundation, and to redirect the focus of translation studies scholars to features of development contexts that have largely been neglected up to now. Simultaneously, I have tried to translate development, to conceptualize the inter-systemic semiotic substrata underlying development and to challenge development scholars concerning their thinking about the inter-systemic semiotic substructure underlying and contributing to the development phenomena they are studying.

2. FUTURE

The implication of the thoughts presented in this book is a rethinking of translation studies as such, a project in which I am not alone—as I have pointed out in Chapters 4 and 5. I hope that translation studies will be freed from the linguistic and literary bias that limits its focus. I am not arguing for a severing of the links with language and literature altogether. Instead, I am arguing that we should add more links. I am suggesting that we should think about translation from a complexity of perspectives that will allow us to see a much larger complexity of phenomenon to study. As my good friend Sergey Tyulenev has reminded me time and again in personal discussion, we should remember that the word *translation* merely means "carrying over" and that the scholars who are studying the linguistic and literary carryings over may not be allowed to hijack the word. There are many more carryings over to be studied.

In the empirical work I have presented, I studied local and small-scale processes, imitating the very ant of Latour. I believe that translation studies should trace the painstaking tying of knots and forging of connections that construct the social until we are able to see the big picture rather than starting with the big picture.

I also think that translation studies scholars need to delve much deeper into the philosophical and epistemological assumptions underlying their work. I am quite aware, and have been told so to my face, that philosophy and theory are, at least in some circles, outmoded ways of going about scholarly endeavors. I am not convinced about these arguments, mainly because the more one talks about situated or contextualized knowledge, the more important it becomes to put your own—often unrecognized—philosophical and theoretical assumptions on the table. The waves of postmodern thought that we have experienced over the last few decades have taught us valuable lessons, but it has not severed the links in our thinking to what has gone before. Therefore, whether we realize and acknowledge it or not, we have philosophies and theories that influence our thought. I choose to be up front about this matter.

I also think that translation studies scholars need to cooperate much more with scholars from other disciplines to understand how translation relates to its subsystems and how it is a subsystem in itself and relates to larger systems. Perhaps, looking at it from the perspective of inter-systemic interaction, translation studies could become a real interdiscipline or transdiscipline drawing all other disciplines together, from mathematics and physics to philosophy and religion through its interest in the very nature of inter-systemicness or inter-systemic interaction. We do, however, need to work out the implications and problems surrounding such a suggestion.

I hope that the thoughts contained in this book will exercise an impact in developing contexts, and particularly in Africa. I hope that it will provide translation studies scholars with enough of an agenda and a conceptual framework to be able to study translation phenomenon in their contexts and on its own terms. For instance, translation studies scholars in developing contexts need not lament or make excuses for illiteracy or semiliteracy in their contexts. Rather, they could study the particular forms of intersystemic semiotic interaction that are prevalent in their contexts. In this way, literacy as a norm of Western values can stop being an impediment in translation studies and become part of the focus of translation studies in developing contexts.

Furthermore, I hope that this book will contribute to challenging translation studies scholars in Africa to make two moves. The one is for them to consistently question the Western bias in their theorizing of their data, in this contributing toward an African agenda for translation studies against the background of the postcolonial project in Africa. The other is for them to consistently question their focus on literary texts and the formal economy as the only or dominant focus for them and their students. I am not claiming that translation studies scholars in Africa should develop an insular agenda or focus solely on the informal economy. It should be an assumed fact that Africa is a hybrid context. What I argue for is that translation studies in Africa should reflect this hybridity in all its complexity.

I dream of a day that it will be possible to conceptualize translation in categories of African thought. Is it true that African thinkers have contributed nothing to world thinking? If Chinese or Indian scholars could find conceptual spaces or frameworks in their traditions and have enriched translation, why not Africans? If one thinks of South American translation studies scholars who have contributed the notion of cannibalism, do African translation studies scholars really have nothing to contribute? I challenge my African colleagues to join me in the quest to understand the complexity of Africa in dialogue with others from all over the world. I suggest we start reading African philosophers, sociologists, literary scholars, political scientists, anthropologists, physicists, chemists, and so on in order better to understand the context in which we work and the possible contribution of our intellectual tradition. I also hope that translation studies will not be a late or new colonizer of the African mind.

3. PAST

As Latour says, I have laid the connections, made the links, tied up the arguments to black boxes, and woven the web. The proverbial baby has been delivered, and the umbilical cord has been cut. It has to live its own life now—and what would become of it is impossible to predict. And as its proverbial parent, I cannot but let it go, knowing pretty well its deficiencies and the weakness of some of the knots that I have tied. Thankfully, I am simultaneously blissfully unaware of some of the larger problems concerning the tying of knots and will only become aware of them when someone deems it worthwhile to start questioning the baby.

I started out by calling this project a quest, a search for identity, perhaps healing, or understanding. Did I attain this goal? I do not know. But the road to identity has proved to have many more turnoffs than I initially imagined, and it acquired a few more as I went along. Healing, even self-forgiveness, have turned out to be elusive, or part of a process into which I have little insight. The process of understanding has proven to be like driving through the mist—one moment it is clear, the next moment you cannot see anything, and most of the time, it is more or less hazy. As many other Africans, I stand amazed at the complexity of "the African psyche", capable of magnanimous conduct as seen in that of Nelson Mandela as well as the most abhorrent conduct such as the neighbors who cut down the macadamia trees of small farmers in Kenya (Maathai, 2009, pp. 150–154).

I both hope and despair for Africa. I laugh and cry for Africa. I am rich and poor living in Africa.

For now, the contract has been signed, the sabbatical report is submitted and the wheels of production are rolling. Ready or not, here it comes!

That is the way it is.

Notes

NOTE TO THE INTRODUCTION

1. From the complexity stance that I take in this book, I view space as both physical or material space and social (constructed) space.

NOTE TO CHAPTER 1

1. I am aware of the fact that the term *Old Testament* is contested. I have merely followed Brueggemann's use.

NOTE TO CHAPTER 2

1. I use the term *language* here not as a logical system but in a pragmatic, performative sense as Searle did.

NOTE TO CHAPTER 3

1. Comment on one of my articles by an anonymous peer reviewer.

NOTE TO CHAPTER 5

1. I acknowledge Monwabisi Ralarala, one of my PhD students, for coining this term.

NOTE TO CHAPTER 7

1. In the South African context, due to the legacy of apartheid, people of mixed descent are mostly referred to as colored or brown, not as black. A debate is raging about this matter, and I am not able to choose a preferred designation in this regard.

References

Adam, P. & Foray, D., 2001. An introduction to the economy of the knowledge society. Maastricht: MERIT.
Agassi, J., 2007. The chancing features of the body-mind problem. *Journal of Physiology*, 101, pp. 153–160.
Agenda 21, n.d. *Division for Sustainable Development, United Nations Department of Social and Economic Affairs*. Available at: http:www.un.org/esa/dsd/agenda21/index.shtml. [Accessed 14 May 2012]
Akrich, M., Callon, M., & Latour, B., 2002a. The key to success in innovation. Part I: The art of interessement. *International Journal of Innovation Management*, 6(2), pp. 187–206.
———, 2002b. The key to success in innovation, Part II: The art of choosing good spokespersons. *Journal of Innovation Management*, 6(2), pp. 207–225.
Andrews, E., 2005. The role of semiotics in the study of language, linguistics and communication: An overview. *Glossos. The Slavic and East European Language Research Centre*.
Arduini, S. & Nergaard, S., 2011. Translation: A new paradigm. *Translation* 1 (Inaugural issue), pp. 8–15.
Atkinson, P., Delamont, S. & Housley, W., 2008. *Contours of culture: Complex ethnography and the ethnography of complexity*. New York: AltaMira.
Axelrod, R., 1984. *The evolution of cooperation*. Rev. ed. New York: Basic Books.
Bak, P., 1996. *How nature works: The science of self-organised criticality*. New York: Copernicus.
Baker, M., 1996. Corpus-based translation studies: The challenges that lie ahead. In: H. Somers, ed. *Terminology, LSP and translation: Studies in language engineering in honour of Juan C. Sager*. Amsterdam: John Benjamins, pp. 175–186.
———, 2006. *Translation and conflict. A narrative account*. New York: Routledge.
———, ed., 2010. *Critical readings in translation studies*. New York: Routledge.
Bakhtin, M.M., 1982. The dialogic imagination: Four essays. Austin: University of Texas Press.
Bandia, P., 2008. *Translation as reparation: Writing and translation in postcolonial Africa*. Manchester: St Jerome.
Barnett, R., 2003. *Beyond all reason: Living with ideology in the university*. Buckingham: Society for Research in Higher Education and Open University Press.
Basamalah, S., 2007. Translation rights and the philosophy of translation. Remembering the debts of the original. In: P. St-Pierre & P. Kar, eds. *In translation—Reflections, refractions, transformations*. Amsterdam: Benjamins, pp. 117–132.
Bassnett, S. & Bush, P. eds., 2006. *The translator as writer*. London: Continuum.
Bassnett, S. & Lefevere, A., 1990. *Translation, history and culture*. London: Pinter Publishers.

Bassnett, S. & Trivedi, H. eds., 1990. *Post-colonial translation: Theory and practice*. New York: Routledge.
Beinhocker, E.D., 2010. Evolution as computation: Implications for economic theory and ontology. Draft paper. Santa Fe: Santa Fe Institute. (A later version of this paper was published in 2011 as: Evolution as computation: Integrating self-organization with generalized Darwinism. *Journal of Institutional Economics*, 7(3), pp. 393–423).
Benshalom, Y., 2010. Performing translation. In: J. St. André, ed. *Thinking through translation with metaphors*. Manchester: St Jerome, pp. 17–46.
Bickhard, M., 2009. The interactivist model. *Synthese*, 166, pp. 547–591.
Brett, E., 2009. *Reconstucting development theory*. London: Macmillan Palgrave.
Brinkley, I., 2006. *Defining the knowledge economy. Knowledge economy programme report*. London: The Work Foundation.
Brinkley, I. & Lee, N., 2007. *The knowledge economy in Europe: A report prepared for the 2007 EU Spring Council*. London: The Work Foundation.
Brisset, A., 2005. The search for a native language. Translation and cultural identity. In: L. Venuti, ed. *The translation studies reader*. New York: Routledge, pp. 343–375.
Brueggemann, W., 1997. *Theology of the Old Testament: Testimony, dispute, advocacy*. Minneapolis: Fortress Press.
Bührig, K., House, J. & Ten Thije, J., 2009. Translational action and intercultural communication. In: K. Bührig, J. House & J. Ten Thije, eds. *Translational action and intercultural communication*. Manchester: St Jerome, pp. 1–6.
Callon, M., Lascoumes, P. & Barthe, Y., 2011. *Acting in an uncertain world. An essay on technical democracy*. Cambridge, MA: MIT Press.
Calvert, P., 2005. Changing notions on development: Bringing the state back in. In: J. Haynes, ed. *Palgrave advances in development studies*. London: Palgrave Macmillan, pp. 47–64.
Castells, M., 2000a. *The rise of the network society. The information age: Economy, society and culture*. 2nd ed. Oxford: Blackwell.
———, 2000b. *End of millennium. The information age: Economy, society and culture*. 2nd ed. Oxford: Blackwell.
———, 2004. *The power of identity. The information age: Economy, society and culture*. 2nd ed. Oxford: Blackwell.
Chambers, R., 2007. *Ideas for development*. London: Earthscan.
Chen, M., 2007. Rethinking the informal economy: Linkages with the formal economy and the formal regulatory environment. In: B. Ghua-Khasnobis, R. Kanbur & E. Ostrom, eds. *Linking the formal and informal economy: Concepts and policies*. Oxford: Oxford University Press, pp. 75–92.
Chesterman, A., 1997. *Memes of translation: The spread of ideas in translation theory*. Amsterdam: Benjamins.
———, 2006. Questions in the sociology of translation. In: J. Ferreira Duarte, A. Assis Rosa & T. Seruya, eds. *Translation studies at the interface of disciplines*. Amsterdam: Benjamins, pp. 1–27.
———, 2008. On explanation. In: A. Pym, M. Shlesinger & D. Simeoni, eds. *Beyond descriptive translation studies: Investigations in homage to Gideon Toury*. Amsterdam: Benjamins, pp. 363–379.
Cilliers, P., 1998. *Complexity and postmodernism: Understanding complex systems*. London: Routledge.
———, 2005. Complexity, deconstruction and relativism. *Theory, Culture & Society*, 22(5), pp. 255–267.
Coetzee, J., 2001a. Modernization theory: A model for progress. In: J. Coetzee, J. Graaff, F. Hendricks & G. Wood, eds. *Development: Theory, policy and practice*. Oxford: Oxford University Press, pp. 27–43.

———, 2001b. A micro-foundation for development thinking. In: J. Coetzee, J. Graaff, F. Hendricks & G. Wood, eds. *Development: Theory, policy and practice.* Oxford: Oxford University Press, pp. 119–139.

Coetzee, J., Graaff, J., Hendricks, F. & Wood, G. eds., 2001. *Development: Theory, policy and practice.* Oxford: Oxford University Press.

Cohen, J. & Stewart, I., 1994. *The collapse of chaos: Discovering simplicity in a complex world.* London: Viking.

Collins, 2006. *Collins English dictionary.* Glascow: HarperCollins Publishers.

Cooke, P., 2003. *The regional development agency in the knowledge economy: Boundary crossing for innovation systems.* Prepared for European Regional Science Association Annual Conference—"Peripheries, Centres, and Spatial Development in the New Europe", Jyväskylä, Finland, August 27 to August 30, 2003.

Coveny, P. & Highfield, R., 1995. *Frontiers of complexity. The search for order in a chaotic world.* New York: Fawcett Columbine.

Cronin, M., 2006. *Translation and identity.* London: Routledge.

———, 2007. Double take: Figuring the other and the politics of translation. In: P. St-Pierre & P. Kar, eds. *In translation—Reflections, refractions, transformations.* Amsterdam: Benjamins, pp. 253–262.

Crutchfield, J., 2009. *The dreams of theory.* Santa Fe, NM: Santa Fe Institute.

Dasgupta, P., 2007. Trafficking in words: Languages, missionaries and translators. In: P. St-Pierre & P. Kar, eds. *In translation—Reflections, refractions, transformations.* Amsterdam: Benjamins, pp. 57–72.

Davenport, P., n.d. *Universities and the knowledge economy.* Available at: http://communications.uwo.ca/President_PDFs/Screen_PDFs/IT-CUKE.pdf. [Accessed 25 January 2013]

David, P. & Foray, D., 2001. *An introduction to the economy of the knowledge society.* Unpublished report for the Maastricht Economic Research Institute for Innovation and Technology.

Davids, I., 2007. The global context of development and its effect on South Africa—A macro approach. In: F. Theron, ed. *The development change agent: A micro-level approach to development.* Pretoria: Van Schaik, pp. 23–40.

Davis, M., 2006. Planet of slums: Interview with Mark Davis by Nathan Gardels. *New Perspectives Quarterly,* 23(2), pp. 7–11.

Deguet, J., Demazeau, Y. & Magnin, L., 2006. Elements about the emergence issue: A survey of emergence definitions. *Complexus,* 3, pp. 24–31.

Delvaux, E., n.d. *The challenge of the informal economy.* Geneva: International Labour Organization.

Derrida, J., 1973. "Différance." Speech, phenomena and other essays on Husserl's theory of signs." Trans. D.B. Allison. Evanston: Northwestern University Press, pp. 129–160.

Devey, R., Skinner, C. & Valodia, I., 2006. "Second best? Trends and linkages in the informal economy in South Africa." Draft of paper read at a conference: Accelerated and Shared Growth in South Africa: Determinants, Constraints and Opportunities, 18–20 October 2006. Birchwood Hotel and Conference Centre, Johannesburg, South Africa.

Donaldson, R. & Marais, L., 2012. Small town, geographies. In: R. Donaldson & L. Marais, eds. *Small town geographies in Africa: Experiences from South Africa and elsewhere.* New York: Nova, pp. ix-xviii.

Du Plessis, L.T., 2000. South Africa: From two to eleven official languages. In: K. Deprez & L.T. Du Plessis, eds. *Multilingualism and government: Belgium, Luxembourg, Switzerland, Former Yugoslavia, South Africa.* Pretoria: Van Schaik, pp. 95–110.

Dutt, A. & Ros, J. eds., 2008. *International handbook of development economics.* Cheltenham: Edward Elgar.

References

Eco, U., 2001. *Experiences in translation*. Toronto: University of Toronto Press.
Emmeche, C., 2004. At home in a complex world: Lessons from the frontiers of natural science. In: K. Van Kooten Niekerk & H. Buhl, eds. *The significance of complexity. Approaching a complex world through science, theology and the humanities*. Burlington, VT: Ashgate, pp. 21–46.
Epstein, J. & Axtell, R., 1996. *Growing artificial societies. Social science from the bottom up*. Cambridge, MA: MIT Press.
Erasmus, M., 2011. *Training community interpreters and translators in South Africa: Conceptualising a curriculum*. Bloemfontein, South Africa: University of the Free State.
Even-Zohar, I., 2006. The position of translated literature within the literary polysystem. In: L. Venuti, ed. *The translation studies reader*. 2nd ed. New York: Routledge, pp. 199–204.
Fischer, L., 2009. *The perfect swarm. The science of complexity in everyday life*. New York: Basic books.
Florida, R., 1995. Toward the learning region. *Futures*, 27(5), pp. 527–536.
———, 2005. *Cities and the creative class*. New York: Routledge.
Flynn, P. & Van Doorslaer, L., 2011. On constructing continental views on translation studies: An introduction. *Translation and Interpreting Studies*, 6(2), pp. 113–120.
Francescotti, R., 2007. Emergence. *Erkenntnis*, 67, pp. 47–63.
Free State's Regional Steering Committee, 2010. *Free State Self-evaluation report: OECD Reviews of Higher Education in Regional and City Development*. Paris: OECD.
Freund, B., 2010. Development dilemmas in post-apartheid South Africa: An introduction. In: B. Freund & H. Witt, eds. *Development Dilemmas in Post-Apartheid South Africa*. Durban: UKZN Press, pp. 1–31.
Gaffney's Local Government, 2009. *Gaffney's local government in South Africa*. Johannesburg: Gaffney Group.
Gambier, Y. & Van Doorslaer, L. eds., 2009. *The metalanguage of translation*. Amsterdam: Benjamins.
Gentzler, E., 2008. *Translation and identity in the Americas. New directions in translation theory*. London: Routledge.
Ghandi Kingdon, G. & Knight, J., 2003. Unemployment in South Africa: The nature of the beast. *World Development*, 32(3), pp. 391–408.
Giddens, A., 1984. *The constitution of society: Outline of the theory of stucturation*. Berkeley: University of California Press.
Gillespie, A., 2001. *The illusion of progress. Unsustainable development in international law and policy*. London: Earthscan.
Goudzwaard, B. & De Lange, H., 1995. *Beyond poverty and affluence: Toward an economy of care*. Grand Rapids, MI: Eerdmas.
Graaff, J., 2001. Theorizing development. In: J. Coetzee, J. Graaff, F. Hendricks & G. Wood, eds. *Development: Theory, policy and practice*. Oxford: Oxford University Press, pp. 5–9.
Graves, M., 2009. The emergence of transcendental norms in human systems. *Zygon*, 44(3), pp. 501–531.
Griffin, D., 2002. *The emergence of leadership. Linking self-organization and ethics*. London: Routledge.
Griffin, D. & Stacey, R. eds., 2005a. *Complexity and the experience of leading organizations*. London: Routledge.
———, 2005b. Introduction: Leading in a complex world. In: D. Griffin & R. Stacey, ed. *Complexity and the experience of leading organisations*. London: Routledge, pp. 1–16.

References

Guldin, R., 2010. Metaphor as a metaphor for translation. In: J. St. André, ed. *Thinking through translation with metaphors*. Manchester: St. Jerome, pp. 161–191.
Gutt, E., 2000. *Translation and relevance: Cognition and context*. Manchester: St. Jerome.
Halverson, S., 2004. Assumed translation: Reconciling Komissarov and Toury and moving a step forward. *Target,* 16(2), pp. 341–354.
———, 2008. Translations as institutional facts: An ontology for "assumed translation". In: A. Pym, M. Schlesinger & D. Simeoni, eds. *Beyond descriptive translation studies: Investigations in homage of Gideon Toury*. Amsterdam: Benjamins, pp. 343–362.
Handelman, H., 2005. Ethnicity and ethnic conflict. In: J. Haynes, ed. *Palgrave advances in development studies*. London: Palgrave Macmillan, pp. 160–180.
Hart, K., 1972. Informal income opportunities and urban employment in Ghana. *Journal of Modern African Studies,* 11(1), pp. 61–180.
Hassink, R., 2005. How to unlock regional economies from path dependency? From learning region to learning cluster. *European Planning Studies,* 13(4), pp. 521–535.
Hatim, B., 1997. *The translator as communicator*. London: Routledge.
Hatim, B. & Mason, I., 1990. *Discourse and the translator*. London: Longman.
Hauser, C., Tappeiner, G. & Walde, J., 2007. The learning region: The impact of social capital and weak ties on innovation. *Regional Studies,* 41(1), pp. 75–88.
Hayami, Y. & Godo, Y., 2005. *Development economics: From the poverty to the wealth of nations*. 3rd ed. Oxford: Oxford University Press.
Haynes, J., 2005. Religion and development. In: J. Haynes, ed. *Palgrave advances in development studies*. London: Palgrave Macmillan, pp. 138–159.
———, 2008. *Development studies*. Cambridge: Polity.
Heard, D., 2006. A new problem for ontological emergence. *The Philosophical Quarterly,* 56(2), pp. 55–62.
Heilbron, J., 2010. Towards a sociology of translation: Book translations as a cultural world system. In: M. Baker, ed. *Critical readings in translation studies*. London: Routledge, pp. 304–316.
Heniuk, V., 2010. Squeezing the jellyfish: Early Western attempts to characterize translation from Japanese. In: S. André, ed. *Thinking through translation with metaphors*. Manchester: St. Jerome, pp. 144–160.
Hermans, T., 1999. *Systems in translation: Systemic and descriptive approaches explained*. Manchester: St. Jerome.
———, 2007. *The conference of the tongues*. Manchester: St. Jerome.
Hettne, B., 2005. Discourses on development. In: J. Haynes, ed. *Palgrave advances in development studies*. London: Palgrave Macmillan, pp. 26–46.
Heylighen, F., Cilliers, P. & Gesheson, C., 2007. Complexity and philosophy. In: J. Bogg & R. Geyer, eds. *Complexity, Science and Society*. Oxford: Radcliffe Publishing, pp. 117–134.
Hofstadter, D., 1979. *Gödel, Escher, Bach: An eternal golden braid. A metaphorical fugue on minds and machines in the spirit of Lewis Carroll*. London: Penguin Books.
Holland, J., 1995. *Hidden order. How adaptation builds complexity*. New York: Basic Books.
———, 1998. *Emergence. From chaos to order*. Reading: Helix Books.
Holmes, J., 2002. The name and nature of translation studies. In: L. Venuti, ed. *The translation studies reader*. 2nd ed. London: Routledge.
Hoogendoorn, G. & Nel, E., 2012. Exploring small town development dynamics in rural South Africa's post-productivist landscapes. In: R. Donaldson & L. Marais, eds. *Small town geographies in Africa: Experiences from South Africa and elsewhere*. New York: Nova, pp. 21–34.

Houghton, J. & Sheehan, P., 2000. *A primer on the knowledge economy. CSES Working Paper No. 18*. Melbourne: Victoria University of Technology.
House, J., 1997. *Translation quality assessment: A model revisited*. Tübingen: Gunter Narr.
Hudson, R., 1999. The learning economy, the learning firms and the learning region: A sympathetic critique of the limits of learning. *European Urban and Regional Studies*, 6(1), pp. 59–72.
Ibourk, A., 2012. *Contribution of labour market policies and institutions to employment, equal opportunities and the formalisation of the informal economy: Morocco*. Geneva: International Labour Organization.
IDP-Gariep, 2002. *Gariep Municipality: Integrated development plan*. Unpublished municipal report.
IDP-Kopanong, 2003. *Kopanong Municipality: Reviewed integrated development plan 2003–2006*. Unpublished municipal report.
IDP-Pixley Ka Seme, 2010. *Pixley Ka Seme district Municipality: Summary of the integrated development plan (IDP) for 2010/2011 financial year*. Unpublished municipal report.
IDP-Ukhahlamba, 2004. *Ukahlamba District Municipality: Integrated development plan review 2004/2005*. Unpublished municipal report.
IDP-Umsobomvu, 2010. *Umsobomvy Local Municipality: Integrated development plan 2010/2011* Unpublished municipal report.
IDP-!Xhariep, 2012. *Xhariep District Municipality: IDP and budget process plan for 2012/2013*. Unpublished municipal report.
IISD, 2012. *International Institute for Sustainable Development*. Available at: http://www.iisd.org/sd/. [Accessed 11 January 2013]
ILO, 1972. *Incomes, employment and equality in Kenya*, Geneva: International Labour Organization.
———, 2007. *Success Africa: Partnership for decent work—improving people's lives*, Geneva: International Labour Organization.
———, 2009. *The informal economy in Africa: Promoting transition to formality: Challenges and strategies*, Geneva: International Labour Organization.
Inggs, J. & Meintjies, L. (eds.), 2009. *Translation studies in Africa*. London: Continuum.
Jäger, G. & Van Rooij, R., 2007. Language structure: Psychological and social constraints. *Synthese*, 159, pp. 99–130.
Jakobson, R., 2004. On linguistic aspects of translation. In: L. Venuti, ed. *The translation studies reader*. 2nd ed. London: Routledge, pp. 138–143.
Johnson, N., 2009. *Simply complexity. A clear guide to complexity theory*. Oxford: One World.
Jousse, M., 2000. *The anthroplogy of geste and rhythm*. Trans. E. Sienaert & J. Conolly. Durban: Mantis Publishing.
Kauffman, S., 1995. *At home in the universe. The search for the laws of self-organisation and complexity*. New York: Oxford University Press.
Klapwijk, J., 2008. *Purpose in the living world? Creation and emergent evolution*. Cambridge: Cambridge University Press.
Korten, D., 1990. *Getting to the 21st century: Voluntary action and the global agenda*. West Hartford, CT: Kumarian Press.
Kotzé, D. & Kotzé, P., 2007. Understanding communities and enabling people—A holistic approach. In: F. Theron, ed. *The development change agent: A micro-level approach to development*. Pretoria: Van Schaik, pp. 76–99.
Kraay, A., 2011. *Exploring the role of translation in (informal) community development*. Unpublished MA mini-dissertation. Bloemfontein, South Africa: University of the Free State.
Kruger, H., 2012. *Postcolonial polysystems: The production and reception of translated children's literature in South Africa*. Amsterdam: John Benjamins Publishing Company.

Latour, B., 1987. *Science in action: How to follow scientists and engineers through society*. Cambridge, MA: Harvard University Press.
———, 2000. When things strike back: A possible contribution of 'science studies' to the social sciences. *British Journal of Sociology*, 52(1), pp. 107–123.
———, 2007. *Reassembling the social. An introduction to actor-network theory*. Oxford: Oxford University Press.
Lavassa, A., 2009. Art as metaphor of the mind: A neo-Jamesian aesthetics embracing phenomenology, neuroscience and evolution. *Phenomenology and Cognitive Sciences*, 8, pp. 159–182.
Le Roux, P. & Graaff, J., 2001. Evolutionist thinking in the writing of Marx, Parsons, Rostow, and Giddens. In: J. Coetzee, J. Graaff, F. Hendricks & G. Wood, eds. *Development: Theory, policy, and practice*. Oxford: Oxford University Press, pp. 45–61.
Lefevere, A., 1990. Translation: Its genealogy in the West. In: S. Bassnett & A. Lefevere, eds. *Translation, history and culture*. London: Pinter Publishers, pp. 14–28.
Legassick, M., 2010. *The politics of a South African frontier: The Griqua, the Sotho-Tswana and the Missionaries, 1780–1840*. Basel: Basler Africa Bibliographien.
Lewis, D. & Mosse, D. eds., 2006. *Development brokers and translators. The ethnography of aid and agencies*. Bloomfield, CT: Kumarian Press.
Lewis, R., 2007. Language and translation: Contesting conventions. In: P. St-Pierre & P. Kar, eds. *In translation—Reflections, refractions, transformations*. Amsterdam: Benjamnis, pp. 27–38.
Leydesdorff, L., 2006. *The knowledge-based economy: Modeled, measured, simulated*. Boca Raton, FL: Universal Publishers.
LSM, n.d. *South African Audience Research Foundation*. Available at: http://www.saarf.co.za/LSM/lsms.asp. [Accessed 21 February 2013]
Lund, F., 2008. *Integrating local economic development and social protection: Experiences from South Africa*. Geneva: International Labour Organization.
Maathai, W., 2009. *The challenge for Africa: A new vision*. London: Heinemann.
MacKenzie, M., 2010. Enacting the self: Buddhist and enactivist approaches to the emergence of the self. *Phenomenology and Cognitive Science*, 9, pp. 75–99.
MacKinnon, D., Cumbers, A. & Chapman, K., 2002. Learning, innovation and regional development: A critical appraisal of recent debates. *Progress in Human Geography*, 26(3), pp. 293–311.
Makhado, M., 2010. *The context of translation: A auto-ethnographic study of English/Tshivenda translators*. Unpublished MA mini-dissertation. Bloemfontein: University of the Free State.
Mapengo, M.B., 2011. *Broadening the dimensions of translation theory: An exploration of the implications of incorporating the views of Xitsonga translators and users of translated texts*. Unpublished BA Hons research project. Bloemfontein, South Africa: University of the Free State.
Marais, H., 2011. *South Africa pushed to the limit: The political economy of change*. Cape Town: UCT Press.
Marais, J., 1997. *Representation in Old Testament narrative texts*. Leiden: EJ Brill.
———, 2010. I have rhythm therefore I am: Exploiting the linguistic anthropology of Marcel Jousse in exploring an African curriculum for translation studies. *The Interpreter and Translator Trainer*, 4(1), pp. 33–46.
———, 2011. Can Tymoczko be translated into Africa? Refractions of research methodology in translation studies in African contexts. *Southern African Linguistics and Applied Linguistics*, 29(3), pp. 375–383.
Marion, R., 1999. *The edge of organization: Chaos and complexity theories of formal social systems*. London: Sage.
Martín De León, C., 2010. Metaphorical models of translation: Transfer vs imitation and action. In: J. St. André, ed. *Thinking through translation with metaphors*. Manchester: St. Jerome, pp. 75–108.
Mbembe, A., 2001. *On the postcolony*. Berkeley: University of California Press.

Mead, G., 1969. *Mind, self & society from the standpoint of a social behaviourist.* Chicago: University of Chicago Press.
Meylaerts, R., 2011. Translational justice in a multilingual world: An overview of translation regimes. *Meta,* LVI(4), pp. 743–757.
MIDP V, 2012. *Unit for language facilitation and empowerment: MIDP V.* Available at: http://humanities.ufs.ac.za/content.aspx?id=515. [Accessed 15 January 2013]
Miller, J. & Page, S., 2007. *Complex adaptive systems. An introduction to computational models of social life.* Princeton, NJ: Princeton University Press.
Milton, J. & Bandia, P. eds., 2009a. *Agents of translation.* Amsterdam: Benjamins.
———, 2009b. Introduction: Agents of translation and translation studies. In: J. Milton & P. Bandia, eds. *Agents of translation.* Amsterdam: Benjamins, pp. 1–18.
Mitchell, M., 2009. *Complexity. A guided tour.* Oxford: Oxford University Press.
Molefe, A., 2011. *Re-conceptualising interpreting and translation.* Unpublished B.A. Hons research project. Bloemfontein, South Africa: University of the Free State.
Monti, E., 2010. Metaphors for metaphor translation. In: J. St. André, ed. *Thinking through translation with metaphors.* Manchester: St. Jerome, pp. 192–210.
Montuori, L.A., 2008. Foreword: Edgar Morin's path of complexity. In: *On complexity.* Cresskill: Hampton Press, pp. vii–xliv.
Morgan, C., 1923. *Emergent evolution.* London: Williams and Norgate.
Morgan, K., 1997. The learning region: Institutions, innovation and regional renewal. *Regional Studies,* 31(5), pp. 491–503.
———, 2004. The exaggerated death of geography: Learning, proximity and territorial innovation systems. *Journal of Economic Geography,* 4(1), pp. 3–21.
Morin, E., 2008. *On complexity.* Cresskill, NJ: Hampton Press.
Morrison, M., 2006. Emergence, reduction and theoretical principles: Rethinking fundamentalism. *Philosophy of Science,* 73, pp. 876–887.
Moss, T., 2007. *African development: Making sense of the issues and actors.* London: Lynne Rienner Publishers.
Motsie, K., 2010. *Multicultural communication and translation in integrated marketing communication: Informal advertisements.* Unpublished MA mini-dissertation. Bloemfontein, South Africa: University of the Free State.
Munday, J., ed., 2007. *Translation as intervention.* London: Continuum.
———, 2012. *Evaluation in translation: Critical points of translator decision-making.* London: Routledge.
Muñoz-Calvo, M. & Buessa-Gómez, C., 2010. *Translation and cultural identity: Selected essays on translation and cross-cultural communication.* Cambridge: Cambridge Scholars Publishing.
Nauta, W., 2007. *Ethnographic research in a non-governmental organization: Revealing strategic translations through an embedded tale.* West Hartford, CT: Kumarian Press.
Nida, E., 2004. Principles of correspondence. In: L. Venuti, ed. *The translation studies reader.* 2nd ed. London: Routledge, pp. 153–167.
Nord, C., 2001. *Translating as a purposeful activity. Functionalist approaches explained.* Manchester: St. Jerome.
Nouss, A., 2007. Translation and mettisage. In: P. St-Pierre & P. Kar, eds. *In translation—Reflections, refractions, transformations.* Amsterdam: Benjamins, pp. 245–252.
Nussbaum, M., 2011. *Creating capabilities. The human development approach.* Cambridge, MA: The Bellknap Press of Harvard University.
Nussbaum, M. & Sen, A., 1993. *The quality of life.* Oxford: Clarendon Press.
Olivier de Sardan, J., 2005. *Anthropology and development. Understanding contemporary social change.* London: Zed Books.
Otsuka, K. & Kalirajan, K. eds., 2011a. *Community, market and state in development.* New York: Palgrave Macmillan.

———, 2011b. Community, market and state development: An introduction. In: K. Otsuka & K. Kalirajan, eds. *Community, market and state development*. New York: Palgrave Macmillan, pp. 3–10.

Oxford Dictionary, n.d. *Oxford Dictionary Online*. Available at: http://oxforddictionaries.com/. [Accessed 30 July 2012]

Payne, A. & Phillips, N., 2010. *Development*. Cambridge: Polity Press.

Powell, W. & Snellman, K., 2004. The knowledge economy. *Review of Sociology*, 30, pp. 199–220.

Presidency, T., 2006. *Clarifying the Second Economy Concept*. The Presidency Policy Co-ordination and Advisory Services. Available at: http://www.thepresidency.gov.za/docs/pcsa/social/briefsynopsis.pdf. [Accessed 07 February 2013]

Prigogine, Y., 1996. *The end of certainty. Time, chaos and the new laws of nature*. New York: The Free Press.

Prozesky, H. & Mouton, J., 2001. The participatory research paradigm. In: J. Coetzee, J. Graaff, F. Hendricks & G. Wood, eds. *Development: Theory, policy and practice*. Oxford: Oxford University Press, pp. 537–552.

Puuka, J. et al., 2012. *Higher education in regional and city development: The Free State, South Africa 2012*. Paris: OECD.

Pym, A., 1998. *Method in translation history*. Manchester: St. Jerome.

———, 2006. On the social and the cultural in translation studies. In: A. Pym, J. Schlesinger & Z. Jettmarová, eds. *Sociocultural aspects of translating and interpreting*. Amsterdam: Benjamins.

Queiroz, J. & El-Hani, C., 2006. Semiosis as an emergent process. *Transactions of the Charles Pierce Society*, 42(1), pp. 78–116.

Quoc Loc, P., 2011. *Translation in Vietnam and Vietnam in translation: Language, culture, identity*. Available at: http://scholarworks.umass.edu/dissertations/AAI3482720. [Accessed 3 August 2012]

Rabbani, M., 2011. *The development and antidevelopment debate: Critical reflections on the philosophical foundations*. Surrey: Ashgate.

Ranis, F. 2011. Crossing borders: A tribute to Yajiro Hayami. In: K. Otsuka & R. Kalirajan, eds. *Community, market and state in development*. New York: Palgrave-Macmillan, pp. 11–13.

Rhoades, G. & Slaughter, S., 2004. Academic capitalism and the new economy: Challenges and choices. *American Academic*, 1(1), pp. 37–59.

Rist, G., 2002. *The history of development: From Western origins to global faith*. 2nd ed. London: Zed Books.

Rogerson, C., 1996. Urban poverty and the informal economy in South Africa's economic heartland. *Environment and Urbanization*, 8(1), pp. 167–179.

———, 1997. Local economic development and post-apartheid reconstuction in South Africa. *Singapore Journal of Tropical Geography*, 18(2), pp. 175–197.

———, 2004. Ten years of changing development planning in South Africa. *IDPR*, 26(4), pp. 355–358.

———, 2007. 'Second economy' versus informal economy: A South African affair. *Geoforum*, 38, pp. 1053–1057.

———, 2008. Consolidating local economic development in post-apartheid South Africa. *Urban Forum*, 19, pp. 307–328.

———, 2010. Local economic development in South Africa: Strategic challenges. *Development Southern Africa*, 27(4), pp. 481–491.

Rogerson, C. & Preson-Whyte, E., 1991. South Africa's informal economy: Past, present and future. In: C. Rogerson & E. Preston-Whyte, eds. *South Africa's informal economy*. Cape Town: Oxford University Press, pp. 1–7.

Romm, N., 2001. Critical theoretical concerns in relation to development: Haberman, modernity and democratization. In: J. Coetzee, J. Graaff, F. Hendricks &

G. Wood, eds. *Development: Theory, policy and practice.* Oxford: Oxford University Press, pp. 141–152.

Roodt, M., 2001. Participation. civil society, and development. In: J. Coetzee, J. Graaff, F. Hendricks & G. Wood, eds. *Development: Theory, policy and practice.* Oxford: Oxford University Press, pp. 469–481.

Said, E., 1993. *Culture and imperialism.* New York: Vintage Books.

——, 1994. *Orientalism.* New York: Vintage Books.

Salemink, O., 2006. Translating, interpreting and practicing civil society in Vietnam. In: D. Lewis & D. Mosse, eds. *Development brokers and translators.* Bloomfield, CT: Kumarian Press, pp. 101–126.

Samson, M., 2004. *Organizing in the informal economy: A case study of the municipal waste management industry in South Africa.* Geneva: International Labour Organization.

Samuels, J., ed., 2005. *Removing unfreedoms: Citizens as agents of change in urban development.* Warwickshire, England: ITDG Publishing.

Sawyer, R., 2005. *Social emergence: Societies as complex systems.* Cambridge: Cambridge University Press.

Schäffner, C., 2010. Cross-cultural translation and conflicting ideologies. In: M. Muñoz-Calvo & C. Buessa-Gómez, eds. *Translation and cultural identity: Selected essays on translation and cross-cultural communication.* Cambridge: Cambridge Scholars Publishing, pp. 107–128.

Schenk, C., Blaauw, D. & Viljoen, K., 2012. *Unrecognised waste-management experts: Challenges and opportunities for small business development and decent job creation in the waste sector in the Free State.* Geneva: ILO.

Searle, J., 1995. *The construction of social reality.* New York: The Free Press.

——, 1998. *Mind, language and society.* New York: Basic Books.

——, 2010. *Making the social world: The structure of human civilization.* Oxford: Oxford University Press.

Sebeok, T., ed., 1986. *Encyclopedic dictionary of semiotics.* Berlin: Mouton de Gruyter.

Seibt, J., 2009. Forms of emergent interaction in General Process Theory. *Synthese,* 166, pp. 479–512.

Sen, A., 1999. *Development as freedom.* New York: Anchor Books.

Shaw, T., 2005. The global political economy. In: J. Haynes, ed. *Palgrave advances in development studies.* London: Palgrave Macmillan, pp. 249–267.

Simeoni, D., 2007. Translation and society: The emergence of a conceptual relationship. In: P. St-Pierre & P. Kar, eds. *In translation—Reflections, refractions, transformations.* Amsterdam: Benjamins, pp. 13–26.

Simon, S., 1990. Translating the will to knowledge: Prefaces and Canadian literary politics. In: S. Bassnett & A. Lefevere, eds. *Translation, history and culture.* London: Pinter Publishers, pp. 110–117.

——, 2007. 'A single brushstroke'. Writing through translation: Anne Carson. In: P. St-Pierre & P. Kar, eds. *In translation—Reflections, refractions, transformations.* Amsterdam: Benjamins, pp. 107–116.

——, 2012. *Cities in translation: Intersections of language and memory.* London: Routledge.

Singh, R., 2007. Unsafe at any speed? Some unfinished reflections on the 'cultural turn' in translation studies. In: P. St-Pierre & P. Kar, eds. *In translation—Reflections, refractions, transformations.* Amsterdam: Benjamins, pp. 73–84.

Smith, K., 2002. *What is the 'Knowledge Economy'? Knowledge intensity and distributed knowledge bases.* Maastricht: United Nations University.

Smuts, J., 1926. *Holism and evolution.* London: Macmillan.

Spivak, G., 2007. Translation as culture. In: P. St-Pierre & P. Kar, eds. *In translation—Reflections, refractions, transformations.* Amsterdam: Benjamins, pp. 263–276.

St. André, J., ed., 2010a. *Thinking through translation with metaphors*. Manchester: St. Jerome.
———, 2010b. Passing through translation. In: J. St. André, ed. *Thinking through translation with metaphors*. Manchester: St. Jerome, pp. 275–294.
St-Pierre, P., 2007. Introduction. In: P. St-Pierre & P. Kar, eds. *In translation—Reflections, refractions, transformations*. Amsterdam: Benjamins, pp. 1–10.
St-Pierre, P. & Kar, P. eds., 2007. *In translation—Reflections, refractions, transformations*. Amsterdam: Benjamins.
Stacey, R. & Griffin, D. eds., 2005. *A complexity perspective on researching organizations: Taking experience seriously*. London: Routledge.
———, 2006. *Complexity and the experience of managing in public sector organisms*. London: Routledge.
Steiner, T., 2009. *Translated people, translated text. Language and migration in contemporary African literature*. Manchester: St. Jerome.
Strauss, D., 1978. *Inleiding tot die kosmologie*. Bloemfontein, South Africa: SACUM.
Stumpf, S., 1975. *Socrates to Sartre. A history of philosophy*. New York: McGraw-Hill.
Sturge, K., 2007. *Representing others: Translation, ethnography and the museum*. Manchester: St. Jerome.
Susam-Sarajeva, S., 2002. A 'multilingual' and 'international' translation studies? In: T. Hermans, ed. *Crosscultural transgressions: Research models in translation studies, II: Historical and ideological issues*. Manchester: St. Jerome.
———, 2006. *Theories on the move: Translation's role in the travel of literary theories*. New York: Rodopi.
Swart, I. & Venter, D., 2001. NGOs and churches. In: J. Coetzee, J. Graaff, F. Hendricks & G. Wood, eds. *Development: Theory, policy and practice*. Oxford: Oxford University Press, pp. 483–495.
Taylor, I., 2005. Globalisation and development. In: J. Haynes, ed. *Palgrave advances in development studies*. London: Palgrave Macmillan, pp. 268–287.
Taylor, M., 2001. *The moment of complexity: Emerging network culture*. Chicago: University of Chicago Press.
Theron, F., ed., 2007a. *The development change agent: A micro-level approach to development*. Pretoria: Van Schaik.
———, 2007b. The change agent-project beneficiary partnership in development planning—Theoretical perspectives. In: F. Theron, ed. *The development change agent: A micro-level approach to development*. Pretoria: Van Schaik, pp. 41–75.
———, 2007c. The development change agent: A micro-level approach to development. In: F. Theron, ed. *The development change agent: A micro-level approach to development*. Pretoria: Van Schaik, pp. 1–22.
Theron, J., 2011. *Non-standard workers, collective bargaining and social dialogue: The case of South Africa*. Geneva: International Labour Organization.
Toner, P., 2008. Emergent substance. *Philosophical studies*, 141, pp. 281–197.
Torop, P., 2002. Translation as translating as culture. *Sign Systems Studies*, 30(2), pp. 593–605.
Toury, G., 1986. Translation. In: T. Sebeok, ed. *Encyclopedic dictionary of semiotics*. Berlin: Mouton de Gruyter, pp. 1107–1124.
———, 1995. *Descriptive translation studies—and beyond*. Amsterdam: John Benjamins.
———, 2010. Some recent (and more recent) myths in translation studies: An essay on the present and future of the discipline. In: M. Muñoz-Calvo & C. Buesa-Gómez, eds. *Translation and cultural identity: Selected essays on translation and cross-cultural communication*. Cambridge: Cambridge Scholars Publishing, pp. 155–171.
Trivedi, H., 2007. Translating culture vs. cultural translation. In: P. St-Pierre & P. Kar, eds. *In translation—Reflections, refractions, transformations*. Amsterdam: Benjamins, pp. 277–287.

Tymoczko, M., 2002. Connecting the two infinite orders: Research methods in translation studies. In: T. Hermans, ed. *Crosscultural transgressions. Research models in translation studies II: Historical and ideological issues.* Manchester: St. Jerome, pp. 9–25.

———, 2006. Reconceptualizing Western translation theory. Integrating non-Western thought about translation. In: T. Hermans, ed. *Translating others.* Manchester: St. Jerome, pp. 13–32.

———, 2007. *Enlarging translation, empowering translators.* Manchester: St. Jerome.

———, 2010. Western metaphorical discourses implicit in translation studies. In: J. St. André, ed. *Thinking through translation with metaphors.* Manchester: St. Jerome, pp. 109–143.

———, 2013. *Neuroscience and translation.* Manchester: St. Jerome. (Forthcoming)

Tyulenev, S., 2010. Translation as smuggling. In: J. St. André, ed. *Thinking through translation with metaphors.* Manchester: St. Jerome, pp. 241–274.

———, 2011a. *Applying Luhmann to translation studies: Translation in society.* London: Routledge.

———, 2011b. Translation as a factor in social teleonomy. *Traduction, Terminologie, Rédaction,* XXIV(1), pp. 17–44.

———, 2012. *Translation and the Westernization of eighteenth-century Russia.* Berlin: Frank & Timme.

Uchiyama, A., 2009. Translation as representation: Fukuzawa Yukichi's representation of the "Others". In: J. Milton & P. Bandia, eds. *Agents of translation.* Amsterdam: Benjamins, pp. 63–84.

Van Huyssteen, J., 1986. *Teologie as kritiese geloofsverantwoording.* Pretoria: HSRC.

———, 2004. Evolution and human uniqueness: A theological perspective on the emergence of human complexity. In: K. Van Kooten Niekerk & H. Buhl, eds. *The significance of complexity. Approaching a complex world through science, theology and the humanities.* Burlington, VT: Ashgate, pp. 195–215.

Van Kooten Niekerk, K. & Buhl, H., 2004a. Introduction: Comprehending complexity. In: K. Van Kooten Niekerk & H. Buhl, eds. *The significance of complexity. Approaching a complex world through science, theology and the humanities.* Burlington, VT: Ashgate, pp. 1–18.

———, eds., 2004b. *The significance of complexity. Approaching a complex world through science, theology and the humanities.* Burlington, VT: Ashgate.

Van Wyke, B., 2010. Imitating bodies and clothes. Refashioning the Western concept of translation. In: J. St. André, ed. *Thinking through translation with metaphors.* Manchester: St. Jerome, pp. 17–46.

Venuti, L., 1995. *The translator's invisibility: A history of translation.* New York: Routledge.

Waldrop, M., 1992. *Complexity: The emerging science at the edge of order and chaos.* London: Viking.

Webb, J., Tihanyi, L., Ireland, R. & Sirmon, D., 2009. You say illegal, I say legitimate: Entrepreneurship in the informal economy. *Academy of Management Review,* 34(2), pp. 492–510.

Wittgenstein, L., 1958. *Philosophical investigations.* Oxford: Basil Blackwell.

Wolf, M., 2011. Mapping the field: Sociological perspectives on translation. *International Journal of the Sociology of Language,* 207, pp. 1–28.

Xaba, J., Horn, P. & Motala, S., 2002. *The informal sector in sub-Saharan Africa.* Geneva: International Labour Organization.

Yates, D., 2009. Emergence, downward causation and the completeness of physics. *Philosophical Quarterly,* 29(234), pp. 110–131.

Yule, G., 1996. *The study of language.* 2nd ed. Cambridge: Cambridge University Press.

Index

activism 93, 142–4; activist 93, 144
actor-network 24, 34, 44, 47, 59, 97; *see also* network; node
Adam 174–5
adaptation 32–3, 126, 132, 139
advocacy 142, 145
Africa 1–10, 119, 190–1, 196, 208–9; African 1–3, 5–9, 19, 89, 91, 133, 154, 183, 202, 208; South 2–7, 57, 69, 91, 119, 136, 146–7, 151–2, 162, 166–8, 180, 188, 190–2, 195–6, 198–9, 201–2, 204, 206; sub-Saharan 178, 180, 195
Agassi 47
Agenda 21, 146, 161
agent 11, 24, 27, 31, 33–5, 44, 55, 58, 62, 67, 89–90, 92, 94–5, 113–4, 132–5, 144, 169, 171, 178, 182, 187; agency 7, 11, 34, 43, 58, 60, 62, 72, 77, 89–95, 109, 111–15, 120, 132, 144, 192
Akrich 59–60, 96
Andrews 98
anthropology 17, 24, 44, 71, 84, 94, 111, 121, 131–2, 184
Arduini 15–6, 22, 77
Atkinson 20, 24
Axelrod 42, 91–2
Axtell 24, 37

Bak 26, 40–1
Baker 41, 43, 77, 89, 91–2, 112, 143
Bakhtin 130
Bandia 6, 41, 79, 89–91, 94, 113, 171, 187
Barnett 203
Basamalah 103
Bassnett 77, 79
Beinhocker 50

Benshalom 79
Bickhard 49, 50
binary 6, 9, 17–18, 20, 22
biology 10, 19, 27–8, 41, 49, 53, 63, 67, 69, 100, 111; biological 10, 23, 28–9, 38–9, 48–51, 53–4, 57, 67, 71, 76, 91–2, 96, 100–1, 104–6, 110, 113, 139–40, 181
border 8–9, 11, 25, 40, 71, 81, 91, 100, 122, 131–2, 146–47, 151–55, 166, 206; boundary 71, 98, 100, 131, 178
Brett 121–5, 127, 132, 139–40, 142
Brinkley 171, 173–4
Brisset 187
Brueggemann 25
Bührig 89
Bush 79

Callon 17, 24, 143
Calvert 134
capitalism 114, 120–1, 124–5, 139–40, 142–3, 177, 190; capitalist 120, 124–5, 190
Castells 18, 123, 128, 141–2, 161, 167, 172, 178–9, 184, 191, 194
causal 41, 50, 52, 67, 87, 90, 95, 111, 114, 122; causality 11, 24, 26, 34–6, 41–2, 49, 59–60, 114; downward causation 28, 36, 49–51, 54, 56–7, 67, 111–12, 131
Chambers 130, 135
chaos 18–20, 25, 32, 34, 36, 38–40, 48, 51, 105; edge of 21, 28, 32, 39–45, 80–1, 97–8, 133, 141, 143
chemical 10, 23, 28–9, 38, 40, 48–50, 52–4, 63, 71, 76, 85, 92, 96, 100–1, 104, 106, 110, 113, 181

Chen 188–94
Chesterman 36, 38, 90, 114
Cilliers 22, 26–7, 63, 80
cluster concept 84, 86–8
Coetzee 125–31
Cohen 19, 22, 30, 35, 47, 53
Collins 99
complex 2, 4, 7, 10–11, 15–19, 21–37, 39–46, 48–50, 57–60, 62, 69, 71, 77–8, 84–9, 92, 94–9, 102–6, 112–14, 120, 122–3, 127, 131–2, 134–5, 137, 175–6, 206; complexity 4–5, 9–11, 15–51, 55–57, 59–60, 62, 67, 71–2, 74–6, 78, 80–1, 84–95, 97, 98, 100, 102–5, 109–10, 113–15, 119–20, 122–3, 125–6, 130, 140–2, 146, 199, 205, 207–8, 210
complicated 25
compute 10, 18, 37, 44; computation 24, 36, 37, 41, 44, 45
connection 18, 23, 29, 38, 56, 59, 61, 69, 96–8, 105, 130, 137, 181, 184, 200, 207, 208; connecting 7, 21, 32, 59, 61, 97, 168, 179; connector 33, 60
constrain 23, 27, 50–1, 55, 57, 59, 64, 66–9, 92, 168; constraints 11, 28–9, 39, 132, 145–6, 180
constructivism 10, 29, 66, 92; constructionist 5, 29; constructivist 29, 66, 71
contingent 17, 22–3, 41, 74, 80, 83, 86–8, 205; contingency 31–2, 74, 85, 105, 141–2
Cooke 172, 174, 178
Coveny 18–9, 28, 30–1, 34, 37
Cronin 74, 89–90, 95, 111, 122, 128, 169
Crutchfield 50

Dasgupta 89
Davenport 175
David 172, 174
Davids 128
Davis 134, 191
deductive 87–9, 104–15, 113; deductively 36, 113
Deguet 51
Delvaux 190
deontic 64, 68, 70
dependency 127, 167
determinism 19, 21–23, 92, 127; deterministic 23, 34, 112, 127

development: capabilities approach 122, 135–7; developmental 7–8, 28, 39, 133, 135, 143–4, 166, 181; developmentalists 140; innovation 90, 133, 172–7, 179; local economic 11, 145–7, 151, 153–4, 162, 167–8, 179; policies 152–3, 161, 168–9, 206; sustainable 8, 129, 189, 191; underdeveloped 121, 125; underdevelopment 126, 127, 133
Devey 188, 190, 192
dialogic 85, 130, 140, 182
disorder 2, 21, 24–5, 36; see also order
Donaldson 146, 165, 187
dualism 23, 63, 72; dualist 10, 23, 49, 69, 190; duality 28, 37
Du Plessis 148
Dutt 121, 190–1, 195

Eco 98, 100
ecology 84, 128; ecological 10, 21, 26, 29, 54, 66, 92, 110, 112, 114
economy 7, 11, 29, 107, 122–3, 128–9, 136, 140, 143–5, 155, 158–9, 171–85, 187–204; economics 7, 19, 24, 27, 57, 70–1, 111, 120, 122, 125, 127, 132, 171, 177–8, 184, 188, 205; economists 122, 140, 189; informal 7, 11, 95, 144–5, 153–4, 162–4, 168, 184, 187–204, 206, 208; knowledge 11, 128, 145, 171–5, 177, 179–81, 184–5, 206; market 123, 125, 127, 140, 162, 174, 177, 192, 195, 196, 198, 201
El-Hani 52, 111–12
emerge 10–1, 23, 26, 28–9, 31–4, 37, 39, 42, 48–59, 62, 67–8, 70–2, 74, 81, 84, 88, 94–5, 100, 106–8, 110–11, 120–1, 131, 143, 205; emergence 10–1, 18, 22–4, 28–9, 31, 33, 36–7, 42–59, 62–3, 65, 67, 69–72, 87, 88, 93, 95, 98, 107–13, 131, 135, 146, 190, 195, 205; emergent 10–1, 29, 31, 33–4, 36–7, 41, 43, 46–7, 50–4, 56–9, 69, 72, 76–7, 87–8, 93–4, 96, 101, 106, 110–12, 114, 122; emergentists 7, 18, 48, 67; emerging 2, 10, 15, 29,

Index

50–1, 53–4, 57, 67–8, 72, 87, 106, 110, 147, 173; ephemeral emergent 57, 58, 110
Emmeche 28–9, 36, 39, 49
entropy 27, 32, 36; see also *negentropy*
Epstein 24, 37
equilibrium 20, 31–2, 38–41, 43–4, 49, 57, 59, 80, 97; disequilibrium 32, 35; nonequilibrium 26, 31–2, 43–4, 81, 102
Erasmus 198
essentialism 76, 92, 142; essentialist 2, 86, 92; essentialize 5–6, 143
ethnography 3, 82, 147; ethnographic 5, 8, 9, 81–2, 153–4, 184
Even-Zohar 32, 44
evolution 19, 23, 30, 38–9, 48, 52, 54, 82, 125; evolutionary 24, 41, 127; evolutionist 54, 124, 127, 133, 139, 142; evolving 50, 94

Fischer 30, 52
Florida 168, 172, 175–7
Flynn 6
Foray 172, 174–5
foreignization 40, 42–3
Francescotti 51–3
Free State's Regional Steering Committee 151, 177
Freund 126
fundamentalist 10, 133

Gaffney's Local Government 149–50
Gambier 16
genotype 28, 37; *see also* phenotype
Gentzler 7, 77, 89, 95, 113–14, 168, 171, 187
geography 4, 174, 175–6, 178
Gesheson 26
geste 94–5
Ghandi Kingdon 192
Giddens 37, 58
Gillespie 121, 128, 142
globalization 90, 114, 122, 128, 177; globalizing 92, 95, 127
Godo 127
Goudzwaard 138
Graaff 125, 127, 129
Graves 48, 52
Griffin 62, 93–5
growth 35, 91, 98, 124–5, 127–8, 130, 136, 140, 142, 152, 168, 173, 189, 190–2, 195

Guldin 80–1
Gutt 79

Halverson 68, 70
Handelman 134
Hart 188
Hassink 176
Hatim 77
Hauser 175, 177
Hayami 127
Haynes 122, 126–7, 134, 187
Heard 50, 54
Heilbron 90
Heniuk 79, 81–3
Hermans 16, 27, 30, 89
hermeneutic 8, 130–1, 133, 135, 141–2, 161, 167–8, 175, 206
Hettne 124
Heylighen 15, 18, 21–3, 26, 30
hierarchy 10, 21, 23, 26–9, 33, 47, 50, 67, 72, 110, 112, 178
Highfield 18–9, 28, 30–1, 34, 37
history 2–3, 5, 16, 18, 23–4, 26, 28, 32, 35, 39, 41, 44, 48, 55, 63, 71, 74, 76–7, 79, 82, 84, 89, 91–2, 94, 98, 100, 105, 111, 121–7, 131–2, 138, 142, 144, 151–2, 187; historicity 27, 38
Hofstadter 9, 17, 20–1, 46–8, 50–1, 65, 75, 92
holism 19, 48; holistic 76, 88, 132
Holland 23, 26, 33–4, 47–8, 50
Holmes 16, 74, 77
Hoogendoorn 146
Houghton 172–3, 175, 177
House 40, 89
Hudson 177
hybrid 2, 3, 8, 29, 40, 104–5, 131–4, 139, 201, 208; hybridity 2, 15, 25, 40, 91, 124, 208

Ibourk 190, 193, 195
ideology 3, 6, 8, 16, 31–2, 43–4, 77, 82, 92–3, 100, 108–9, 113–14, 121, 132–3, 144, 146, 151–2, 171, 183, 187
IDP 147, 153–62, 164–5, 170; Gariep 147, 150–1, 160; Kopanong 147, 151, 160; Pixley Ka Seme 147, 154, 156, 158–61; Ukhahlamba 154–55, 158–60; Umsobomvu 160; !Xhariep 147, 151, 153–54, 156–60
ILO 188–9, 191, 193, 195

228 Index

imperialism 121, 127, 139, 142; imperialist 120, 131
indigenization 9, 40, 42–3, 168
individual 17, 20, 27–8, 33, 37, 41, 46, 49, 51, 55–9, 62, 71, 74, 83, 88–90, 94–5, 103, 109–10, 113–14, 120, 125, 127, 130–2, 134–6, 140–1, 153, 168–9, 176–7, 179; individualism 17, 55, 59, 88; methodological individualism 37, 55
Inggs 195
initial conditions 10, 33–5, 57
intentionality 63–7, 70
inter: action 38–9, 97; -ing 38–9, 61–2, 65, 70, 72, 96, 98, 100, 103, 105–7, 109; -ness 38, 61–2, 65, 81, 84, 98, 100, 101, 103, 105–7, 113, 176; phenomenon 84, 100, 103–5; semiotic 91, 98, 102–3, 184, 199, 206; systemic 76, 96–8, 103–5, 113, 179, 205–7; systemicness 104, 179, 207; related 98–9; relationship 61, 98, 100, 103–4, 113
interact 31, 38, 40, 42, 50, 55–6, 58, 62, 71, 110, 174; interaction 7, 11, 18, 23, 28–9, 31–3, 37–8, 41–2, 47, 50–3, 55–9, 62, 65, 70–2, 84, 87, 94–5, 106–11, 114, 120, 131–3, 138, 175, 178–80, 199, 200, 203, 206–8; symbolic interaction 58, 62, 68, 84, 94, 110
interdiscipline 85, 207; interdisciplinary 7, 29, 30, 88, 111, 122, 140, 143, 184, 203
interpreting 68, 110, 131, 133–4, 145, 151, 154, 163–5, 167–9, 178, 188, 198, 203; interpreter 89, 162, 183, 199, 202
irrational 20, 22, 47, 83, 87; see also rational
irreducible 53, 56, 112; see also reduction; non-reducible

Jäger 52
Jakobson 16, 100–3, 105, 113, 206
Johnson 18
Jousse 11, 53, 67, 94, 106, 110, 112, 184, 200
juxtapose 70, 88, 93, 115; juxtaposition 26, 43, 78

Kalirajan 122–23
Kauffman 2, 21, 29, 31, 35, 37, 39–40, 47, 51, 98
Klapwijk 52–3
Korten 128
Kotzé 128, 131, 135
Kraay 198–99
Kruger 195

Latour 8, 18–22, 24–6, 29, 34, 36, 38, 42, 47, 58–62, 66, 70–1, 76, 82, 89–90, 93, 96–7, 100, 105, 110, 113, 120, 134, 136, 143–44, 168, 203–4, 207–8
Lavassa 49
Lee 174
Lefevere 49, 77, 79
Legassick 112, 13
Le Roux 129
level: macro 114, 123–5; micro 128–9, 135
Lewis 9, 91, 96, 114, 131, 134, 143
Leydesdorff 122, 172
link 8, 20, 23–4, 29, 31, 33–4, 36, 38, 41, 44, 58–61, 67, 70–1, 78, 83, 90, 95–7, 120–1, 156, 168, 177, 179–81, 184, 189, 191, 194, 199, 200, 202, 204, 206–8
linear 17, 24–6, 41, 57, 114, 126–7, 135; see also nonlinear
LSM 197–8
Lund 146, 168, 191, 193, 195

Maathai 2, 7, 131, 192, 209
MacKenzie 50
MacKinnon 177
Makhado 196–7
Mapengo 82
Marais 9, 25, 53, 94, 110, 146, 165, 187, 190, 195
Marion 32
Martín De León 81
Mason 77
material 11, 29, 48–9, 51, 53, 55, 57–60, 68, 70, 84, 100, 110, 119–20, 125, 130, 136, 138–9, 174, 176, 178, 180, 183, 197, 203, 205; materialistic 28, 51–2, 57, 59, 140; materiality 49, 60, 68–9, 72
Mbembe 7, 22, 133
Mead 48, 52, 55, 67, 94
mediate 62, 79, 91, 134, 141; mediation 91, 134, 168, 177; mediator 60, 203

Meintjies 195
meme 38, 91
metaphor 9, 43, 77, 83, 98–100, 108
metaphysics 47, 50, 54, 60
Meylaerts 153, 168
MIDP V 165
Miller 25, 27, 37, 39, 42, 47
Milton 6, 41, 89–90, 94, 113, 171, 187
Mitchell 17–9, 26–7, 29, 32, 34–6, 39, 51
modernization 90, 125–7, 139, 171, 187, 190
Molefe 82
monist 10, 23, 29, 69; monism 72, 112
Monti 81
Montuori 19
Morgan 48–9, 175–6, 178
Morin 19–26, 38–9, 46, 78
Morrison 52, 54
Moss 120, 126
Mosse 9, 96, 114, 131, 134, 143
Motsie 197–8
Mouton 129
multi: lingual 8, 11, 62, 69, 120, 153, 162, 166, 168, 188, 194, 201; lingualism 130, 153–54, 162, 164–65; multilinguistic 167, 201; modal 65, 110, 184; modality 164, 184
Munday 89
Muñoz-Calvo 92

narrative 2, 21, 89, 91–2, 103, 128, 141
naturalism 52, 112; naturalistic 67
Nauta 134
negentropy 21, 32, 36, 38; *see also* entropy
Nel 146
neoliberal 123, 129; neoliberalism 127, 190
Nergaard 15–6, 22, 77
network 18, 25, 50, 58, 59, 61, 71, 97, 128, 161, 171, 173–4, 177–9, 181–5, 188, 196–7, 199, 200, 202, 204; *see also* actor-network; node
Nida 77
node 20, 33, 59–61, 71, 97, 178, 183–4; *see also* actor-network; network
nonlinear 11, 17, 21, 25–6, 30, 33–7, 41, 51, 57, 60, 87, 99, 102, 114, 122, 135, 144, 205; *see also* linear

Index 229

non-reducible 53–4, 57, 205; *see also* irreducible; reduction
Nord 40, 43
Nouss 103
Nussbaum 121–2, 124–5, 129, 135–7, 163

Olivier de Sardan 7, 130–34, 139, 161, 167, 175
ontology 10, 57, 60–3, 66, 70, 97, 102; ontological 50, 52, 55–6, 67
order 16, 18–9, 21–2, 24–5, 28, 31–4, 36–40, 51, 58, 104–5, 140; *see also* disorder
oral 91, 103, 110, 112, 121, 131, 145, 151, 153, 183, 186, 188, 201–3, 206
organize 28–9, 38, 40–1, 50–1, 56–7, 61, 115, 177–8; organization 22–5, 28–9, 32, 37, 39, 49–51, 56–7, 78, 111, 126, 159, 173–5, 181, 185, 188; organizational 93, 115, 176; *see also* self-organization; self-organized criticality
Otsuka 122–3
Oxford Dictionary 99

Page 25, 27, 37, 39, 42, 47
paradox 3, 20–2, 25–6, 37, 39, 46, 62, 70, 74–5, 78, 83, 85, 89, 94, 114, 130, 141, 152, 205; paradoxical 5, 9, 15, 17, 21–3, 26–7, 29, 37–40, 43, 46, 51, 56, 59, 71–2, 78, 81, 89, 94, 98, 106, 115, 130
particular 4–5, 9, 11, 20–3, 25, 28–9, 31–2, 46, 49, 56, 62, 64, 70, 74, 76, 78, 82–3, 87–8, 90, 96, 106–7, 115, 122–4, 131, 133, 135, 137, 139, 144, 146; particularity: 39, 47, 85; particularism 4
Payne 129
phase transition 39–40
phenotype 28, 37; *see also* genotype
Phillips 129
physical 10, 23, 26, 28–9, 40, 48–51, 53–4, 56, 63–4, 66–7, 69, 71–2, 76, 85, 92, 96, 100–1, 104–6, 110, 112–13, 126, 136, 172, 203; physics 19, 27, 30, 35, 40, 52, 63, 79, 100, 110, 207–8
positivism 46, 49; positivist 22, 84
postmodern 2, 4, 85, 88, 91, 95, 205, 207; postmodernism 15, 17, 20,

27, 47, 74, 81; postmodernist 9, 75, 77, 80, 83, 141
Powell 129
power 2–5, 7–10, 17–8, 22, 50–2, 63–4, 66–8, 79, 90–1, 93, 119–20, 122, 124, 127, 132, 135, 139, 141, 143, 147, 152, 154–5, 161, 164, 167, 174, 177–8, 187, 193
Presidency 190
Prigogine 21, 26, 32, 41
prisoner's dillemma 42
process 4, 9–11, 18, 23–4, 26–7, 32–4, 47–50, 57–62, 64, 68, 70, 79–80, 84, 86, 90, 94–5, 97–100, 105, 109–10, 124, 126, 131–4, 139, 141, 146–7, 152, 154, 156–8, 161, 163–4, 168, 172, 175–8, 181, 193, 207, 209
Prozesky 129
psychology 19, 24, 44, 61; psychological 10, 23, 28–9, 48–51, 54, 57, 63, 65, 71, 84, 92, 95–6, 100–1, 106, 113, 142
Puuka 139, 151, 177
Pym 89–90

Queiros 52, 111–12
Quoc Loc 83

Rabbani 123–4, 131, 140–1, 169
Ranis 132
rational 94, 126; rationalistic 88, 126; rationality 3, 20–1, 46–7, 88, 92, 134, 141; *see also* irrational
reduction 17, 29, 31, 56, 63, 189, 191; reduce 10, 17, 19, 22, 24, 26, 28, 31–2, 47–9, 52–4, 56, 58, 62–3, 67, 71–2, 77, 83, 98, 107–8, 112, 123, 126, 136–7, 142, 158, 175; reducible 52, 58, 62, 70–1, 84, 106, 122; reducing 70, 77, 91, 111, 140, 173–4; reductionist 10, 15, 19, 20, 22, 26, 28–30, 34, 40, 42, 46–7, 49, 52–3, 69, 77, 80–1, 84–8, 91, 95, 107–8, 111, 114, 123, 130; reductive 15, 20, 30, 86; reductionism 9, 11, 15, 18, 22, 25–6, 28–31, 35, 46, 48–9, 52–3, 56, 59, 72, 83–4, 205; reductionistic 22, 26, 59, 122; *see also* irreducible, non-reducible
relatedness (including interrelatedness) 17, 20, 25–7, 57, 62, 99, 113; relationship (including interrelationship) 5, 9, 11, 17–8, 20–5, 27–31, 34–5, 37–40, 43–5, 48–63, 67, 72, 75–6, 78, 81, 83, 86–7, 89–90, 92, 94–107, 110–11, 113–14, 121–23, 126, 132, 138–40, 143, 159–60, 177, 188, 191, 202, 204; relational 86, 113; relationality 52, 96
relative 5, 65, 173, 200; relativism 124, 139, 142–3; relativity 18, 123–4, 126
Rhoades 175
Rist 120–5, 138–42, 163, 179
Rogerson 168, 190, 192
Romm 129
Roodt 129
Ros 121, 190–91, 195

Said 119, 121, 124, 139, 141–3, 164
Salemink 134
Samson 189–90
Samuels 191–2
Sawyer 18–9, 23, 44, 48, 55–9, 62, 71, 110
Schäffner 90, 92
Schenk 192, 194
Searle 7, 10, 23, 47, 49, 52, 54, 58, 62–71, 89, 96, 205–6
Sebeok 98
Seibt 50
self-organization 28, 30–1, 36, 39, 50–1, 95, 98; *see also* organize
self-organized criticality 28, 31, 40–2; avalanches 40–1; sand 40, 41; *see also* organize; self-organization
semiotic 7, 11, 38, 47, 52, 54, 58–60, 62, 64–5, 69–72, 76–7, 81, 84, 91, 95–8, 100–13, 120, 133, 135, 176–7, 179, 181, 199, 203–4, 206, 208; intersemiotic 91, 98, 103–4, 109, 181, 199, 206; intrasemiotic 98, 101; semiosis 62, 67–9, 71, 102–3, 112; semiotically 83, 203; semiotics 8, 46, 62, 64–5, 67, 69–72, 76–7, 81, 83–4, 95, 96, 98, 100, 102, 110–14, 171–72, 204–6
Sen 125–6, 129, 135–6
Shaw 134
Sheehan 172–3, 176–7
Simeoni 75

Index

Simon 77, 92, 187
simplicity 19–20, 30, 35, 142
Singh 89
Skinner 192
Slaughter 175
Smith 57, 172, 174–6
Smuts 19, 48
Snellman 172
social: action 89, 132; capital 129, 168, 176–7, 196, 199, 202–3; change 8, 127, 132–3, 139, 168; Darwinism 121, 139; effect 91, 114; emergence 48, 54, 58, 62–3, 110; environment 126; fact 11, 68; interaction 55, 59, 62, 87, 138, 206; phenomenon 10–1, 23, 55–6, 58, 62–3, 65, 67, 69, 72, 84, 89, 93, 110, 113; reality 11, 29, 31, 34, 44, 47, 52, 54–9, 62–4, 66–72, 77, 84, 89, 91–3, 100, 107–14, 119, 125, 131, 144, 146, 178, 187–8, 194, 205; science 5, 8, 15, 19, 24, 26, 35, 56, 60–1, 67, 93, 111, 142; structure 37, 56, 58, 110–11, 131, 135; system 18, 27, 35, 40, 55–7, 72, 90, 95, 107, 120
society 2, 3, 5–8, 17, 19–20, 28, 33–4, 37, 46–7, 49, 55, 57–9, 63, 65–7, 69, 72, 78, 90, 94–6, 110–11, 114–15, 120–127, 131–4, 136–7, 139, 142–3, 161–2, 165, 168–9, 171–3, 177–9, 188, 193–5
sociological 43, 48, 55, 58–60, 72, 90, 96, 100, 125, 127; sociology 7, 9, 16–17, 19, 31, 37–8, 54–5, 59–61, 77, 84–5, 92, 96–7, 108, 113–14, 120, 122, 128
space 3–4, 6, 8–9, 27, 31–2, 37, 44, 54, 62, 65, 69, 72, 75, 77–9, 83, 85, 88, 92, 95, 98–9, 109, 111, 113, 128, 131–5, 152, 154, 158, 175, 177–9, 184, 203, 206, 208
Spivak 91
St André 79, 81, 89, 108
St-Pierre 89
Stacey 62, 93–5
Steiner 93, 195
Strauss 75–6
Stumpf 17, 74
Sturge 5, 54, 82, 171
substratum 23, 25, 29, 49, 51–3, 62, 71–2, 84, 87–8, 100, 106–7, 109–11, 113, 122, 136, 203, 205; substructure 23, 51, 69–70, 72, 120, 140, 146, 174, 176, 203, 205–6
supervenience 51, 63; supervene 51, 56, 72; supervenient 10, 51, 59
superstratum 29, 52, 88
Susam-Sarajeva 4, 90, 146, 171, 187
Swart 128, 198
system: sub 31, 40, 44, 56, 58, 62, 70, 72, 84, 102–3, 106–7, 109–10, 121, 206–7; complex adaptive 4, 26–8, 30–4, 37, 39–40, 42, 44, 46, 59, 61, 96–7, 99, 102, 104, 106, 112–13, 135, 206; complex 21, 25, 28, 31, 34, 36, 41, 57–8, 132, 176; complex systems theory 16, 23, 23, 27, 29, 36

Taylor 15, 18, 32, 38–9, 106, 128
thermodynamics 27, 32, 34, 36, 38
Theron 128–29, 134–35, 189–90, 195
Toner 54
Torop 98
Toury 16, 32, 92–3, 98, 100
transdiscipline 115, 207; transdisciplinarity 24, 26; transdisciplinary 17, 19, 71
translation: communal 168, 182–3, 206; as rewriting 32, 44, 49, 78–81, 103, 110; philosophy of 10, 16, 32, 37, 115; turns in 44, 75, 77–8, 83, 90, 93, 95, 108, 111, 113
travel theory 90, 171
Trivedi 77, 89, 104
Tymoczko 2, 4–5, 7, 9, 16, 29, 36, 65, 77, 79, 81–9, 93–4, 104–5, 111–14, 168, 183, 193–4, 199
Tyulenev 21, 30, 62, 72, 77–80, 85, 89–90, 96, 98, 100, 104, 114, 171, 207

Uchiyama 187
universal 4–5, 17, 20, 22–3, 49, 74, 94, 124, 140–2, 205; universalist 88; universalism 4, 17; universality 3, 25, 39, 41, 47, 94, 113–14, 141; universally 137, 141; universalizing 5
universe 10, 63, 65–6, 130–1, 177

Valodia 192
Van Doorslaer 6, 16

Van Huyssteen 18, 24, 47, 66
Van Kooten Niekerk 18, 23, 28, 34
Van Rooij 52
Van Wyke 79
Venter 128, 198
Venuti 32, 40, 204

Waldrop 19, 47
Webb 193
Wittgenstein 36, 86–8, 94, 104, 113

whole 6–7, 10, 17–20, 22–4, 26–7, 30–1, 33, 36–8, 41–2, 44–5, 47–8, 51–55, 58, 61, 65, 69–70, 72, 75–6, 78, 86–7, 97, 107–8, 112
Wolf 90

Xaba 190

Yates 53–4
Yule 98